SHEER FICTION

VOLUME THREE

BOOKS BY PAUL WEST

Fiction

Love's Mansion

Lord Byron's Doctor

The Place in Flowers Where Pollen Rests

The Universe, and Other Fictions

Rat Man of Paris

The Very Rich Hours of Count von Stauffenberg

Gala

Colonel Mint

Caliban's Filibuster

I'm Expecting to Live Quite Soon

Bela Lugosi's White Christmas

Alley Jaggers

Tenement of Clay

Non-Fiction

Portable People

Sheer Fiction (Volume One)

Sheer Fiction (Volume Two)

Out of My Depths: A Swimmer in the Universe

Words for a Deaf Daughter

The Snow Leopard

The Modern Novel

The Wine of Absurdity

Byron and the Spoiler's Art

I, Said the Sparrow

SHEER FICTION

VOLUME THREE

PAUL WEST

McPherson & Company

Copyright 1994 by Paul West. All rights reserved.
Manufactured in the USA. First Edition.

 # 31278248

Library of Congress Cataloging-in-Publication Data
(revised for vol. 3)

West, Paul
  Sheer fiction.

  1. Fiction—20th century—History and criticism.
I. Title.
PN3503.W44 1987   809.3'04   86-33252
ISBN 0-914232-82-7
ISBN 0-929701-38-0 (v. 3)

Published by McPherson & Company, Publishers, Post Office Box 1126, Kingston,
New York 12401. The first printing has been made possible in part by grants from the
literature programs of the New York State Council on the Arts and the National
Endowment for the Arts, a federal agency. Designed by Bruce R. McPherson. Typeset
in Times Roman by Studio Graphics.   1 3 5 7 9 10 8 6 4 2

Some of these essays and reviews first appeared in the following periodicals, and
permission to reprint them is gratefully acknowledged: *At Random, The Authors
Guild Bulletin, Book World (The Washington Post), Boston Phoenix, Chicago Tri-
bune, City Lights Review, Conjunctions, Dimensions (A Journal of Holocaust Stud-
ies), GQ, Harper's, The Los Angeles Times, The Nation, The National Review,
Parnassus, The New York Times Book Review, The New York Times Sophisticated
Traveller, The Paris Review, The Review of Contemporary Fiction, The Southern
Review, The St. Petersburg Times, Twentieth Century, The Voice Literary Supplement.*
The essays on Mary Butts and Joanna Scott were written expressly for McPherson and
Company and the Ashville School. The essay "A Vision of Bright Cannon-Fodder"
is the preface to *Words for a Deaf Daughter* and *Gala*, published in one volume by
Dalkey Archive Press.

CONTENTS

Preface
7

I: Essays

Remembrance of Things Proust
11

Thomas Mann, Englishman
21

Night 1002: When It All Goes Down
34

The Absurd Revisited
49

A Vision of Bright Cannon-Fodder
54

Where Novels Come From
59

Judge Not
66

Back to My Desk
71

Shoptalk
75

Middle River Stump Jump
77

Literary Lions at the Public Library
80

Tan Salaam and the Aga Khan
87

Enemy Coast Ahead
90

Borrowed Time
92

II: Reviews
97

Jean-Jacques Rousseau   Jean Genet   Alain Robbe-Grillet
André Gorz   Samuel Beckett   Beckett and Giacometti
Frederic Prokosch   Walter Abish   Joanna Scott
John Barth   William T. Vollmann   Zulfikar Ghose
Leslie Marmon Silko   Anne Rice   Richard Price
Mary Butts   Lawrence Norfolk   Michael Ayrton
Doris Lessing   Michael Moorcock   Miguel Angel Asturias
Hermann Hesse   Milan Kundera   Tom Wolfe
Santa Claus of Middle Earth   Octavio Paz   Geoffrey Moorhouse
Charles Sprawson   Art and the Double Life
Johann Wolfgang von Goethe   A. Alvarez   Jiri Weil
The Book of Alfred Kantor   Hitler and Canaris
Helmuth James von Moltke   Kristallnacht   War as a Soap

Preface

Anyone patient and daring enough to have dipped into the two preceding volumes of *Sheer Fiction* without being deflected from examining a third will notice an increase here in the number of essays. I have been reviewing less, though perhaps at greater length, and doing more pieces that explain the huffs, scrapes, and stances I have blundered into.

Readers will notice how the notion "sheer" backslides a little in this collection, permitting a small ghetto, or burghetto, that encloses books about the Nazi era, in which I have taken a developed interest ever since being bombed by the Luftwaffe. I have indeed, while researching the Stauffenberg plot (and Hitler's revenge) in library stacks, gagged at the water cooler, as when reading about the goings-on, the *doings,* in Plötzensee execution jail. Of the books in this cornered group, only Jiri Weil's novel is fictional; I wanted to bring together books, and events, that sundered my mind in extraordinary, terrible ways, far beyond the *licet* of fiction, so far that fiction about such things seemed blasphemous. I became interested in something so preposterous, so gross, it seemed to have had to be made up by someone insane. So the creative mind leaks away into the infinity of pain and horror, knowing that regimented racism stops the novelist in his/her tracks. The phrase *"non-*fiction" comes in time to have a blood-curdling dignity one cannot gainsay. In the end we confine ourselves to two kinds of symbolisms that should fuse. I remember that symbolism used to mean the throwing together of two things that remained apart: *syn-ballein.* Thus the effable met the ineffable. I wonder about what happened at the Little Big Horn after the massacre, when squaws thrust their sewing awls through dead Custer's eardrums to make him hear better in the next life.

P.W.
25 December 1993

7

I

Remembrance of Things Proust

A PASTY-FACED, LANK-MUSTACHED INVALID IN FURS accosts the viola player and asks if they will play the entire work again. He will pay them generously. We are at the Concert Rouge in the Rue de Tournon, Paris. It is November 1916, and Marcel Proust, age 45, has fallen in love with the string quartet of the Belgian composer, César Franck. A few nights later, the members of the Poulet Quartet enter a taxi that already contains both a tureen of mashed potatoes from a posh Parisian nitery and, beneath an enormous eiderdown, Proust himself.

At his apartment, they play the Franck twice while Proust lolls on his bed, enraptured; he then pays them with fifty-franc bills tugged from a Chinese box and, exclaiming his delight, motions the quartet downstairs to four waiting taxis. With some fried-up mashed potato and enough Champagne, he has turned his world to gold. The Poulet Quartet will come again and again, wondering if Proust has more money than the world has music, while he himself wonders not about money but about the shortness of one life divided into the world's masterpieces. This is the long division of Proust the music-lover, the sum of his rapturous devotions. He is always under pressure, not all of it self-imposed.

Proust was asthmatic and learned early what all narcissists know: that disease is finally the most imposing of all the art forms. Long before he would begin to lose his hair, weakness and choking drove him in upon himself, into the famous cork-lined room at 102 Boule-

vard Haussmann, where, looked after by his matchless maid, Céleste,
he began to write in bed the most astounding super-novel of our day.
Disease was Proust's muse, goading and inspiring him; and to read
him, even a bit, is to taste and tweak mortality, to become your own
bedridden grandee snob with most of Paris at your beck and call
and the whole of human memory to pluck at as if you were some
ravished anthologist of the night, a brilliant child with the world for
a windup toy.

"The Midnight Sun," his friends called him, because, even as a
youth, he kept weird hours, sucking on nightlife like an addict. Gre-
garious and witty, he frequented the salons of the Princess Mathilde
and Madame de Caillavet, learning how to conduct himself in the high
reaches of Saint-Germain society, where chic was manna. He gossiped
interminably with servants and young girls, went to theater and broth-
els and sent friends the longest letters they had ever received. He went
out and about, a pampered, cheerful sybarite whose true life—that of
a demoniacally shut-in artist—could not begin until he retreated, in
1909, to pursue his copious recall of all he had seen and been in the
preceding years. And none too soon. He had thirteen years to live, and
he was only 38.

He had trained himself, though. He could not retreat effectively
to his bedroom without having something sizable to retreat from, and
he had all that. He had taught himself how to be alone, how to bring
the world to his bedside, how to make illness a catalyst and inspiration
a flail. He had colossal memory, almost intolerable sensitivity and an
ear like a trap. He had learned from Ruskin how to float on his own
prose, and from the freakish dandy Robert de Montesquiou how to
cherish and exploit the most perverse parts of his personality. He was
a dream analyst, a trance-conjurer, a scandal-savorer, a girl-fondler, a
boy-cuddler, a matron-stroker, a snob maven, a dealer in smart re-
marks and a prodigious theorist of love.

Now only rarely did he slink off to the Ritz to inspect a lineup
of eligible new kitchen boys and bellhops. Pederasty took a backseat,
as it were, as he made more and more of what he had cached and
codified. He became a fusspot, a dawdler, one who believed in memories as inexhaustible objects of contemplation. He discovered a truth
not true for all: that a sumptuous, agile mind needs only one remem-

bered thing—one toddy sipped, one hankie sniffed, one gorgeous rump unblinked at—which it then devours lifelong, not merely making a meal of it but converting it into a private universe, ever fattening, never lost.

Proustian memory is not an act of will, however; it is involuntary, coming to life under stimuli unknown and wholly unreliable, not investigative but meandering swanlike across a smooth and indifferent opaque surface. For Proust, memories come unbidden or not at all. He does not ferret them out, but once he has them he builds them into mighty pagodas of nostalgia, transforming moments into aeons, syllables into tropics, heartbeats into tantrums of constant desire.

First, then, this creepy, mauve, dulcet man was a caravan, flaunting himself; then a magic carpet always blown homeward, from the raucous periphery to the cork-lined womb. He fed on himself, knowing that to write a short story you force a camel through a needle's eye, and to write a definitive conspectus of your own time you force a whole epoch through the cerebral cortex of a high strung man-about-town.

As soon as we read him, his memory becomes ours. As soon as we have read him, our own memories become more alive than usual, infected, or infested, by his. By becoming the entity known as the Narrator (who is not altogether Marcel Proust), Proust becomes more than himself. And we, by surrendering ourselves to the Narrator's power at each reading, go beyond ourselves while the book teaches us not so much how to remember as how to behave when we do.

For instance, when the Narrator begins "Time and again I have gone to bed early," his name is already lost in time, and the following seven volumes of *A la Recherche du Temps Perdu (In Search of Lost Time)* are written or uttered by someone with whom we have a pretend familiarity, knowing him as we sometimes know pets or children. His blanked-out name stands for the blanked-out part of his life. It is as if we were all icebergs, yearning for the missing or invisible seven-eighths. For non-French readers, Proust is like Christopher Robin saying his prayers at the foot of the bed, daring the Almighty his soul to take as he drifts away into never-never land, hoping to awaken next morning *complete* and *intact*.

According to some readers, Proust's method is passive; to others, it is brisk and energetic, almost Promethean. Proust has it both ways, both sloth and quest. Now the couch potato wins, now the go-getter. You have to be both in a trance and mentally busy to recall a total past, warmly alive again, as the Narrator is; you sip tea and nibble madeleine cakes at your aunt's, and an entire episode comes back, all the close-ups that bring a whole atmosphere with them.

But let's be realistic. Not much of the 3,000-page book comes from the silky undulations of unique memory. More of it comes from tidy, accurate recall, from a memory not only photographic (it omits nothing) but pedantic too (it *insists*). So *In Search of Lost Time* has a double weave. A good deal of it is mystical speculation, such as the following:

> In Vinteuil's music, there were thus some of those visions which it is impossible to express and almost forbidden to contemplate, since, when at the moment of falling asleep we receive the caress of their unreal enchantment, at that very moment in which reason has already deserted us, our eyes seal up and before we have had time to know not only the ineffable but the invisible we are asleep.

And a great deal of it comes under the heading of social, worldly advice. One of the book's characters, Saint-Loup, whom the Narrator has hitherto found kind and tenderhearted, explains how to get a servant fired:

> "What! you mean to say you don't know how to get a fellow you don't like sacked? It's not difficult. For instance, you need only hide the things he has to take in. Then, when they'[re in a hurry and ring for him, he can't find anything, he loses his head. My aunt will be furious with him, and will say to you: 'But what's the man doing?' When he does show his face, everybody will be raging."

So here he is, drinking up his hypersensitive childhood and the music he adores, but also in memory restaging the antics of various social tribes, from Odette the free-floating courtesan and the petit bourgeois Verdurins, mean and clannish, to the unshakable and eccentric aristocrats the Guermantes. One character, Swann, from the upper reaches of the bourgeoisie, links the two tribes, spending much of his time with the Guermantes but marrying Odette. Their daughter, Gilberte, eventually conquers social Everest by marrying a nephew of one of the Guermantes.

If it all sounds gossipy and petty, it is. There is devastating scandal and savage heartbreak; the bourgeoisie may be groping tactlessly upward while the aristos go on corrupting themselves. It's the kind of seething social circus you find in the novels of John O'Hara and Mordecai Richler, in such movies as *The Godfather, I* through *III*, and Bertolucci's *1900*. The aim is to anatomize society with such adroit selectivity as to seem exhaustive. And yet, just as there are the many who belong, there are the few who don't, the outsiders floating about, in Proust's masterpiece rotten and poignant, such as the Baron de Charlus, "who combines feminine hysteria with the attributes of a grand seigneur." Charlus is one who bleeds psychologically, a comic dandy, one of a race accursed," Proust says: the men who love men. Proust the homosexual presents his own lover in real life, Alfred Agostinelli, as the Narrator's Albertine, a woman, and Albertine's death and transit into oblivion form one of the most grievous, agonizing stretches of prose in the entire novel. To Charlus and Albertine we add Swann, whose clearly delineated shift from fop to climber shades over into farce without losing its caustic moral point.

Proust's gigantic novel interweaves many stories and careers; but he is far from content simply to tell a story. He piles characters up against time. He links stories only to parody the old notion that life has no plot, whereas fiction has. Proust is making a barricade, knowing that in prose you can do almost everything—in particular, doodle with society, doodle with memory, and then, having tampered that far, make society mysterious and memory accessible. Those who pride themselves on remembering everything know no longer how to behave in society, and those who behave well can remember nothing worthwhile. It is better to be a dreamer in both worlds. Proust does all this in such minutely detailed fashion that you begin wondering if he will ever get to the point, and then, after he has got there, if he will ever leave it. He takes preposterous pains to omit nothing, and in his manuscripts additions billow out, unfolding like improvised sails.

Perhaps his prose is an analogue of society itself, of the busy anthill fixed in aspic, with what we will never know about other people evoking all that we will never know about ourselves.

And yet to know so much anyway. Swamped in redundancy, we seek to mend our lives by adding to our psychic and emotional load. The modern human emerges from Proust's hands as a beast of burden, gossip's glutton. As if gossip were the profoundest form of research.

You would think that a writer such as Proust, who revels in the quasi-omnipotence of the masturbator, would handle human relationships with comparable control. Not so. he may be able to pluck social classes from the rainbow of history, just as he does the evasive helium balloons of boyhood rapture. But with individuals, especially beloveds, he finds that ecstasy—the emotion that throws you out of yourself into a trance of adoration—depends on distance, loathing even. He controls best the relationships that might but never do come about. Love arrives in spite of itself. A chemical thing, it cannot come to white heat, to full froth, without some kind of impediment. While coming to the boil, the lover fumes, stamps, mutters and deplores, knowing that peak ecstasy will come only after being fended off. Indeed, Proustian love— that polymorphous perverted sublime—thrives best in the absence of the beloved, an oddly medieval process evoking Chaucer's *Knight's Tale,* in which the two lovers, imprisoned in separate towers, watch their idol, Emily, and howl in unison.

Heaven help them. Proust's lovers—especially the Narrator and his epicene Albertine—torture themselves with refusal, denial, lies infidelity, jealousy, not in some simple parody of *"odi et amo"* (to love is to hate) but profoundly recognizing that human appetite is paradoxical. In the brain the center for rage is close to the center for lust, just as the yawn reflex comes from the same place as the loin twitch (yawn hard and your loins will tremble a bit). In a famous exquisite passage, where the lovers' faces linger so close that their eyelashes become entangled, the emotions that surface are not merely those of hyperfine delicacy and intimacy; they are also those associated with entrapment, claustrophobia and nausea. To be so ravishingly close is also to be offended and overpowered. To Proust, love is exasperating: essential yet repulsive, at its best a private and narcissistic growth, at it worst a humiliation en route to the chamber of horrors.

After Albertine dies, the Narrator writhes in agony because he misses the torture she brought him. He misses his jealousy, the force that propelled and heated their relationship amid the erotic mazes created by "intermittences," as he calls them, of the heart. Human identity, even for lovers, is a process rather than a fixed state. So love comes to be a nervous disease, a twitchy conundrum in which cynicism and exaggeration meet and fester. What the Narrator and Albertine undergo in almost Wagnerian terms, Swann and Odette undergo less grandiosely; but all in Proust's novel who meet and join end up in a ghetto gnawing at one another. Love emerges as espionage, sadism, fever, its only compensation being that the lover who looks out for Number One remains in charge, and shapes the affair not into a permanent union but into a voyeur's Venusberg, a terrible toy analogous to society and memory. Life, Proust saw, is dangerous—made easier, sure enough, by an empty teacup and some sugar, a peach fetched from the Ritz or hot sheets and woolen pullovers, but diurnally monstrous.

You finish your reading of *In Search of Lost Time* by telling yourself, yes, he knew the society and civilization of his times better than anyone. But, being neither reporter nor documentarist, he transformed much of what he saw, involuntarily, I think, providing us with a replica of evolution itself. If evolution, as we have recently been told, is not so much a directed eclecticism as a twitching, autonomous, biological fidget, then Proust reminds us of it. To him, memory, society and love go their own ways almost heedless of the ardent individuals seeking to assert themselves amid the three main nets. Memory won't let you remember what you want to. Society rots while aiming high. And love befouls itself for reasons unknown. Who, confronted with so berserk a trinity, would not plump for the life of imagination, for its benign metamorphoses, its milkable profundity?

Encountering the English writer-diplomat Harold Nicolson, stationed in Paris, Proust asked him how he and his colleagues did things. "We generally meet at ten in the morning," Nicolson began; but Proust stopped him: "No, you're going too fast, begin again. You take the official motorcar, you get out at the Quai d'Orsay, you climb the stairs, you enter the committee-room. What happens then?" Avid for the merest detail, Proust can seem helplessly obsessive; but he was infatuated with the texture, the small change, of life, whereas most people—and many novelists—live in a shallow blur.

By 1921, he stumbles and stammers, on one occasion having to ask a waiter some ten times for a mineral water, "Contrexéville." Overdosing himself with opium, Veronal and other narcotics, he sometimes goes for more than a week without food, then troughs on spaghetti or boiled potatoes. Or he eats nothing but ice cream for weeks on end. When he has the strength to hold the telephone, he listens to live performances on his Théatrophone, for which the subscription is sixty francs. He can sing the part of Pelléas from Debussy's opera *Pelléas et Mélisande,* becoming especially fond of the moment when Pelléas proclaims "Ah, I can breathe at last." He seems an accursed man asking to be damned further. Nothing is enough for him. Combining emotions in a heroic fashion, he creates the massive album of an entire society. Life, he tells us, is full of lawless magic that always goes wrong. Dead, and laid out with a large bunch of violets on his chest, he seemed more defunct than other corpses. His face assumed a greenish majesty, one eyelid slightly raised. But Céleste had forgotten her promise to bind his fingers with a rosary brought back from Jerusalem. It mattered little. The Midnight Sun had left behind him a coffer full of artificial light.

II

If there is an exalted view that says literary criticism amounts to more than condiment, handiwipe, substitute, pony, we hear about it only from its exponents, who see criticism as an art form. What they never bother to say is that criticism, occupying time you might spend on the original text, should be at least as well-written as that text. Criticism *presumes,* making love to its own obfuscations (and then wastes even more time and space on elucidating them.)

Such is one problem with Julia Kristeva's little book on Proust, actually a series of lectures given at the University of Kent in a series honoring T.S. Eliot (whose criticism has singular grace and perspicacity). Reading Kristeva, as she tries to puzzle out Proust, I found myself saying Proust does this kind of thing better, deciphering the world far more deftly than she deciphers him. But she does have ideas, all of which come from him.

There is another problem having to do with Proust: we should not try to understand him too well; we should swing with him, allowing his voluptuous analysis of perplexity to be the aesthetic object, allowing it to stand as a unique vase or jug might stand, requiring all of our attention but none of our interpretation. Kristeva tidies him up, makes him zealously deliberate, a man who doesn't so much move with the lunges of his mind as write because he knows what writing is for. The warning has always been there, in his notion of the involuntary memory, which cannot be harnessed to serve. We are its passive ministrants, obliged maybe to make sense of our responses to him but not of his to time, memory, loss: the subjects that chose themselves for him.

This said, we can see Kristeva, psychoanalyst and professor of linguistics, clarifying her own response, especially in the light of Georges Bataille's concept, "the profanation of the mother," which means that, for the mother to become literature, she must die and then be exploited without the usual propriety. She becomes malleable raw material, neither loved nor revered, stuff for brothel chit-chat. (This is akin, perhaps, to the notion that you have good sex with people you most dislike.) Her most attractive idea, however, is that of communion within a cathedral, almost an echo of Gombrowicz's interhuman church. Proust, she argues, creates a sacred place in which our own dreams float in the orbit of his; or we simply adopt his dreams as our own. Here, perhaps again, is Eliot's sacred wood. Here the word is therapeutic. Here dreams are dispossessed of us and given back to us as objects of infinite modulation. I think she feels Proust on her senses with exquisite finesse and doesn't need to hammer or twist him into symmetry under this or that heading, whether it be "polytopia," "textual genetics," or a movement that is "metaphorico-metonymic."

Altogether more telling is her quotation from *Contre Sainte-Beuve*, in which Proust lays it on the line: "we all kill those who love us by the preoccupation we cause in them, by that very restless tenderness which we breathe in and put ceaselessly on its guard." To love someone, he means, is to afflict them, and to abort that love is to emancipate them. Hence there is a guilt of loving and a related guilt of unloving, with the latter easier to bear because it restores love to the level of what Eliot called sexual "eugenics" (and *he* knew). This ambivalence is one of the most interesting things in Proust, who understood better than even Freud the endless metamorphoses of the loved object, whether a person or a place name, a bicycle or a steeple.

Kristeva imparts a good deal of information on the provenance of Proust's masterpiece (Notebook 3 contains eight versions of the narrator's awakening) and the sources of his abstract ideas (Darlu, his old tutor, drawing heavily on Lachelier and Ravaisson). Like some detective, she tracks all the radiating tangential evocations of the famous madeleine without ever realizing that readers' imaginations will please themselves and remain unconstrained. She's a bit Procrustean, hunting *the* Proust. She's good, though, on Proust's gynecology and the way in which, writing *A la Recherche,* he seems to be "making a *dress.*"

Is this book, then, to put alongside the brilliant short studies by Samuel Beckett and the late Howard Nemerov? It's almost subtle and keen enough to be there rather than lost like a razor blade among the deadwood tomes of paraphrasing professors.

[1993, 1994]

Thomas Mann, Englishman

W HY I LIKE HIM, and why he dismays others, it is not hard to say. Mann is weight, vision, elegance, length, and steadiness. He carefully considers everything before allowing himself to become symphonic. He selects and massively elaborates images which not only reverberate into every area of being but also provide him with a structural core which is part of the core of life: the sanatorium; Faustus; Joseph's brothers; Krull the rootless, and the helplessly rooted Buddenbrooks. In almost all of his works you find ancient, primitive patterns of life—disease, ambition, kinship, wandering, and stability, not to mention birth, naming, procreation, and death—intermixed with the patterns man has devised throughout the ages to clothe and disguise them. In millions of words he fuses an almost boundless primitive awareness with a voracious regard for what William James called "the big blooming buzzing confusion" of everyday life. And this fusion is a rare thing: you find it elsewhere only in Shakespeare, Cervantes, Dostoyevsky, Proust, Faulkner, Nabokov and a few others. It amounts to thoroughness of witness and makes Mann's *oeuvre* what every good poem should be: an inexhaustible object of contemplation.

Additionally, of course, there is his didactic, textbook side. he aims to teach men about Man; and our incidental, intermittent moods—levity, gravity, boredom, euphoria, despair, and so on—all come under and are made to serve the almost punitive gravity of his main purpose, which is to celebrate life in the act of proving how deathbound it is.

This is why Mann is great and not just very good. His vision is grand enough to survive all his minutiae, and his reportorial eye is the exact servant of his mind. His total vision is the sum of seeing and of seeing beyond, which is not the same as being observant and a little clairvoyant. Rather, it means becoming expert in, say, something as metaphysical as the facial and the non-facial quality of human faces. He is out to entertain, yes: *en passant;* but he intends mainly to instruct, to give a comprehensive postgraduate course in the physics and faith of being human. It is not surprising that he endorsed Philip Toynbee's description of him as the "Isolated World Citizen." Mann himself knew that he looked like some kind of uncoated Joseph, luxuriously disaffiliated and comfortably all-seeing. Because he could not beat life or death, he joined them both; but he joined nothing else. And Philip Toynbee's calling Mann "almost too good to be true," made the point extremely well. Mann agreed. What he saw was "a mere seven hundred words, the most correct thing which has been said about my existence by anyone in England and perhaps anywhere else. Young Toynbee is right. . . ." But few others have come anywhere so near the truth.

Heavy, portentous, long-winded, flatulent, morbid, belletristic, pontifical, pedantic, pretentious, fantast, and drear: Mann's readers (as well as some of his non-readers) have captiously but understandably called him all these things at one time or another. The spirit or mind (or whatever we choose to call the bedraggled, rain-sodden butterfly that animates us) is too empirical and self-conscious to enjoy Thomas Mann, especially the Mann of the longest novels. Confronted with anything sustainedly transcendental, visionary, or metaphysical, the reader lapses into a fit of twitching uneasiness, sniggers with disdain, and settles down again to something reliable: novels of manners or biographies and histories. Not *The Magic Mountain* (it isn't there, as Everest is), the Marble Cliffs, the Society of the Tower, the plights of the Steppenwolf and the Man without Qualities; and even less the grave plunge into Schopenhauer and Nietzsche. Since Hardy and Lawrence, very few English novelists have addressed themselves to what Englishmen—unlike Frenchmen, Americans, and Germans—uneasily call the human condition. Or to the absolute or the cosmos. The honorable, although not always successful exceptions, have been

John Cowper Powys, William Golding, and Graham Greene. The rule, however, and this is true of critics as well as of novelists, is a baffled, faintly derisive averting of attention from Man, God, and Myth to something immediate and measurable such as consciousness of class and the comedy of humors. Allegorical novels from whatever country have usually been received in England with a kind of shopkeeper's or pawnbroker's narrowness; Robert Penn Warren's *The Cave* no less than, say, Hermann Broch's The *Death of Vergil*. From what I can gather, most of those who enjoyed Günter Grass's *The Tin Drum* did so not because it offered a powerful and suggestive myth or archetype, but because it was in some ways comic, and therefore relatable to the frolics of Amis, Burgess, and Wain.

One new incumbent of the Chair of German in the University of London, tenable at Bedford College, lectured inaugurally on the theme, "Much is Comic in Thomas Mann." After Professor Erich Heller's ironic German, Professor Ronald Peacock's funny one. A change, they say, is as good as a jest. But not much in Thomas Mann is comic, although he has comic scenes. It is typical of the English to try to rescue him from his own apocalypse, to distort him in order to accept him. In this way, presumably, the English can forgive him his long-windedness and his passion for archetypes. One almost wonders if the printer didn't make an error, producing "Comic" when he should have set up "Cosmic," and if the Professor didn't obligingly change his theme.

On the one hand, Professor Peacock says, "a vast amount of work has been expended on interpreting Mann's novels as analyses of modern European man trapped between nihilism and ruthless ideologies. It is of course true. . . ." It is of course nice of him to concede that much. After all, the trapped man is a European, a foreigner over there across the water where they are always getting worked up about angst, commitment, alienation, existence, essence, suicide, and the absurd—words no reader feels obliged to use in arranging or ending his life. So much for Europe. "Of course," Professor Peacock goes on, in that strangely patronizing way the English have of crediting other people with their own banalities, "most people have realized that Mann's last, and unfinished, novel, written in his late seventies, about an elegant-minded confidence man and embezzler, is indeed a comic novel." One wonders who had *not* realized. And then we are informed that

Mann himself told his daughter Erika that the first volume of the *Joseph* series "is rather grand and much is comic, as always." He also on another occasion objected that people always discussed his irony and never his humor, always his version of what he called "the Erasmian smile of irony" and never his version of "the laugh from the heart." There is no doubt of it: Thomas Mann, both in his daily life and in his writing, liked humor and tried to cater to those who wanted to laugh. But, it seems to me, his humor is always handicapped.

He is so self-conscious about it. With him it is not a libertine eruption but a carefully planned foray into the vein. He is always watching himself while he does it; his use of humor is deliberate. He knows that any writer trying to be comprehensive is obliged to provide samples of many human attitudes. In his 1943 address to the Library of Congress he confesses how readings in Laurence Sterne helped to keep him "in the right mood" during the last *Joseph* years. "Naturally," he says, "it was the humorous side of the *Joseph* which profited by this reading. Sterne's wealth of humorous expressions and inventions, his genuine comical technique, attracted me, for to refresh my work I needed something like this." That is revealing. Notice that Sterne's comical technique is genuine (as distinct from his own, which he knows is an act of will) and how wanly, how jadedly, he speaks of "refreshing" his work. This is not the statement of a master comedian helplessly finding everything bulging into fun at the touch of his hand, but rather the aristocratic, punctilious dandy who fussed when the soup was scorched or the butter not quite fresh and who in his novels sought tirelessly for completeness, for a gigantic filigree in which the problem of man would be proven indivisible—the humor from the calamitous, the political and social from the metaphysical. The essentially comic novelist revels in disorder, untidiness and commotion; and clearly Mann is not a Grimmelshausen, a Cervantes, a Smollett, or a Sterne. Instead, he is a master weaver of epic tapestry, like Firdusi the Persian poet he so much admired. Anxious to include everything in his last masterwork, he says of the *Joseph* tetralogy, "the whole work . . . seeks to blend a great many things, and because it receives and imagines everything human as a unity it borrows its motives, memories, allusions, as well as linguistic sounds from many spheres." It is the same search as we find in *The Waste Land* and *Finnegans*

Wake and it is, above all, what Mann said he himself was: "desperately German."

It is generally said that the German mind is all of a piece; it breeds polymaths and abolishes compartments. And Mann himself speaks of the aesthetic, the moral, and the socio-political as inseparable from one another. There is, he says, a human totality which brooks no denial. Small wonder that he links the epic spirit ("it wants the whole") to the novel, requiring a cosmic irony that is an irony of the the heart, "a loving irony." This is the opposite of English taste, which makes humor a social thing, whereas Mann—calculating and plotting his epic novel, loading it and embellishing it—evolves a strategical humor that is cosmic: something robust enough and impersonal enough to counter his cosmic morbidities yet not so robust as to demolish characters already deficient in vigor. To match his study of the *Tendenz zum Abgrund* Mann has to seek for contrast; but he rarely seems to be having any fun himself. The depths must laugh and profundity must smile, as Goethe says, but only because all seriousness springs from death. In *The Transposed Heads* Nanda dismisses Schridamann's death wish as mere lovesickness. This is not so much comic relief as, on Mann's part, a reduction to manageability—a counter motif in the impersonal pattern. Again, he describes the *Joseph* tetralogy as "a humorous, ironically softened—I am tempted to say a 'bashful' poem of man." The story has been distanced, tempered, towards the monumentality of myth. "The attainment of the mythical viewpoint," Mann says, "is of decisive importance in the life of the narrator; it signifies a peculiar enhancement of his artistic mood, a new serenity in recognizing and shaping . . . ." And this impersonal obligation is what, in *Joseph in Egypt,* transforms the erotic content into something mythical: through his two dwarfs, Mann connects the erotic with the pernicious and thus, as he explains, hopes to reconcile us to Joseph's chastity. It is a deliberate, tactical move, and hardly the outpouring of any spirit of fun or embodiment of guffaw. Mann is a planner; and his humor, far from impulsive or spontaneous or even violent, is architectonical. It is a means of control, not an eruption. It is implicit in his statement that he follows the dates of Genesis "with semi-jocular faithfulness." To be semi-jocular is to be no more than a joke's ghost.

Mann himself expounded and justified his way of using humor. Almost like Nietzsche, aching to bring science and art closer together, he emphasizes what he calls the critical element and cites Dmitri Merejkowski on Pushkin and Gogol. In Pushkin we find unconscious creativity: the fecund mind spilling and distributing itself from sheer richness. The emotion is allowed its head; the episode or portrait becomes an act of euphoric, almost voluptuous self-indulgence. Pushkin, like someone in Mann's own Berghof, becomes a law to himself, a specialist in engrossment and expansion. But he fails to evolve and apply standards that do not derive from the speciality he has drifted into. His work remains homogeneous. And in this, Mann says, he fits both Schiller's notion of the naïve and Merejkowski's notion of poetry.

On the other hand, what Schiller calls the sentimental and what the Russian philosopher finds distinguishing Pushkin from Gogol— criticism—is precisely what Mann finds modern and seeks to practice in his own writing. It is typical of Mann to seek a corrective to the mythical, relentlessly poetic, essentially German side of himself. But notice: he does so after a calculated appraisal; his intelligence is advising his creative impulse. And his resort to criticism—to a creative consciousness such as Gogol's—shifts his work from homogeneous to heterogeneous with great success, but the humor which is the means of that shift, which is the *moyen de possession,* remains a deliberately planted integer, as unlikely to captivate the reader as to dominate the text. "Look," it seems to say: "I am an instance of humor; I show you that Thomas Mann is not an accidental or an oblivious writer. I am here, almost in the spirit of a Brechtian narrator, to stop you from lulling yourself into complete empathy. This is fiction, myth: Thomas and Anna Buddenbrooks, Kröger, Castorp, Settembrini, Lotte, Goethe, Aschenbach, Joseph, and Krull—they are not real, any more than Faust was real. They are motifs in a symphonically conceived demonstration; they are diagrammatic. They are no more people than the sounds of Beethoven are human emotions. And when they work or eat themselves to death, or when the glutton is rebuked by the offer of a Lenten snack, or when Thomas Buddenbrook dies of an abscessed tooth and a surfeit of Schopenhauer, or when Krull makes his faces, or when Christian Buddenbrook mimics, or when Lotte confuses Werther's kiss with Goethe's, or when Thomas Mann with his usual grace finesse insinuates himself into the telling as Serenus Zeitblom or heavily says he subscribes to the tradition of the Emperor Carolus, then you are being admitted to the spectacle of Thomas Mann deciding it is time to be satirical, mocking, ironic, farcical, derisive, grotesque, facetious, and so on."

There are always inflections in the voice and they are those of an elaborately deliberate performer who knows he has behind him a whole German tradition of earnestness and solemnity. Mann unbends but he hardly ever relaxes. He knows so acutely what levity is for that he himself does not participate in the laugh. Professor Peacock goes so far as to align Mann with Rabelais, but this is clearly a slab of English fog. What he calls Rabelais's "colossal capacity for playful comment and movement, disporting itself in a riot of verbal creation" is as far from the relentless, fastidious march of Thomas Mann as from that of Henry James. That is my point; in part. Rabelais is the improviser; like Pushkin, he lets the whim of the moment lead him and somehow contrives to make the reader aware of this. If Rabelais, Pushkin, and, say, Joyce are Dionysian writers who yield showily to sudden accesses of mental and verbal energy, Mann and James and Proust give the impression of always writing to a pattern of always observing a pre-determined decorum of tone: always subjecting the notion of the moment to a cool part of the mind. In a word: Apollonian. Mann's humor is that especially, as well as being bookish and elaborate. It is a conscious and circumspect condescension, like that of T.S. Eliot. It is at its best in *The Magic Mountain* and *Doctor Faustus* where Mann is forging his own myths and images. In The Holy Sinner, on the other hand, which Professor Peacock commends for "a miraculously light touch," Mann is ill at ease because he is trying to combine the irrec-oncilable: a point about the human condition—a point made with baneful gravity—and what is in fact and effect a game with mari-onettes. He cannot have it both ways. These are not merely extremes; they are mutually exclusive extremes. It is like trying to make Punch and Judy stand in for Pilate and Mary. And Mann tries to do this only because, as a German, he is unduly afraid of making his point in the way Schiller called naïve. In trying to fuse genres which are discretely successful in Eliot's *Murder in the Cathedral* and Kafka's *Metamor-*

phosis, respectively, Mann reveals a lack of ease with both Christian myth and medieval Märchen. A less fastidious, a less deliberate writer would not have got himself into this position in the first place. Once again we see Mann's resolve to erase dividing lines. His German passion for unity leads him into bold schemes which he thinks will bring about what he admires in Shakespeare: "the cosmic irony of art." But, in fact, he is too self-conscious to manage what Shakespeare achieved through sheer impersonality and self-exclusion. Shakespeare's dramatic irony becomes part of the world he portrays, whereas that of Mann remains an essential maneuver in his literary performance. Falstaff begins as a caricature and ends up transcending that status; Spinell in *Tristran,* like Fitelberg in *Doctor Faustus,* remains a caricature throughout because Mann, ever as didactic as deliberate, cannot float him free from his initial moorings.

From all this we might think Mann belongs with the novelists and dramatists of the Absurd; but not quite. Whereas they juxtapose in order to express their theme, Mann juxtaposes for technical reasons that have much to do with his being a German trying to fulfill epic pretensions without lapsing into naïveté. But this does link him to the English (of all people), whose comic juxtapositions—in the worlds of Angus Wilson, Anthony Powell, and Joyce Cary—are just as technically strategical as Thomas Mann's: they are a means of managing self-consciousness. Mann tries to be non-German; the English try to forget they are social beings. And both end up being respectively more German, more social, than before. The comedy of Mann and the nervous giggles of those English novelists are too functional to captivate the reader, at whom they are not directed in the first place. The genuine humorist, deep down, must be fond of chaos, must revel in untidiness; and this Mann cannot do. He so lucidly and neatly addresses himself to the business of humor that, like his own Prince in *Royal Highness,* trying to transcend his public role, he only succeeds in magnifying it. Mann's ways of de-Germanizing his work are more German than what he is trying to shed. They are English too—not in the way of Shakespeare and Dickens, whom sheer energy led beyond tactics, but according to the gospel of categories. Humor as a defense, a corrective, and a calisthenic is an essentially English thing; and this is what we find in Mann, going as it does beyond the irony attributed to him and into the region of exorcism: a technique of expulsion by which humor does not irradiate, or melt into, a novel but pits it, punctuates it, forestalls a too willing suspension of disbelief and in other words makes the reader himself acutely self-conscious. He watches the words from the outside, just as the English novelists watch their world of manners, just as Mann's ailing heroes watch theirs. Thomas Mann himself, needing humor against what he thought German naïveté, did not relish chaos enough to be outrightly funny. His very recourse to all the forms of humor—irreverence, satire, bawdy, caricature, cartoon, badinage, deflation, hyperbole, pun, bathos, sarcasm, mockery, juxtaposition—is ascetic: he watches like Baudelaire in the sexual act; he watches himself doing it and regrets the necessity. Just as his heroes regret having to have bodies.

In the long run, humor—whether that of Rabelais, Shakespeare, Dickens, or Pushkin—involves its creator in its operations and exposes him for what he is. Humor cannot remain cerebral, cannot be conceived aloofly. Take, for instance, Dickens's comment in *A Tale of Two Cities:*

> It was the best of times, it was the worst of times, it was the
> age of wisdom, it was the age of foolishness, it was the
> epoch of belief, it was the epoch of incredulity, it was the
> season of Light, it was the season of Darkness, it was the
> spring of hope, it was the winter of despair.

This sounds aloofly diagnostic, but it is really Dickens in a special mood, self-consciously proving the futility of trying to interpret at all. And the proof does not end where that sentence does; Dickens the man, the temperament, the presence, goes on accumulating behind the verbal accumulation. Humor such as this amounts to a kind of moral infection, its only value residing in Dickens' implied susceptibility to it. Mann's humor, on the other hand, is the literary equivalent of protocol. It sobers us and leaves us suspended: after it has expended itself, there is no one there. After realizing Dickens' point in that dialectical dead-end I have just quoted, we have a strong sense of his presence (the whole statement being a device to draw attention to himself—to personality after analysis has failed). But our no doubt amused response to, say, Dr. Krokowski the psychologist in *The Magic Mountain,* as he stands behind the little table with arms outstretched like Jesus, is to something quite different.

> It turned out that Dr. Krokowski, at the end of his lecture, was making grand-style propaganda for the dissection of souls, and with arms outspread summoned everyone to come unto him. Come unto me, he said, though in other words, ye who are weary and heavy-laden. And he left no doubt as to his conviction that all, without exception, were weary and heavy-laden.

Where the Dickens consolidates itself into genially offered absurdity, so that we feel impelled to exclaim, "Yes! here is a wise mind indeed!" the Mann confronts us with absurdity and then leaves us, like Stendhal's Lamiel, "with nowhere to go." Dickens's little heap of conflicting observations is a mere prologue to himself; we feel the absurdity is as nothing compared with the human ability to report it and yet stay sane. Mann's report has about it a blasé finality which, while alerting us to his presence, deprives us of him at the last word. Dickens, setting his paradoxes in rhythmical and syntactical parallel, constructs a synthesis amounting to zero. Mann, forcing an interpretation from the outset, credits Krokowski with words he did not say (the narrator has to have those words on which to build his ironic, mock-numb conclusion). Trying too hard, Mann smothers the very fatuity he is trying to expose; and we end feeling we might even have been misinformed. So much presentation; so few facts. If you cry wolf all the time, you get a sore throat; and if you cry it so hard, as Mann does here through interpretation, parallel, anaphora, and a report that is really a convenient distortion, no one attends and your reader suspects the situation isn't funny anyway, least of all to you. All he knows is that now and then you resolve to include something grotesque, as if from a pipette.

So Dickens achieves his effect by strategical casualness whereas Mann wastes effects through too much nudging. Life is bizarre enough without having the bizarre forced upon it. It is as if Mann, regarding the epic novel as *"une mer à boire,"* dumped salt into it at regular intervals, just to make sure. That is what comes of cherishing Goethe's dictum that irony "Is that little grain of salt which alone renders the dish palatable."

As I say, Mann is more than a little English in the strategies he practices with his private self. Happier in the role of humorist than when laughing, he subjects his conceptions to a firm but somehow impersonal hand. Like the typical Englishman E.M. Forster—heart not cold but somewhat "undeveloped"—Mann has a fully developed manner but is curiously reticent. He is self-deprecatory in the sense of minimizing himself in a routine way. As if the self could not face the light of day and had to remain wrinkled up, squinting out from the folds: nervous, brittle, almost coy, and always aloof. This is very English. And Mann, acutely aware of the German alliance between psychology and metaphysics, between anecdote and myth, between Life and Thought, does minimize himself. He does not know which idea to utter. Uncomfortable at not having the all-encompassing idea but also at belonging to a tradition of all-encompassing ideas, he reserves himself in an idiosyncratic way which is not, as people so readily say, that of irony (for irony implies an intended opposite) but that of the man who doesn't mean what he says yet doesn't mean its opposite either. Mann's manner is one of embarrassment before the inexplicability of life. "Isn't life," he seems to say with Katherine Mansfield's young girl, "Isn't life . . . ." Like her, he cannot supply the complement.

His niceties, then, are cosmic and functionally different from those of the English. At first glance, Mann saying "I do not have much faith, nor do I believe very much in faith," might suit the English. A man who says this should be content with the sort of work that Novalis said Goethe's was: "He is in his work what the English are in their goods: highly simple, neat, comfortable and lasting. He [Goethe] accomplished for German literature what Wedgwood did for the world of English arts. . . ." But Mann is too German for that, too seraphic. And this is where he parts company with the English and adopts the reticences and Mona Lisa smiles of the man who, making elaborate connections between ideas and anything else, cannot admit defeat. What in Mann would have been an oasis of honor in a desert of ennui, or a non-committal *que sais-je?* like Ionesco's or Beckett's, becomes a dialectical exercise that is sometimes quite barren.

Mann might have done well to emulate Chekhov, whom he extolled in his last essays. Chekhov did not try to go beyond mere depiction, and his depiction is neither ironic nor embarrassed. Mann, however, anxious to show the total of life, injects humor and then feels self-conscious to the point of heavy-handed evasiveness. No wonder *Felix Krull* seems a release: he can just invent and concoct; he doesn't have to think. The picaresque is the necessary idiom of those who cannot make sense of life and therefore, without a thought, drink what Camus called the wine of the absurd and eat the bread of indifference. Mann's familiar young man, leaving home and family and venturing into the unknown region of the outside world, this time and almost for the first time embodies much of Mann himself, content to survive and enjoy and not to reason why. When the riddle of the universe cannot be answered (and that is always) then surely, the novel indicates, a whole culture and its history from Genesis to Kuckuckian post-Einsteinian physics is enough.

I have been arguing (desultorily, I know) that although Mann's symbolism and myth are less congenial to current English tastes than tastes before 1945, his resort to humor as a means of dispelling or exploiting his embarrassment is in fact curiously English and affords English readers a spurious way into his novels. In the process I have, willy-nilly, harped on Mann's only weak point; if indeed it is weak at all. It only looks weak when we pretend, as I think Professor Peacock does, that it is an important part of his work. It is wiser, I think, to regard Mann's almost spinsterly amusement at himself as a by-product of his mighty endeavors. Let us note it, and pass on. Mann reminds me not of Jane Austen or Saint Teresa but of Anarcharsis who, hearing that the sides of ship were four fingers thick, said that the passengers were just that distance from death. Such a thought may well scare the English reader back to deck tennis or quoits whereas Mann, "desperately German," broods further, pushing through the four inches of *das Boat*. That is what I mean above all: there is no protection in his work; nothing to distract us or to soothe; nothing to put—for long, at any rate—between ourselves and his sense of death and his sense of life. Hence my caveat.

Mann's unrelenting effort to write the novel of scope—something like a German *Moby-Dick* or a German parallel to The *Brothers*

Karamazov—is alien not to the achievement of Hardy, Lawrence, and perhaps E.M. Forster, who already seem writers of a distant time, but to the small-mindedness and petty dimensions of those—novelists and critics and readers—who have succeeded those three and their contemporary devotees without inheriting from them. To those who will listen, without evolving coy ways of misconstruing what they hear, Mann speaks with a majestic importunity belying his reserve. It would be a shame if sympathy with him and his purposes lapsed into the keeping of university professors of German and of other specialists. It would have been worthwhile to speak out if only to resist one attempt to characterize Mann as a "comic" writer (which is like calling Aesop an historian or Goethe a crystallographer). There is no point, as I see it, in trying to write novels according to principles less thorough than his (as Günter Grass proves, taking up where Mann left off and, if anything, taking on even more). We must, I repeat, see those principles plainly and not distort them to suit our whims.

The snow-sequence in *The Magic Mountain,* generally acknowledged as one of Mann's most magnificent pieces of writing, has an equally magnificent counterpart in the snow-valley scenes in D.H. Lawrence's *Women in Love.* Hans Castorp, enveloped in the white darkness, falls asleep, dreams vividly, and wakes again, awakened to the antinomies of life and death. In *Women in Love,* which argues for something very close to Mann's own "friendliness to life," Gerald Crich dies in the snow, having irrevocably committed his life to the deathliness of industrial Western society. In each instance a symbol is offered, an epiphany or vision is suggested. Such offers and such suggestions may not be the stock-in-trade of the literary sociologists or the froth-headed fun-mongers who often pass for novelists today, but they must in large part be that of imaginative novelists. This, I contend, is the way to reach the authentic Thomas Mann. The questions have not changed. No cosmic assessor has endorsed or refuted any of the conflicting answers. The boat of Anacharsis is still what it was. Imagination is still with us (isn't it?). And so too, through the uses of imagination, is Thomas Mann's embarrassment by the universe and the uninvited snows.

[1969]

Night 1002:
When It All Goes Down

O PEN SESAME: As you near checkout, with its overtones of death, the trim domain called Supermarket offers you a look into the unruly. Sixty-nine cents gives you permanent rights over a vertical trapdoor placarded with such enticing legends as the girl who gave birth while skydiving (the baby was born in free-fall); the Borneo tribe doomed after eating a young Swiss scientist who had AIDS; a cave that cures arthritis; and a space alien (already drawn in color on the front page) who cured a teenager's acne. You do not even have to pay, not if the line at checkout is long enough. You have time to scan the rest, from the child wholly allergic to light (with regular exposure she would lose the tips of her fingers and toes, her nose and ears) to the Austrian baby born with horns, from Paulette Schaedel whose home is stuffed with model pigs, 740 says the report, to the seventy-four-year-old blond widow whose golden hair provided the cross hairs in World War II bombsights. Most folk that I've seen scan and then buy, lured into a further relationship with the marvelous. This is how the abstracted supermarket shopper tunes up his or her senses, calling back Sindbad and Aladdin, if they ever indeed left us, moving on from daily mundanity to a permanent 1002nd Night in which we all become part of something wilder than ourselves. We turn into sports of nature, prodigies of lust or charm, suffering hyper-Dickensian coincidences. By proxy, we get out of hand.

For some, more specialized than most supermarketeers, this sixty-nine-cent rag revives the icons of Jacobean drama or the Gothic English-German novel, but even such rarefied recognitions as these dangle from the same peg of the antihumdrum. And here it all is, packed in tight, a tribute to our faith in the unpredictable. Life is not only queerer than we think it is; it is queerer than we can imagine. Edna Sulvang's cat ate her savings, $1200, because it was suffering from pica. Bigfoot, most lately seen by Robert France of Vandergrift, Pa., smells like rotten eggs. Chinese diggers have found a tomb containing a woman some two thousand years old whose brains cells and other tissues respond to induced stimuli so much that doctors are trying to clone her, splicing her DNA with DNA from a living organism. As Harold Nicolson said, only one man in a thousand is boring, and he's of interest because he's a man in a thousand. But the assumption begins to form that, even though everything is wonderful if studied thoroughly enough, some things just have the edge anyway. Created by humans, or gods, they redound to the gods' credit.

II

SAILING BEYOND: Of course, if you save the sixty-nine cents you can make up your own events, from the paraplegic boy scout who gives his hundred-year-old mother a cesarean with a kazoo in a blazing blimp to the Oxford-educated gecko who dictates an Encyclopedia Galactica whenever fed on fresh plaque from human teeth. This is what Cortázar called "sailing beyond the limit," after which comes sailing beyond all previous sailing beyond it, in quest of some Platonic ne plus ultra that cannot exist. Coleridge, that arch-fancier of Fancy and Imagination, that fondler of the difference between the two, would have called the outrageous entries in our sixty-nine-cent rag works of Fancy, which is to say imagination without grandeur or seriousness. And Doctor Johnson would have lumped them along with the brainchildren of the poet Cowley as heterogeneous images yoked by violence together. All very well to knock such things, but the universe itself is no paragon of taste or decorum. More to the point is the popularity of these neomagical rags, making us wonder if they exist and thrive because what's in books no longer offers the magical, the outrageous, the preposterous, the distorted, at least not those read by the average shopper. Popular literature has become humdrum, and so is minimalist fiction; it is Latin American fiction that these rags are closest to, but then it is anthropology that is closest to Latin American fiction, closer than it is to any other "-ology."

The vision of the novel as an instrument for detecting the rise and fall of a social class is one thing, but the vision of the novel as the source of the preposterous is another, and far older. One of the perils that literature is heir to is the risk that it may try to be too responsible, that writers may try to make it so, after the example of Camus, Sartre, and others, whereas it exists as much to regale and stagger us as to preach and curb. Our sixty-nine-cent *Sun,* edited from Boca Raton and printed in Canada, together with its siblings, is solidly in the business of providing myth and legend, fantasy and folk tale, in lamentable prose, to be sure, but all the same it gives the mind and the senses a run for their money.

Whenever I pick one up, I have the weird feeling that I am once again reading the classics, Ovid or Lucian, *Beowulf* or Malory, not least because, in fleeing the norms, this popular press confirms them. Like Homer and Virgil, who also lived in a world that included star-nosed moles, waltzing mice, and kelp that grows as much as eighteen inches a day (not to mention cats with pica and children whom daylight fries). I feel I am in touch with one of literature's older impulses, pre-industrial of course, and I suspect that, even if you fed all the lurid stories from all the tabloids for a year into a computer, established highest common factors and so forth, you would only have identified a few categories and proved the monotony within the seemingly endless variety. What's important here is the basic respect for life's incalculability, for its sheer generative élan. Life is wondrous, and people like to be told so without having to perform the hard graft of nonstop observership. So they resort to preposterous things in tabloid form to remind themselves of the same message. If reverence for life has gone underground, and I mean life as an end in itself, heedless of human desires, then the tabloid wondermags, in their Ripley's Believe It or Not fashion, bring it back into the light again. In one sense these newspapers are mystical, always paying zoological or cytological homage whether or not their editors know it, and feeding the vast insensate curiosity out there where folk like to believe in the *happenable*. Why, it could almost be. Maybe it was. It will surely happen one day, anyway, even if it hasn't happened yet. There is a humility behind this attitude: we don't know everything, it says, and we never will.

III

HELEN'S DOUCHE: Go now to what looks like the other extreme: high culture, highbrow; I say *looks* because Euripides was a popular highbrow, almost a demystifying lyricist. In his play *Trojan Women*, there is no source for what happens in Michael Cacoyannis's film version, in which Irene Pappas plays Helen, all too briefly. If you are reading or watching Euripides, you get Hecuba telling Menelaus to avoid looking at Helen, his wife, "lest she captivate you with longing." Helen, she says, is a witch. "I know her; so do you and all her victims." At this point Helen enters "beautifully dressed." And she gives Menelaus hell. What Cacoyannis gives us is the Trojan women frantic with thirst, observing Helen's guard backheel a pan of water beneath the bottom plank of the otherwise stone shack in which she is being held. Between the horizontal planks we see Helen first snatch the pan, then shuck her robe, and stand in it. Now she squats. She appears to sluice her face, her hair, her shoulders, then the rest of her body. Although some of the water splashed out when she tugged the pan toward her, there is enough left in which to bathe the rest of her. She remains at the squat until a fusillade of stones from the Trojan women makes her retreat to the back of the shack. Perhaps, as they see her (not as clearly as we from our chairs), she seems to be doing something even lewder. From what we see of their view of her, we might well conclude that the Trojan women see her at the squat, as if relieving herself, no doubt bathing her parts: something more than merely dipping them. As the scene opens, Menelaus exclaims at the brilliance of the sun on "this day in which I shall get possession of my wife" and, soon after, Hecuba says, "she [Helen] sets homes aflame." (Cacoyannis's version is even stronger in that he has Hecuba say *that fire comes from her* to burn homes, "magic for death.") Whatever we imagine, along with the Trojan women who have been refused water to drink, Helen is cer-

tainly getting herself ready to make her entrance, and apparently she
has the finery with her, scorning the "rags and tatters" Hecuba says
she should have worn. But go back a moment.

Let us say that Helen has to somehow dampen down the preter-
natural heat she is famous for. Cacoyannis has her go hard to work,
maybe even coax herself to some kind of climax. She doesn't rush.
Helen is Venus observed, washing her lips and vagina. The women go
berserk, but Helen washes away, perhaps recalling this or that man,
and when she at last comes out and says "Menelaus" in hello, it is with
a purring contralto pillow tone, from the very center of a woman
delighted still to be in heat. Pappas does it with sleek carnality, driving
Menelaus out of his mind all over again. Off he goes with her, raving
about "a vile death for a vile woman," but Cacoyannis has resumed all
her shameless history in that one greeting, so brash and thoughtless.
The sluicing scene is so powerful because no one says anything; all
you hear is the trickle of water as Helen dilutes her most personal
oozings, and you imagine the water in the pan clouding up minute
after minute while the women and Menelaus wait. It's a form of fore-
play, an erotic dawdle. It's a quotation from a brothel scene with the
man washing himself at some discreetly placed basin, except that this
is a woman doing it, ill-screened from an audience of women standing
behind the husband she cuckolded.

To say at least some of these things is to risk seeming overpowered by aphrodisiac (Helen's own excuse, when she says it was all
Aphrodite's fault); but that is not the response of the Trojan women
or of Euripides. It is the fault of Cacoyannis, who wants the action to
stir the viewer in as intimate a way as possible, so that the story of
Helen and Menelaus upsets us not in a modern way so much as in a
way that only nowadays can be talked about. He makes of his viewer,
certainly the male one, a Peeping Tom, mainly because of what he
doesn't show, though his hints come on strong (one's first view of
Helen, for instance, is of brown eyes in their oval slits looking through
a gap between two planks). In no time at all, as with the girl who gave
birth while skydiving or the Borneo cannibals doomed after devouring
Gerald Voisard of Geneva, we are sailing beyond the limit, getting
past the plausible into some twilit zone of original imagining: going
further than the actual text warrants, not (I think) in order to compre-

hend it better but to flesh out in full its hints at dislocation, which is what you have when things that don't belong together team up or when things that do don't.

Consider an impetus that exceeds the traditional limits of control, or even the imaginable ones—Let there be light, and there was light. Scientists call such events *singularities,* meaning the event itself is extraordinary, but the word is misleading, and I should perhaps stay with "dislocation," although Poe's Perverse or De Quincey's Involute are easier to say. We are talking about experiences that seem insufficiently lush, in which the universe's gamut of possibility has not come to bear, and in turn about how humans repair the lack, which they do with various means: hysteria, libido, mutilation. The classical scholar G.S. Kirk speaks enlighteningly in *The Nature of Greek Myths* (1975) about "a sacred interval in the flux of profane experience" and the way in which certain myths "give some kind of 'total perspective'" that links the participant with the primordial generative power of the cosmos. He then goes on to suggest that the disruption, or dislocation, of familiar patterns is in itself life-enhancing and liberating. Greek myths, he argues, are not strong on dislocation, whereas Amerindian ones are, and he cites the one that Lévi-Strauss made famous in *Mythologiques.* The Bororo Indians' young man Geriguiaguiatugo rapes his mother in a forest, for which transgression his father eventually strands him atop a cliff, from which he escapes with the help of a magic stick given him by his grandmother. He then reaches the summit, where he kills some lizards and hangs a few of them around his waist as reserve supplies; but the dead lizards attract vultures who eat them and part of the young man's fundament as well (really his bowels). So he makes a prosthetic fundament (artificial bowels) from a sort of mashed potato. And so on. It is not difficult to invent the headline a sensation-rag would concoct for such a deed.

Put, say, the girl who gives birth while skydiving, Cacoyannis's Helen, and Geriguiaguiatugo together and what emerges is not something atavistic, irrational, or fantastic (though it incidentally has some of these qualities) but something closer to the Absurd or to what Chaucer knew as "aventure or cas." *Nature,* if you like, and a *natura naturans,* in other words finding out what it is like by doing whatever comes naturally. I mean Nature developing an identity by doing what it does next, according to whatever teleology is built into it; according to whatever it selects when we say something is "selected for." True, there is a severely practical aspect to the birth in space, to which skydiving clubs ought to attend (they should hand out specific instructions), but what boggles the mind is the dislocation of the birth from its usual surroundings. Helen's father Zeus was a god of gods, and when she asks her guard for water it's not as if Irene Pappas is doing it. She is natural power tickling herself pink. And young Geriguiaguiatugo is trapped between two worlds, one surgical and colostomical, the other mythic, no doubt having to do with the first colon created. This is not an area of which we can "know" anything, but we can feel an enormous amount about it without quite knowing why—except for recognizing at the same time the sometimes successful transits of evolution. In each case, I suggest, we are getting an image so vivid that we no longer know, or care, what it is an image of. Artaud wanted such things in both theater and literature. So did De Quincey and Poe. God, some wag said, is on the side of the strongest artillery; by the same token, technological humans like to join themselves to processes whose cause (if any), as distinct from their methods, eludes us.

This may be reverting to the habits of our ancestors (atavism), but it is more: it is trying to get behind those habits to the first instance of wonderment, and, say, the first fish to come up on land, the first dinosaur to fly. Of course, where we have no knowledge and may never have it, we invent, contriving to chill ourselves with metaphysical awe that remains partly cozy because we have it down on paper, under control, at least until we begin to entertain it thoroughly in our heads, pondering without being utterly scientific a birth-cry in the near vacuum of a certain altitude (then wondering about the first baby to be born in an ejectible cockpit-pod), or Helen's smugness inasmuch as Aphrodite still hasn't deserted her in spite of all those death sentences, Helen must *know* she is going to win out and spend her old age with Menelaus in peace and quiet, so she dawdles over her douche, she's not human at all, and that's why Menelaus, Zeus's son-in-law, is going to walk to the Elysian Fields alive. As for Geriguiaguiatugo, he makes one wonder at the metaphorical nature of the mashed potato he uses when he is being godlike.

IV

THE EXECUTION OF ADMIRAL WILHELM CANARIS, head of the German Foreign Intelligence Service: I now approach my theme from another angle, recalling my researches. All too often I, the fiction-writer, found the historians had already written my fiction for me. For instance, Hugh Trevor-Roper writes about Canaris's 1945 execution in Flossenberg concentration camp. "He was strangled," Trevor-Roper says, "in six stages, with a noose of thin wire." If we look at the definitive work on Canaris, Heinz Höhne's *Canaris,* published in Germany in 1976, we find that the garrison medical officer, Fischer, who was present at the execution, reported: "The condemned men were herded across the yard to the gallows, one by one. They were made to mount a small pair of steps. Then the noose was placed round their neck and the steps pulled away from under them." Canaris went first. One SS witness says, "The little admiral took a very long time—he was jerked up and down once or twice," whereas Fischer merely states that Admiral Canaris died a "staunch and manly death." Trevor-Roper's six-stage strangling came from an article in *Human Events* (no. 14, 3 April 1946) based on secret-service reports of which no details are provided. Secret service or no, I think the notion of piano wire came from erroneous accounts of the hanging in Plötzensee of eight conspirators on 8 August 1944. All but one or two accounts of the Plötzensee hangings mention piano wire, but the eyewitnesses are clear on the point: what was used was cord, hempen and thin. It is true that the Plötzensee eight were hanged on butcher's hooks affixed to a girder, and that the hooks came from a local butcher. But those six stages for Canaris, his piano-wire noose, and the piano-wire nooses attributed to Plötzensee, come to us out of vengeful embellishment, as if decent humans, obliged to write about such atrocity, feel obligated to make the atrocious seem even worse, to shift it all the way up into an absolute both pornographic and stark.

Deinosis the Greeks called it, this habit of seeing things at their absolute worst, and I can see why indignation—the true voice of God, as someone said—wants to exaggerate. In fact, Nazi hanging was a mode of strangulation sometimes taking twenty minutes; it was in no way an attempt to break the neck, which it is supposed to be in more enlightened regimes. Loath as one is to do so, one has perhaps to give some credit to the Nazis at Flossenburg for trying to curtail the dapper little dog-loving admiral's last agony, unless they were just trying to move things along because four other condemned men awaited their turn. If you have to paddle in this bloodbath you run across minor, demented points of pride edging over into compassion; for instance, carefully kept statistics indicated that the average time in executions by guillotine between the opening of the door to admit the victim and the actual descent of the blade was only seven seconds. One can forgive historians, I suppose, for wanting to make the bad seem worse (although Trevor-Roper, on the same page of the Collier edition as he cites six stages and that noose of thin wire, says that General Fromm, who had Stauffenburg and others shot, was himself *hanged*—but he was in fact *shot,* as all the authorities agree, in Brandenburg prison on 17 September 1946). Sophie Scholl, the theory goes, suffered less than Canaris because she was beheaded and he was hanged. Yet who can say when an agony *begins?* Because we do not know, because we know that pain is also a mental thing, we allow ourselves a good deal of latitude in apprehending such awful things, and I am not sure that a protracted execution is not the most hideous epiphany of all, amply fitting G.S. Kirk's notion of "a sacred interval in the flux of profane experience" and indeed, in the most ironic way conceivable, conferring "some kind of 'total perspective.'" Perhaps this is why the historians get woolly and operatic, zeroing in on piano wire because the offending nation is that of Beethoven and piano wire has more dulcet connotations than thin cord. In their vivid way they are not succumbing to relativism but waxing creative, like the believe-it-or-not rags, like Cacoyannis and Geriguiaguiatugo.

V

THE DILATED EYE: I am talking about the opening-up of an art form wide enough so that the cosmos can pour into it or, if not that, then the uninhibited awareness of the person reading, viewing, listening. It may be, at least on etymological grounds, a form of ecstasy: when, say, the work "throws" the author "out" of it, or when the work throws the person apprehending it out of him- or herself. All the rules and conventions lapse, and you suddenly realize that the New York Met's version of Poulenc's opera *The Dialogues of the Carmelites* is different in at least one respect from that of the Canadian Opera Company: as the singing nuns go to the guillotine, the Met offers a truly shocking thump of the blade whereas the Canadian version offers only a rattle as of drumsticks being shuffled. The guillotine at the Met would behead a bison with ease whereas the Canadian one might put paid to a snowman only.

So with *Shoah:* if you are going to have a nine-hour film about extermination camps, then you really need one that puts you aboard a death train every ten minutes or so, and this is what the film does, whereas the screenplay does not. The film abounds in repetitions and longueurs either edited out of the script or never there in the first place. Reading the words, you would never get that sense of being mentally disemboweled as, once again, the train halts short of Treblinka, goes through the gates of Auschwitz, or heaves gently through greenery or the Polish plain.

As the tolerant reader may divine, I am making my allusive way toward the almost mind-stopping recognition of what it is like to be in the thick of life: to be at the mercy of the mathematical, cytological caprice of the life process; to be human amidst that which is nonhuman but nonetheless has brought us forth. It is what comes to mind when we try to establish the nature of God, the First Cause, the Prime Mover, or whatever. We have met it in Poe, in "The Imp of the Perverse," when we read:

> But out of this *our* cloud upon the precipice's edge, there grows into palpability, a shape, far more terrible than any genius, or any demon of a tale, and yet it is but a thought, although a fearful one, and one which chills the very marrow of our bones with the fierceness of the delight of its horror . . . it involves that one most ghastly and loathsome of all the most ghastly and loathsome images of death and suffering which have ever presented themselves to our imagination—for this cause do we now the most vividly desire it.

It is not your everyday velleity by any means, but you have met it elsewhere, if not in Francis Picabia's *L'Oeil Cacodylate,* then in De Quincey's four-page meditation on a sketch of the Great Nebula in Orion (M 42) in the course of which, anthropomorphizing like mad, De Quincey scares himself to death. If to make art is not to copy the world but to copy the Creator's ways, then to some extent we allow ourselves to copy those ways when we contemplate death or disease, and briefly, although with the delicious loathing that Poe and De Quincey whip into a foam, we assume the role of godlike destroyers, both squirting and zapping, both fructifying and annulling, both a power and something unnameable, as baffling to the astronomers as to the theologians. How perverse of us thus to mimic a perverse universe, but such is the ultimate nursery game, to be seen at its least vehement in Beckett's *Watt,* when Sam and Watt feed frogs, thrushes, and plump young rats to the ravenous rats that glide up and down their pants-legs and " hang upon [their] breasts." It is on these occasions, Sam says, that he and Watt come "nearest to God." Much more pretentious is Hemingway's notion that the hunter bestows the gift of death, which amounts only to safari Naziism. One of its most dignified appearances occurs in Georges Bernanos's *Diary of a Country Priest,* as the priest grapples with the fact of his cancer, and one of its most allegorical in Camus's *The Plague.*

We do not have one word for this ghastly liberty although thousands of books have been written about it in deference to it. The ancient Greek gods often meddled directly in human lives, so that their perversity often decided a human life; but over and above even them was *ánángke,* an impersonal necessity, upholding order in the universe, and faced with it even the gods were helpless. What I am talking about is close to *ánángke,* but I intend the imaginative penetration of it either in quotidian life or in works of art (at junctures carefully set up as zones of anomie, in which an imaginative reader, viewer, listener, can let almost anything happen). The result, I suggest, is not very different from the frisson a savage might feel during an especially ecstatic dance in the course of which he or she slides into a nonhuman frenzy. Call it safety valve in art or life. Call it even a kind of homeopathy, by which you dose yourself with stuffs that mimic in miniature the symptoms of a vast disease. In this case, of course, you take the stuffs (metaphors, most probably) and hope the miniature version will become indistinguishable from the big one: the portrait will become its double, as Artaud might say. And, for an afternoon or a nanosecond, you feel you are behaving like a full-blown deity; like a full-blown whateveritwas that started things off.

Of course this is hopeless anthropomorphism, which would not be so bad if the disease were wholly mental, since the ostensible remedy itself is no more than that. But no, the disease is physical too, entailing our decline and disappearance, not for any given reason beyond the fact this is the gait, the habit, that matter has settled into. Perhaps there is a logic to the argument that runs: all bred breeders have to die, whereas an unbred nonbreeder need not. Perhaps Galileo was, in a limited sense, right when he said that death made sense because old people have to move out for the new. All it would take to put paid to that is one permanent generation such as we have not had except in direst imagination.

VI

A GRAVE OF FLAMING SUNSHINE: The characters we create remind us what it is like to have lips, say, and to sit in a quiet room testing their inner and outer lines with the tip of the tongue, or eyes that can be palped with the fingertips. What a thing to have knees and ankles, heart behind the ribs, a cleft in one's rear and various holes in one's face. This is the thin end, to be sure, not in same league as having a passion to know the nature of the First Cause, but related. And what of the god-given skill, empathy, so often prated about but rarely practiced?

Take Roland Barthes's early book on Michelet (1954). What, he asks all through, did it feel like to be Michelet? Obsessed by the fear of premature burial, he had the coffins of his first wife and his father reopened, and the body of an uncle scarified, just to be sure. Michelet wanted his own body to be exposed to the sun until it decayed. Well, says Barthes, "we know that such a death was in part stolen from Michelet: not only is his wish apocryphal, but instead of the grave of flaming sunshine which he was to have at Hyères, Michelet's widow chose to give him an official and elaborate mausoleum at Père Lachaise." There he lies in the headstone, his head to one side, on his face an expression of tamed exasperation while, bestriding him, an aloof buxom Juno in the raw pink of health flings a finger at heaven while looking away from him at about two o'clock from the noon-line of his legs. She has what one would call an imperial face and a fleshy forearm. She doesn't matter, though, whereas Barthes's phrase "the grave of flaming sunshine" does, expressing Michelet's yearning better than Michelet ever did, even if going a bit too far for the sake of a cogent phrase. It is a wonderful phrase because it flirts with oxymoron, proffering an enclosure as the only open solar death that one can have. After thus irradiating him, they would have to bury him, presumably, to see if he came back to life: the reverse of burial followed by exposure.

I found a dead baby salamander with exquisite yellow tracings just like code on its black flanks, as if it were some formula on legs, designed to walk the world until at last deciphered. I stood it back on its legs and left it in the sun. In no time it had shriveled like a Hiroshima shadow down to the metal coping it had stood upon, an organic decal like a leaf to thin and bleach until only a smear. "What is it like to be *you?*" asks a character in William Golding's *Free Fall,* putting what seems to me one of the most valuable questions any author can mess with. Perhaps we are better at that than at asking what is it like to be ourselves, no doubt because we fear coming up with something commonplace about a tummy upset, sciatica, a twitching nerve in the eyelid. If so, aren't we wrong? My left thumb doesn't' like to stay in its socket. It wanders, and the range of sensations its tiny rectifiable dislocations prompt amazes me. An opposable thumb gone wrong? What priceless raw material, as it were, on hand.

On a much less exalted plane there is the crudely executed drawing I found on the flyleaf of a book (Berry Fleming's The *Fortune Tellers)* on the chest of drawers in a Washington, D.C., hotel room. A fancy hotel, this, with gold faucets in the bathroom; it was obviously a resort of horny diplomats. I was there at the expense of a well-known newspaper, down in D.C. to watch Victor Hugo travestied on stage in *Les Misérables.* I felt like Aladdin, but an Aladdin who had not even spoken, when I turned the page and saw this urgently executed *pasa doble* with its one flukey perfect breast-fed nipple, its

bizarre hint of

coitus through the navel, its chubby-faced satyr of a man, and the strange impression it gave that he had, here and there, wiped the ball of his pen clean before going on. Here is how the inscription ran, or leaked:

Tu Eres una
Puta Conita—Las
piernas tienes abiertas
y te cojes asi.

Both the slapdash squiggler or copperplate panegyrist and his Puta Conita had gone, but they left the room somehow warmed, more with their awkwardness than with their lust. I was their voyeur, by aventure or cas. Who else had opened the book? If anyone, had they noticed that it said 10¢ in the top righthand corner? Had he handed her the book with the drawing in it? Had she smiled at the compliment and handed the book back? Or had he written it to the air, in a masturbation fantasy? Or had he addressed his words to the book itself? I felt closer to him and his P.C. that evening than to Victor Hugo, and I kept imagining different scenarios for the event.

NOTE

Greek *ekstasis* was originally a medical word meaning "dislocation of a joint" and inferably dislocation of the mind, which is to say either putting it where it has no habit of being or keeping it where it is but as something different. The mycologist R. Gordon Wasson has suggested that *ekstasis* was the state of mind achieved by someone initiated into the Eleusinian Mysteries, a cult central to the Greek religious experience for a thousand years. Initiates drank an ergot solution containing psychotropic alkaloids. In the 1940s a Swiss chemist synthesized some of the alkaloid's lysergic acids ("lysergic" means "obtained by hydrolysis from ergot") and described their potent psychotropic effects, especially those of the one called lysergic acid diethylamide (L.S.D.) Among those reputed to have been initiated at Eleusis was Plato. Recreational or sacrilegious use of these drugs came later, in 415 B.C., when Alcibiades used them at his private parties.

I am suggesting that the arts can induce comparable states of mind at the same time as enabling the participant to retain a much greater degree of control and discrimination. Of course it is precisely this kind of experience that minimalism eschews, to its blatant loss, whereas the holistic kind of art I am discussing is nothing if not maximal, akin perhaps to what Paul Valéry intended by his word "implex": when the mind is raised to its maximum apprehensive power—not a far cry from the old war cry of "mind-expanding," but without the de rigueur narcosis.

[1991]

The Absurd Revisted

W E DO NOT HEAR as much of the Absurd as we used to; in cold storage in Kierkegaard and Camus, the term has lapsed from vogue, still of course evoking anything that is *surdus,* meaning irrational or senseless and so, by unkind extension, backward or deaf (*sourd* is "deaf" in French). The ab means "utterly," but I wonder if anything is utterly absurd. The human condition is too mixed for that. Camus defined the absurd as the gap between the mind that yearns and the world that lets it down, by which usually we intend death, the way in which the universe looks after itself and has no response to our individual fates. But to complain that the universe, so to speak, doesn't treat us as well as it does itself is to liken the human to the cosmic, and not that justifiably. Semi-facetious allusions apart (yes a human can be a white dwarf, even a red giant), you and I are quite unlike the universe: not expanding or contracting or pulsating, nor made up of clusters of galaxies strewn throughout a vacuum, nor even as constant as suns, as untidy as an open cluster, or, for that, as organized as a molecule, as inscrutably omnivorous as a black hole. Indeed, even where the universe might seem a bit absurd—with its so-called "wobbles" in the genetic code, with six ways of making one essential chemical but only one of making another chemical just as essential—it still gets by, through a predominance of successful chances.

We are not the small version of that; the universe is an absolute, which means it needs nothing but itself, whereas we humans want to be without lack, as Sartre says. You could, I suppose, work out an exact ratio of component parts, likening molecules to hypothetical planets round many, many stars, and human individuals to suns, families to clusters, clans to galaxies; but the universe, made of the same stuff as we, is what includes us, and continually re-uses us. We cannot sever ourselves from it to become unobligated exceptions. All we can do is heed what we have in common with suns, as we heed what we have in common with elephants or clouds without becoming elephantine or cloudy, and cease being infatuated with metaphors that take us from the body to the body politic, from a body of thought to bodies celestial. Our special gift, it seems, is to be the universe's way of pondering (and disliking) itself, and that gift brings hazards with it, including disliking the way the universe uses us to formulate a dislike of itself it can ignore without using us at all.

Even worse, if you settle for the human microcosm vis-à-vis the cosmic microcosm, you first of all run into Beckett's nastiest aphorism and get wounded by it: "The mortal microcosm cannot forgive the relative immortality of the macrocosm." The word "relative" evinces our indignant ignorance, but doesn't remind us that anyone who makes microcosms, and wants them accurate, has to reckon with this: Each microcosm adds itself to the macrocosm (it has nowhere else to go), so an accurate microcosm has to include—in little, of course—all the microcosms that have been added, are being added, will be added to the great big cosm itself. Halt everything, you say; no more microcosms added until mine's finished. Impossible: just as the expanding edge of the universe outstrips the astronomer's telescopes, so does the constant surfeit of microcosms outstrip the micro-cosmetician who, in the very act of trying to sum up, both thwarts himself and renders others obsolete. A less than tolerant view of how our little versions go astray is Dylan Thomas's juxtaposition of Llaregub and Llarebyg, which reverse into "Buggerall" and "Biggerall," in other words nothing and everything. The universe at large does funny things: galaxies collide or deform one another; every now and then, a subatomic particle called the anti-sigma minus hyperon goes the wrong way; and, each year, in a putative room full of radium atoms, one dies, but why that particular one we have no idea. The universe does funny things within us too, making children age at enormous speed until a ten-year-old is bald and toothless, or making a mongol here, a cretin there, or making me inherit from my mother's side of the family migraine attacks which must have had a first sufferer somewhere in the family tree, saddling my sister with a quarter-sized nevus on her writing hand (a port-wine plateau of scab that bled), and making my niece a celiac case, unable to metabolize gluten.

The analogy we need beyond word, simile, metaphor (all of them analogies) is between the race and the universe, and by that token, although not as old, we are level-pegging, although surely we will never keep pace, not we humans, afflicted with the primitive old brain that the famous Broca called the limbic system. If, as individuals indignant about the prospects for our race, we call ourselves absurd, then we have a case of sorts, and in the main only ourselves to blame. The universe is not subject to its own conscious will, whereas we are subject to our own, and it is only the universe's good luck to be so big we haven't been able to dominate it all, we who should not ape the violence of the stars themselves but exercise whatever degree of self-control we have, never mind how slight. Our ironic fate is to be—in the thick of the All—not only implicated, but conscious, and unable all the same to see that, although the universe includes our race, the universe itself is not included in anything, much as we cannot see that, although the race includes us all, the race is not the same as any individual, is predicated on transcendence, not on soothing parallels. Galileo has it clear in his *Dialogue on the Two Great Systems, giornata I* where he says:

> As for those who so exalt incorruptibility, inalterability, I believe they are brought to say these things through their great desire to live a long time and through the terror they have of death. And not considering that, if men were immortal, these men would not have had an opportunity to come into the world. They would deserve to encounter a Medusa's head, which would transform them into statues of jasper or of diamond, to make them more perfect than they are. . . . And there is not the slightest doubt that the Earth is far more perfect, being, as it is, alterable, changeable, than if it were a mass of stone, even if it were a whole diamond, hard and impenetrable.

If you buy that, you relegate the absurd to social or stylistic incongruity, which includes, I suppose, wanting the universe to behave towards us like a caring parent doomed to die before us, and glad that we can carry on the seed, the blood, the unappeasable longing never to vanish, for all eternity, into the uncaring but endlessly receptive chemistry of the cosmic machine. If, as a race, we cared as much about survival as we do *qua* individuals, we would behave racially better, much as other races on other planets have been doing for ages, deterred by contempt from communicating with us, even over a distance colossal enough to keep us at bay.

The pessimism of cosmologist Fred Hoyle, whose delight in the universe does not extend to humankind (breeding and brawling), sets him apart from those euphoric, high-energy theorists who rule the roost and look on the bright side, but somehow never manage to persuade un-organized humanity to behave any better. That is what's absurd: to have the inkling without being able to make it count. While we talk about getting our house in order before the hypothetical time-limit ascribed to violent technological societies, stars evolve and die all the way along the curve of the Hertzsprung-Russell diagram of star-formation, immune and remote; Nero might just as well be an astronomer, rather than nothing at all, admiring the heavens while the matrix of mankind goes up in smoke. Second things put first can ravish us even in the depths of our shame. The race will go to the wall, not better, but better-informed, which is like saying a can-opener doesn't work but has a lovely shine.

Afflicted with an awareness that can be aware of itself, the human being is the only creature of its kind on the planet. Endowed with a mind forever posing questions it cannot answer, the human either settles for the leap of faith or settles the mind with some form of mindlessness. (Ignatius Loyola: the sacrifice of the intellect is the one in which God most rejoices.) Suicide seems to put the mind out of its agony, and so, sometimes, does chronic paganism. But not for Camus, who finds suicide too confessional, a crass and gross self-betrayal, and paganism too intermittent a drug for a rational animal. No: beyond nihilism, suicide, spuriously soothing guesses at the meaning of life, the human must reason his/her way to the point at which one says yes to the Minotaur, the eventual and ineluctable destroyer, and from there on (the terms vary) sustains an incessant act of revolt, refusal, defiance, disdaining both bromides and appeals. In this way, although hemmed in by a dense, alien, almost mathematical matrix of non-stop phenomena, the mind works with what it has, watching the natural world with almost opinionless attentiveness, making the most of things rather than the best, and staying put with tenacity and acumen. We are the only models of us.

This program is easier for the creative artist than for others. If the mind is redundant vis-à-vis the cosmic imponderables, it may have a role in ministering to itself; after all, the absurd—the gulf between desire and fact—exists only in the human mind, and that may make "brainworkers" of us all.

[1994]

A Vision of
Bright Cannon-Fodder

ALTHOUGH THE SUBJECT OF *Words For A Deaf Daughter* could not read the book while I was writing it, and still has been unable to read it some twenty years later, she did participate in the writing, by which I mean she sat on my knee, or nearby, while I wrote. It suited her especially that I was writing on the backs of envelopes slit open; something homespun and undignified in that appealed to her, not least because it was on such paper that she did her own extraordinary daubs and composed what passed with her for prose. The original manuscript sits in a steel drawer in a university library now, an uncouth bundle of pencilled, ball-pointed, crayoned handwriting joined, quite often, by Mandy's scrawls and squiggles: a garish obbligato in the margin, sometimes on the middle of the page. Often enough, in her ecstatically ebullient way, she would snatch a page from me and run away with it, giggling.

She knew what was going on was about her, and she even staged a barbaric correspondence with my editor at Harper and Row (as the house called itself then). When the book first came out, she carried a copy to school and made a nuisance of herself, not quoting but brandishing the thing at her teachers. After all, her picture appeared in it, and some of her drawings (one of which graces a new edition's jacket). It is moving to contemplate such a view of the book, a view that maintains and perpetuates Book as a mysterious item, forever to be fingered and pondered, never wholly to be fathomed. I have nothing to add to the record its pages keep; the experience of writing such a book while its invoked recipient messed about with it fed into the book's subject all along, and I know that, because she nudged me or grabbed a sheet, I lost phrases, had to terminate sentences prematurely, and literally forgot what she'd done ten minutes earlier in favor of some escapade more recent. My familiar, equipped as always with brush and crayon, pencil and fountain pen, was an unquiet host, but also an inexhaustible object of contemplation. The book trembled like mercury as she breathed on it, skewed away sideways as she tormented its author, and mutated second after second. What I really needed was a team of accomplices, to divert her and steady me, but she and I fudged it up alone during alert mornings, and fuzzy afternoons when we both inclined to doze; if you look at the holograph you can see where we goofed and the handwriting kept pace, index to fatigue. It was the most frustrating writing experience of my life, but unique in that the writing provoked into happening things that slid straight into the book, like molten ore settling into a mold at unthinkable speed. It kept being over before it had begun, and it kept beginning again before it had started. An experiment, it was a hectic transcription, and I sometimes pretended I was Busoni, shifting Bach organ music into music for piano; certainly living by my wits, a monster of diabolical balance. I could have written my book after midnight, as I do nowadays, filling its chalice during a dead calm; but that would have been too serene a performance, minus the badgering, the torment, the impromptu brilliance of Amanda herself, gadfly, angel, the most preposterous of all persons from Porlock.

Since then, *Words* has had various incarnations and some embarrassing jackets, though its numerous reviews have been astounding. It has become a teaching text and a manual for parents (though, I would think, an erratic and expressionistic one). It began as an essay in the now defunct *New American Review,* chosen by Theodore Solotaroff (who turned the book down for the New American Library, which was when Frances McCullough of Harper and Row glommed on to it). The copy I sent off to Gollancz in London was that rarity, a carbon copy of the typescript, and a smudgy one at that. I still feel, for obvious reasons, an addiction to the physical artifact of those two hundred messy handwritten pages tied together with string: an ideal bundle for John Stuart Mill's housemaid to light the fire with. Emotion drenches those pages as it does any re-reading—this, however, isn't one of the books I tug out of the shelf in the small hours to see how I was writing in those days. It has turned out to be the record of a heyday, of her finest hours.

After twenty years, the voluminous correspondence has tapered off; I had never realized how many people out there had been in the same fix and needed to share their findings. Yet, to me, the book ranks not as useful or epistemological, but as art, verbal art, creating and exploiting that special form of the epistle which seems dramatic: the letter to someone who will never read it, although the rest of the world can. That knife's edge scores me still, because you have to write with passionate scrupulosity, knowing the world has the advantage of the person addressed, whose effability exposes her literal "infancy"—which is the state of not being able to speak. To write in and about such a situation or emergency requires unflinching sensitivity, and I fault myself for not having been unflinching and sensitive enough. I set down what I could, determined to set something down, much in the mood of the German composer Stockhausen, whose "Out of the Seven Days" tells what it was like to live alone in his house for a week with nothing but water to sustain him. *Existenz-musik,* I would call it. Perhaps *Words* is *Existenz-prose.* Is-ness barography. Whatever it is, it cannot be read or judged by conventional standards and requires a generous adjustment in taste, going as it does toward the cry, the shout, the incessant appalled murmur we all emit but fail to heed.

Only the other day, I heard (significant verb) how American Sign Language expresses the word "pasteurize": by passing your hand *past your eyes.* That, like many ingenuities of the handicapped, enthralls me and makes my world wider.

II

When I finished *Gala,* six years after *Words,* Harper and Row asked me for a brief preface, but not without first asking me if I would classify *Gala* as non-fiction, which it is not. I refused, although offered more money for misdescribing my book. Only to me, perhaps, was it vital to insist on minute distinctions.

Readers will recognize, or think they recognize, two of the characters in *Gala,* and rightly. But Milk and Deulius, as such, exist only within *Gala's* pages, whereas whom and what I extrapolated them from exist non-fictionally, as do others of the novel's characters, while yet others are outright imaginary. The mix, as sidewalk colorists say, is all my own work, a tapestry or mosaic that was in my head long before I wrote either book. Both books came out of the same ferment, and *Gala,* in its different register, is a true emotional sequel to the other. What I do in it is to stage the scenario of wish-fulfillment; the wish abides, and the book partly fulfills it on the level of imagination. I have often thought that one should be able not only to describe something but also to recover (or create) anticipations of it. If there were life forms on Mars, unknown, one should be able to imagine them correct in every detail. *Gala* is a planet indeed, a pipedream rendered into prose, perhaps under the auspices of De Quincey, whose "The Affliction of Childhood" afflicts me yet.

As I wrote in 1976, the traditional prefatory note to a work of fiction denies that the characters resemble people living or dead. In this case I am obliged, selectively, both to deny it and admit it, and to add that some of those who were alive in 1976 are now dead. The reaper has been through my squad. All I can add is that I tried to invade imaginatively situations I know quite well, and in doing so to win or exact some freedom of response, of conjecture and intrusive epitome, of license to transpose or combine, otherwise illicit. That is in part what art is for, as well as being a means of trying to create something perfect. I think of this book, as Mark Seinfelt reminded me the other day, as an "auto-fiction": its stimulus, or occasion, I know profoundly at first hand; its pattern, much noticed by scientists, is a dream that I signed.

Drawing the star charts in color was a soothing joy, but I have never been able to find them since; their spring binder must have carried them off among those very stars for verification by the synod of the galaxies. I still search, but in vain. Like so many treasure islands, that binder of pleasure had floated away. In my 1976 introduction, I wrote that any sequel to *Gala* would "probably be neither memoir nor novel but a prose poem dense as a neutron star, one flake of which, metaphorically speaking, would weigh a million tons and cut through any of us as if we were air." Perhaps when I find the binder I will write the sequel to the sequel. Or, when I write the sequel, the binder will come back to hand. The two books together are intended to state that I and others were here and our imaginations too.

[1993]

Where Novels Come From

I HAD NEVER HEARD of the Rat Man of Paris until two friends came back from France saying, Do we have a story for you. And they did. I no sooner knew of that stumblebum of the boulevards, flashing his rat from beneath a shabby raincoat, Columbo style, than I began developing him. True to my breed, I didn't set off for Paris or anywhere else. I *dreamed* him up, although I did start reading the most ancient guide to Paris I could buy. I find that a supply of ancient guidebooks provides a useful source of semi-relevant mirage. I hadn't been in Paris for a long time, but I exploited my memories of that stay as much as I could, which included uncouth experiments in obscene French, some of which got me into trouble. I was twenty at the time. I was also pondering Klaus Barbie, and, sure enough, he ended up in the book, a lugubrious revenant whom the Rat Man wanted to guillotine. After the book came out, I got lots of mail from readers who had seen the actual Rat Man, who had paid him to go away; one correspondent told me the Rat Man had thrown a chair at her, and wondered if I would like to incorporate that episode in future editions. I was in Paris only a few years ago, having a wonderful time, and I saw no sign of Rat Man. No one had seen him in ages, and I began to wonder if my book killed him off; or if, obliged to compete with the phantom Spanish novelist who stalks along the same streets, he must

An address given at a *Cleveland Plain Dealer* Author Luncheon in Cleveland, Ohio, April 30, 1991.

have given up—a victim of Juan Goytisolo, the Parisian-Spanish novelist on whom that wispy personage is based.

I must have read publicly from *Rat Man* scores of times, and tried to answer questions about it. Myself, I think of it as a rather simple and straight and, for me, unstylish book—a tale told almost out of character; but most readers find it loaded with innuendo and symbol. The question I am most often asked, especially by students, is what does the Rat Man's final gesture—of thumbs-up—mean. I try not to answer. I myself know what he means, but his way of indicating it (if you can indicate with a thumb) is rather bizarre, although classical scholars—a fugitive breed now resident in tiny cottages on some campuses and extinct at Johns Hopkins—inform me that cultivated Romans used the thumbs-up to denote Polish Him Off. I leave you to do your own conjuring with the Rat Man's thumb. He remains for me, along with Milk of *Gala,* poor Count von Stauffenberg who wanted to kill Hitler and run the new Germany too, and even poorer Polidori whom Byron couldn't stomach and sent packing in the direction of suicide—one of my favorite characters: a variant on the man who doesn't fit into society, who can't really be civilized, who remains a sleepwalking Goth. Nature frightens him, society unnerves him, love demoralizes him, and death just may not last long enough. Oddly enough, there is a sequel to that book, presently called *Rat Man in Manhattan,* all typed up and ready to go. It's a sort of a sequel, anyway—about an adulterous party official who has been in the Gulag and now lives in a tree house in Central Park, eking out a living in sordid nightclubs. I want to work on it a bit more. So, for the present, it sits in a steel box along with other works more certainly doomed, such as the enormous novel about a journey through the human brain, the other novel about World War Two in Poland (which I abandoned on page 373 with a parachutist floating down in mid sentence), and the science fiction novel I did finish, about a planet filched from Humbert Wolfe's (and Holst's) Betelgeuse.

It took me quite a while to get used to having, as it were, alongside me as I worked on new things, this sump or wrecker's yard of the abandoned, the not quite abandoned, the not quite unabandoned, the wrong-headed, the half-dead, the corrigible, the irremediable, the condemned, the pitiably ectoplasmic and the glossily aborted. Then I began to see the sump or wrecker's yard as a receipt for my having paid my dues; it was against this scuff or debris that, privately of course, I was to see my other stuff, the considerable amount that I let go into print. People have tried to look into this Botany Bay of the book, in order to write academically about it, but I have denied them access. Who knows, some of these cadavers may awaken and soften the heart of even the most minimalizing editor.

Since I seem to be revealing the cupboards in my skeletons, I should mention the water-colors I painted of the aforesaid Stauffenberg, in which he has a shiny arm-stump made of aluminum foil and an expressionistically enlarged briefcase done in voluptuous orange and terra cotta. I did them because I kept forgetting which hand he had lost, which eye. I should have been better at this as my own father lost an eye in the first World War, and my sister and I used to take him for walks, proud with him between us, and she and I would each squeeze one eye shut to be like him. After a while, I recall, the three of us, with hands linked, would begin to veer one way or the other, mostly into the road. I sometimes wonder why I use so many contraptions for my novels: models of planes, of swimming pools, close-ups of faces, crude models of hands, et cetera. I was trained as a carpenter at grammar school, having been adjudged too ungifted for art and too dense for Latin. Perhaps I think the verbal will swallow me up quite if I don't tie myself down to something less ethereal. When *The Very Rich Hours of Count von Stauffenberg* came out, I got all kinds of hate mail from Germany and Switzerland, saying, mostly, we have a butcher's hook and some piano wire for you, why don't you leave German heroes (or psychopaths—leave the space blank) to Germans? In Spanish, the book became a bestseller in Latin America, where all kinds of ex-Nazis, like demented moths licking a sparkler, looked for themselves in the index, in which one entry—that for Gruppenführer Rolf Stundt—is wholly fictitious. *The New York Times Magazine,* in its deadly wisdom, asked me to go on assignment to Argentina and other places, interviewing these new fans in their kennels, but I, in my self-saving wisdom, declined, wishing to go on with my career. Peter Falk offered to play the colonel if ever a movie *was* made of this chamber of horrors. A movie was made, with Brad Davis playing Stauffenberg, and a more wooden caricature I have yet to see.

Until *Stauff,* as I affectionately called it, I had written rather short books; all of a sudden I began to do books of at least twice that previous length (though the Rat Man's book is short). I don't think I had suddenly fallen in love with the loose baggy monster; rather, I had recognized the impenitent amplitude toward which I had long been striving. My brain had taken wing, and the essential complexity and abundance of human life had taken me over. An art of stiff upper-lipped allusiveness no longer appealed; it never really had. Fiction is really guessing at people, and I wanted to do the guesswork in full permutational grandeur, creating books that would blot out everything else (for the reader anyway) and create a spell that clung, making him or her enjoy the unraveling so much that, instead of saying the book's title aloud, he or she would prefer to *say the entire book aloud,* all five hundred pages of it, before using a verb, say. You can imagine the mayhem that would produce in university seminars. Ah, what do *Remembrance of Things Past* and *Bleak House* have in common? First version takes a few seconds; the next takes days. Oh to be lost in literature and not notice one's own death.

At some point after 1984, when I lay in Intensive Care for a month reading Beckett's *Malone Dies,* I began to listen to music while writing. I did my Hopi novel, *The Place in Flowers Where Pollen Rests,* while hearing and rehearing some Busoni Sonatinas played by Paul Jacobs. I must have heard those things some twelve hundred times. They gave me a plateau, a shelf, an otherworldly berm, to thrive on, cutting me almost numinously off. I suppose it was an experiment, doing that; although I now listen to music of the classical sort while I write, I have never again worked one piece to death, as then. I do listen to Busoni-Bach, Frank Bridge, Villa-Lobos, Hindemith, Roy Harris, Howard Hanson, Delius, Vaughan Williams, Ravel, Debussy, Florent Schmitt, Franz Schmidt, Ussachevsky and Luening, Bergsma, Richard Strauss, David Diamond, Havergal Brian, Korngold, Rubbra, Finzi, and Keith Jarrett. The only Berlioz I can stand is *Les Nuits d'Eté* sung by Tate Baltsa. The only operas I can bear to hear are *Wozzeck, Lulu,* and *The Dialogues of the Carmelites.* I am revealing the silver nitrate on the back of the literary mirror that is me. My mother was a concert pianist and then a piano teacher—I grew up with the sound of music and can take it twenty-four hours a day. Her biggest disappointment was that I became what I have become and not a musician; I can't read a note of music (maybe a little honorable bigotry there), but I am *anima naturaliter musicana,* as I say it in my late-learned Latin. I play my cassettes while writing, perhaps because music is a superior art, and I want to get a steady whiff of its azure-lined breath. I write by rhythm anyway, usually knowing the rhythm of an entire page before I have even written it. How odd that must sound, as if I didn't care what I said or which words I combined. I do, but the manger (or the design or the matrix) the words come into begins as an almost symphonic buzz in my head. Asked to comment on what I found the superb prose of a woman writer, I cast around for analogies and ended up saying "She is like the Cleveland Orchestra."

I should end with that, but I want to tell something about the writing of more recent novels. *Lord Byron's Doctor* came to me in a flash. I remembered the name of John William Polidori, tucked away just once in a critical study I had written of Byron almost thirty years before. It was like the source of Stauffenberg: seeing in a war weekly the face of the Count, a rather crude eyepatch in place, and not the image of my father, though akin. I then wrote fifty pages about Stauff, having him hanged, and then I researched him and found he was shot. So I began again, shifting from third person to first.

I had no image of Polidori at all, but I soon got one from the national Portrait Gallery in London, and I read Polidori's diary, published in bowdlerized form and not too interesting a text. I decided to do another impersonation, giving Polly an almost Werther-like quality, and, in the process beefed up a few other lives as well (such as Claire Clairmont's), although not Byron's, which, if anything, needed literary gemfibrozil. I wanted to call the book *Polidori,* but dark brown publishing wisdom prevailed, and the more explanatory title came into being. *Polly,* I now think, would be even better, much as *In Deep* would be better for my book about learning to swim: *Out of My Depths.* I often get the sense that all the years I have had so far have really been my childhood, and that soon I will grow up and get it right. What is the life of the novelist like? We are like those scavengers of the night who, clad in aluminum worksuits, go and unseal trapdoors in the underbellies of jumbo jets, sucking out human detritus through long plastic tubes like the trunks of elephants denied access to the last graveyard.

It's an emotional formula, but it makes the point, I trust, that we remove from the race what T.S. Eliot, referring to Hamlet, once called the black, perilous stuff. The nightsoil of the mind, the substratum of the dream, all that is spent that not long ago was so alive. Like mercantile psychiatrists selling sausages of human pain.

Enough of that. I want to get back to music and to say that *The Women of Whitechapel* began when I heard Lulu scream in the opera *Lulu* as Jack the Ripper laid his hands on her. Years before, to a student who was having trouble with a piece of fiction (she could only hear a scream), I said: Describe the scream for ten pages. She did. It was brilliant. Now I didn't describe the scream for four hundred and some pages, but I tried to get into my novel the miserable screaming condition of Whitechapel women in 1888. Roughly one and a half women were murdered each night, and all from the same degraded class. Corpses were clogging the wheels of the Thames paddle steamers. The prostitutes of that time were almost a mode of refuse, available for four pence, having in their pockets all they owned, happiest and safest when in jail. As Virginia Woolf says in her essay on Walter Sickert, who in my novel is one of the Ripper trio—the dapper, deft inveigler who lures whores into the bloodbath-carriage. "There is gusto," Virginia says, "in the spending of the poor; they are very close to what they possess." Thus one of my two epigraphs. I take liberties in this book. For instance, one of the slaughtered whores is called Long Liz because she was so short—thus Cockney irony. In my book she's tall because I *want* one of them tall. The so-called Ripper was a trio of a famous doctor, a well-regarded painter (Sickert), and an abominable coachman, name of Netley.

Looking back on the provenance of things fictional, with all the pleasure one has when self-consciously equipped with data, I blink with joy, knowing the so-called facts are mere indices to the rapture of dislocation: when something far-fetched or outlandish, or just plain confected, lifts me out of my sedater self and wafts me to the realm of invention. I remember that "invent" used to mean stumble upon or find, and I wonder at the brigand ambivalence of a mind that has it both ways, both concocting and discovering; indeed, discovering only what it concocts, as if private fantasy were a universal given. Mr. Facing Both Ways may be an apt sobriquet for the novelist, both god and diviner, both artificer and scout. Geulincx, the Belgian philosopher doted on by Samuel Beckett, wrote that where you are worth nothing, you should want nothing. A corollary of that may be that, where you are worth anything, you should demand everything before the sheer factuality of the physical universe gags you for ever.

[1991]

Judge Not

WHEN ASKED IN THE SPRING of 1991 if I would serve as a fiction judge for the National Book Award, I accepted straight away. Asked to propose another name, I gave that of William Gass, who also accepted. Stylists rarely get a chance to judge anything since most of those who officiate in literary affairs in this country labor under the fetishistic delusion that prose ought not to be too pleasurable, for writer or reader. Time and again, one finds prose lauded for its "lean," "terse," "taut," quality, and anything that comes along with an iota of personality or distinctiveness gets blasted. Only puritans, or puritanical liberals, would insist thus on sameness and strictness. People who harp on paucity have a poor sense of the world.

All that summer, works of fiction arrived at the door, and went next to the garage or the dining-room table. By September there were half a dozen more or less permanent residents of the table, being dipped into again and again, admired and prized, ranging from Felipe Alfau's *Chromos,* Mary Caponegro's *The Star Café,* and Elena Castedo's *Paradise,* to Joanna Scott's *Arrogance,* Steven Millhauser's *The Barnum Museum,* and Sandra Schor's *The Great Letter E.* Thank goodness, I thought, for women; otherwise there would be four blanks on the table. Those six books had rhetorical vigor and lexical splendor. Their estimable authors knew that prose is not a mere expository medium but an instrument to play, a voice to sing. No barbarous monotony here, but a straight line back to such illustrious forebears as

Faulkner, Proust, Mann, Woolf, Nabokov, Beckett, and even Joyce. The pleasure principle was bearing fruit after all; but the rejected and semi-rejected books in the garage, gathering dust and housing spiders, made me pause. In about 170 out of some two hundred, I had been unable to find a superb sentence, an unforgettable phrase, a scene that burned home. My choices were not representative of the fiction the country was writing. Too bad for the country, too bad for publishing. Clearly, almost nobody knew good from bad.

The next event in what was to become a sorry process was the first conference call. Gass and I had chosen much the same dozen contenders, but I no sooner gladdened about that than the female judge from Arizona began a tirade about what she called masturbatory writing, which to her taste characterized the West-Gass dozen. She was against that kind of thing, and in any case it had been a long time since a Black writer had won. (Or masturbated.) Wait a minute, I said, given too much to digest: "Are there any other writers you think masturbatory?" She rattled off her list of the damned, mostly the illustrious forebears listed above. Another judge, the supposedly savvy one from the red-hot vacuum of Manhattan wanted to bestow the award on someone who had won it before, to be on the safe side. Previous winners weren't banned from entering or winning, but to make honorific lightning strike twice was too much for Gass and me. It would suggest the judges had no ideas of their own, and wielded only a big rubber stamp. That conference call was untidy and unsatisfactory. One or two judges really admired the twaddle in the garage, were looking for work wholesome, mild, vapid and virtually anonymous, and had no taste at all, being into the bargain rather thinly read. The voice of the woman from the University of Arizona jarred my skull, reminding me of my semester there as visiting novelist. At the first meeting of my MFA workshop, the students *pleaded* to be allowed to talk about Proust, Beckett, Nabokov, all of them proscribed locally. I was moved, and we welcomed in the banished geniuses for fifteen weeks while the winter sun shone. I knew from the outset why half the writing faculty cut me dead.

The five judges moved onward to a second conference call, which Gass missed, and I felt mighty lonely as good books fell by the wayside en route to the magic final five. In the end, after some mathematical misadventures, which I had despondently drawn attention to, we had before us a quintet that Gass and I complained about: it represented our standards, criteria, and lifelong beliefs very little. Only Alfau had gotten through the Chinese Wall of the Babbitts. Schor had actually died during the judging. The other three judges, becoming a phalanx of righteous anti-hedonists, made a gesture: Gass and I could take one of the final five out and put one in. In went Castedo, like Alfau an author of Hispanic origin. That was as far as Gass and I got. The final five now included Charles Johnson's *The Middle Passage,* an inferior, nervously didactic novel I read twice, wondering why it was inferior to Johnson's other books. Surely a black novelist writing about slaves should have written with more apocalyptic force; but clearly such a book appealed to the schoolteacherly tastes of the other three judges.

Anyway, my mind said, leaping back in time, what's wrong with masturbation anyway? Why such fear and loathing in 1991? We weren't discussing fascism or terrorism, but only an octave of self-ablation. I had a keen sense of having wasted my time. People who knew me and what I stood for would gape and ask how in hell I put my name to a list such as that of the finalists. Eighty-nine-year old Felipe Alfau, staring at the TV in his nursing home, was unmoved by his nomination; he had waited too long, having written *Chromos* in 1948. I shallow-graved my chagrin by pondering his novel and inditing that labor of love, the citation for him, which went as follows:

> Finished in 1948, *Chromos* sets an imaginary Alfau dreaming in front of old calendar pictures by the light of a match. Before the flame gutters, a real novel has come to him: a tart and eloquent, sly and feisty kaleidoscope of New York Spaniards, wrought in fire amid the *cante hondo* of the heart by a hunger artist almost lost, unpublished, to oblivion.

I hoped it would be persuasive, but only Gass felt its plea. I began to worry, wishing I'd managed to get Chaim Potok's *The Gift of Asher* Lev into the final five, or Michael Rothschild's *Wondermonger.* Too late. I thought of all the writing I hadn't done from spring to fall. Why have to argue like a demon merely to inject into the judging some elementary esthetic criteria such as obtain in an MFA seminar or even a writing class for seniors? Here were Gass and I, having devoted much of our lives to fiction in a certain mode, being outvoted by a trio of moaxes (a moax is a square). Giving in to middlebrow flummery made no sense at all.

The day I flew in to New York for the judges' meeting, I had a call from Roger Cohen, saying *The New York Times Book Review* had given him my number. Would I talk to him about the judging? I did, spelling out the philistinism and sappiness I had heard on the telephone, and the rabid zeal of the woman from Arizona, who said quite openly that black was going to vote black. If only taste had voted taste. If only there had been enough taste in the judges to discern excellence where it showed. For my estheticism I was later to be denounced as curmudgeon; racist; bigot; but I had dismissed Johnson's book early on, and I had argued for two Hispanics.

You can't win. *De gustibus,* runs the old tag, *non disputandum.* It's no good arguing about taste. It's no good clamoring for A Winner either, then, just for the sake of having one. Maybe all two hundred books should have been divided into three categories: Can't Write At All; Can Write; Writes Well. That, indeed, would be no more slanderous and insulting than the present system. I said a lot of this to Roger Cohen, but he didn't print it. What he did print, though, was enough to make the air electric on the following day, the day of the judges' lunch in an obscure eatery uptown (and not at the Algonquin or the Plaza). The woman from Tucson, who didn't know Gass or his work, misidentified the other male judge as Gass. It all sorted out. Mathematically, if Bill and I had voted someone else as our Number One, and not Alfau, Johnson might not have won; it was that close and pointless. Three of my fellow-judges were angry with me, and spent some time denouncing Roger Cohen too; but I have become inured to middlebrow wrath over the last thirty years and have no intention of coming to heel. If I am to judge, all I ask for is excellence, and I will cry *Chapeau!* When the Arizona judge danced on the table at that night's NBA dinner in the Plaza, was she dancing for literature? Or for loyalty? The Manhattan judge had already confided, his tone of exclusive self-importance, how the *Pulitzer* jury did things, but who by then cared?

Relegated to a table on the fringe of the proceedings for speaking when I had never promised to be silent, I heard out the ceremonies, writhing now and then as the banalities piled up. There was, that year, not even an award for poetry to enliven things (though several publishers had entered volumes of poetry for the fiction contest—a smart and significant idea). There is a rough justice in all this: the majority of prose writers, certainly in English, are stolid, wooden, and tonedeaf; the least they can expect is judges of the same caliber, to confirm them in their sameness. The non-fiction judges ignored some wonderful writing, no doubt because in their role as paralytics they had failed to recognize the able-bodied waltzing by as participants in literature. Those who win, it seems, do so for not masturbating in their public prose. The book trade has to be seen to be behaving itself.

Amid the fall-out and the sleazy terminal moraine of judging, I remember being able to tell some of the truth on the McLaughlin Show. Ms. Scott and Ms. Caponegro were honored by the Academy and Institute of Arts and Letters instead, and Ms. Castedo won the Chilean National Prize for Literature. Mr. Alfau has just published his collected poems. And there is talk on and off the Rialto of a new prize in the offing, to be awarded for style. Of course.

[1993]

Back to My Desk

G ETTING BACK TO MY DESK after a semester's teaching, I find my hands fiddling with an English translation of Salvador Elizondo's *Farabeuf,* which years ago I tried to read in my halting Spanish. Now I am itching to have another look at it. There is also a book to review about swimming, appropriately enough. More enticing than even these there sits a book by Peter Greenaway, entirely about his extraordinary movie, *Drowning by Numbers*—I'm especially interested because a couple of French critics liken my novels to his films, and I guess I see why.

Ultimately you begin to recognize what it is that runs through everything you do, what continues even at your most distracted: *The Novel.* You write it to figure out what the darned thing is, and the result is a self-defining enigma. As soon as you've come up with your definition, have added it to the sum of novelness—*summa fabulissima*—the notion of the novel has changed. So you never know what you're doing, not quite; but you do know that you constantly entertain the yearning to peer long and deep, getting down what it feels like to be all sorts and conditions of humans, not committed to any formula for the novel, but to the energies that shake it into being: the lunge, the saunter, the squint, the eavesdrop, the auscultation, the booby-trap. Perhaps the novel is like plastic explosive, taking safely any shape you give it, but sensitive to spark.

What *are* you doing? I often wonder that as I accumulate pages, and I answer myself that I am writing prose on the occasion of a field full of folk. The novel is amplified story, yes, but also a percussive meditation, a dithyramb about how it feels to be somebody, a contingency sample of the All. The novel is a toboggan made of words sent careening over the brow of a hill to see what happens to it, a stent fixed into a bloodvessel to catch cruising embolisms. I can think of any number of metaphors that satisfy me for half a minute. The novelist is someone who makes a pantomime out of the conversation the mind has with itself. The result is a deponent verb: active in meaning, but passive in form. The reader sits as still as the novelist or composer, unless the novelist be reading aloud, which I suspect the novelist of our 1990s should perhaps not be doing. Perhaps the novel is following twelve-tone music, abstract expressionism; after all, you cannot expect intelligent prose-lovers to watch TV *ad nauseam.* What can you do when an editor in a well-known publishing house declares, as one did in 1991, "I can't stand prose more complex than somebody just saying Hi." The novel is what is new in fiction, what the old novel is evolving into. All I know is that such extremes as we find in Greek tragedy belong in the novel, perhaps to keep mundane and humdrum circumstances company, but scything through them as life scythes through us, dropping us once we have served our genetic purpose. Art cuts across that process, giving us something to justify ourselves by while being treated as mere vessels and conduits by the life force. The novel is no more dedicated to the planet than prose style is to endangered species. The novel is artificial, corresponds to nothing, and, if it has anything to say after all, says it to defy the Creator, saying "You never thought of that, did you, *Kyrie?*"

About the novel there is something hubristic, arrogant; trumpeting imagination, praying to prose. Your novel-ist sits in a brightly lit room full of old newspapers, turning the read into something other. It can be accidental. Wholly dependent on you, like the lightbulbs Russian readers have to carry to unlit libraries. Hey Prousto, we say: we/she are manqués manqués. We come from Detroitus. The novelist going out for a morning walk is terrifying: in one hand he/she grasps the leash-ends of a dozen small model planes whose petrol engines snarl and buzz as the noses leap up and down, yelping like huskies, eager to burst away in different directions. The novelist holds them at bay on their leashes, dreaming up new paragraphs while affronted neighbors gather. The novelist takes a trouvaille and makes a big production of it. Example: hanging on my wall, a souvenir de Paris, a TWA Expedite Baggage label, says the following in copperplate ballpoint: "il ne sait pas ce qu'il manque"—*he doesn't know what he's missing*. I never lock my bag. Hence the comment. I can never find the key. The French crack is a profound remark, whether it means "he doesn't know what he's lost" or "he doesn't know what else he could have." I could make a novel out of that, and one day probably will. Not far from this house lives a literato with a condom collection; my plumber told me about it, and I wonder what on earth you do with such a thing. Extrapolation of such a trouvaille would be a delight. Am I giving anything away? No, my version would never be yours. Blood arrives on the stickum of an envelope's flap, and I guess at the cut lip, the sudden sound that prompted the flinch in the licker. Off we go again, speculating. A lovely Italianate girl at a nearby airport has billiard tablelegs; today, as I pass by her counter, I see she has both wrists in plaster casts. Are her legs dragging her downward, on steps say? Not much, it's a beginning, anyway, and the seething commotion of disparate phenomena begins to come together in a magic carpet whose weave is tangential. I keep by me, usually written on hotel paper, hundreds of little observations, ringed in ink, and I glue the sheets together as if making a sail, sometimes having a dozen of them joined side to side. When I use an item I scribble through it, and in reaching it I eye scores of others. Here, on this homemade cloth of gold, I shuffle microcosms, wondering which of them are novels, which of them four-word phrases sometimes inexhaustible objects of con-templation, as for instance "celibate gusto," which I sometimes use as a teaching example. The phrase just came to me one day, hopped up on to the page to be used. And it was. One day soon a sentence will begin "No stranger to Cleveland and the Midwest," once I have the rest of it. I keep wanting to write about the peanut fart you get when you open those silver-foil bags the airlines give you: bulging they come, vented they sag. We novelists put the world together, as the old symbolists used to do. *Sunballein* means "throw together," either a thing and its word, or a human and its deity.

Is fonseca a dry fountain? Was Nakshidid an ornament of the heart? Whose legs move in the air while he/she contemplates a headstone? Someone sees even in the face of joy a quivering, a quavering, a desire not to die, and so feels incurably sorry for everybody.

[1992]

Shoptalk

ALK USED TO BE of the dying or dead novel, but over the past half-century fiction has come massively alive, getting into things its early practitioners never dreamed of: nouveau roman, anti-novel, magical realism, the novel of the aristocratic self-fondling hauteur, the journal of the fictive life, the novel that exists only to evince the author's mind. We've never had it so good. I see a bold new wave of maximal visionaries, each of them an addict of the gorgeous sentence:

Angela Carter (dead, alas), John Hawkes, Robert Coover, Bradford Morrow, Edmund White, Claudio Magris, Elena Castedo, Charlie Smith, Juan Goytisolo, Alexander Theroux, John Vernon, Steven Milhauser, Guy Davenport, Marie-Claire Blais, David Bosworth, and Jonathan Carroll. I am not forgetting William Gass, James Purdy, Walter Abish, or such dead pioneers as Thomas Bernhard and Julio Cortázar, or the work of such newcomers as Lisa Rose, Carole Maso, Joe Schall, Mary Caponegro, Joanna Scott. See how the books pile up. We have all come out of the terminal moraine left us, like lustrous sherbet, by Beckett, Nabokov, Proust, Borges, and Woolf. We are the second generation of those who, in post-Faulknerian sentences, hymn the fertile muddle. Esthetes. Sentence-fetishists. We, the newly deconstructed, laugh, knowing imagination is a labile organ and always was: Indeed, we take pride in warping the rules, knowing there is one rule only, and that is contrast—a small word next to a big one, a Latin word next to an Anglo-Saxon one, purple next to pale, dithyramb next to laconic, King Lear next to his fool, Beckett's Molloy stuck among the living. We hark back to Hermann Broch, Thomas Mann, Colette.

Rhapsodic, ecumenical formalists, we are less a generation than a lost and newfound tribe sworn to recitative. I think our mode is closer to opera than to so-called realism, closer to narrative poetry than to anecdote. In my own novels I show what it is like to be someone. I plumb the opacity of identity, concerned most of all with emotions that people find ineffable; and this, in the best style available to me, I try to relate to the magic and mystery of living, amid which we toil in spellbound aversion. With almost incredulous horror, I watch the presence among us of evil, day in, day out. Angela Carter was right. The world is a terrifying place, from which the multitudes look away. They should but we coax them to look again, make them see the glory beneath the boredom and the evil.

I am a compulsive fictioneer. Whatever I am doing, my head is always kneading and rekneading givens. I hear voices. I need the world to please keep still, my head is such a ferment; but the world won't oblige, so I craft immutable stationary sentences. Fiction writers pride themselves on creating an invented world, but it is never wholly such; it's always derivative. Try as we do to invent, we keep stumbling into what Coleridge called the is-ness of things. So I look at certain historical ready-mades and try to make a virtue of that necessity, even if my contribution happens to be on the plane of style. To my critics, I say I am imaginatively reconceiving an era, which is to say apprehending it as if I were an imagination fresh-born into it. As I write in *Love's Mansion,* if the tree of life is a eucalyptus, then the novelist is its koala bear.

It is hard to explain what I compulsively do, though many have explained it to me. My dream machines may be derivative from the cosmos, the society, the back yard, but they will at least be added to the sum total of Creation; there is nowhere else for them to go. *Love's Mansion* is a monument, a loving invasion. A dramaturgical or operatic elegy. And an attempt to express some views about war and art, love and imagination, youth and age, death and memory, and most of all, a theme that occupies me a good deal these days: how disease, carving us at random, is the fiercest, most blatant art form. We are the stuff the furies rummage through and break; our bodies are their unwitting Lascaux.

[1992]

Middle River Stump Jump

ELUCTANT TO VOICE A CREDO, because some folk cite credos rather than sample the books that evince them, I nonetheless repeat my conviction that the novel, no less than the poem, voices the gut feeling of being alive, as does the Indian raga, say, getting into the open the muling and puling and whining we feel, as well as the blue-riband elation, the hubristic exuberance. Bach's cantatas do the same. For a long time now, over a dozen books, I have been trying to create images of human completeness, not only of the way the mind talks to itself (most of which vanishes), but also of our mind's, our body's, placement in the cosmic scheme of things. In other words, I try to depict the internal and the universal flux, and to show how the former simulates the latter, possibly the latter the former. If this is the maximal view of what's human, and of what's not, so be it. In order to get somewhere on time, we ignore a vast amount of our context, and for the same purpose we ignore a vast amount of ourselves too. I aim to say *We are like this, see; we are complex and undulating, open-ended and labile, but we think we are under control.* So I offer some solace (coming into the full heritage of our minds and

---

"Middle River Stump Jump" was the nickname of the last B-26 Martin Marauder, so-called because it never left the Martin-Marietta premises at Middle River near Baltimore and was used mainly to test various tricky undercarriage combinations (e.g. two fuselage wheels à la motor cycle, one behind the other; and one under either wingtip) that made for bad landings. I like the idea, at least in aviation terms, of an almost blasé, last-ditch experiment, honoring the plane yet not reluctant to bust it up.

emotions), but also some bad news (disease as an art form practiced by evolution). We do not belong to ourselves anyway, but to chemistry, astronomy, physics; we are also imagination's children, and we all have a chance of adding to Creation something that was not there before us, something uniquely ours. I am a potentialist, always wanting us to make the most of ourselves, to leave a scar on the universe. If we find life absurd, as it is, we can devise something absurd of our own to hit back with (Beckett's piano tuners in *Watt*). Hence, my view of language, as it might be of pigment, the twelve-tone scale, marble, the lens and silver nitrate: it is what I work in, dabbling in the blood of my ancestors, echoing their throats in my style, their urgencies in my mine. And I am especially eager to make things from words that, while part of being articulate, aren't merely expository, explanatory, matter-of-fact. Language is a mystery from which we can make mysteries that were not there before, skulking in the matrix like penicillin, but came into being with us, evincing our uniqueness. To use language thus is a reverent homage to our predecessors, who come to life in every tone we muster.

So: mysterious, unique, microcosmic recitative in honor of forebears, flooding our minds with *us,* leaving it behind us as spoor. The point is: having been created, we re-create ourselves, if we dare, cutting a stylish figure amidst the cosmic overwhelm, facing the deistic clock. The stylist gives you another, secret life, unavailable to most.

II

I believe we are living and writing in the last epoch of human endeavor in which anyone will attend to style. A big snowplow behind us will bring a horde of plainspoken mediocrities utterly indifferent to the things we prize Proust, Nabokov, Beckett for. The advance guard of this horde has already taken up roost in the publishing houses.

I believe in the artificial, the unique, the man-made; I am not much given to worrying about the planet; a red giant sun will doom it eventually and, scientists tell me, it is already too late to mount a departure into space. I want to set down what it has been like to be alive, to get across my own private sense of the universe. Some have called me a Hindu mystic: Certainly I am not here to protect people from the world, but to attune them to it. Most of the stuff that surrounds us is what the British used to call railway reading: you buy the book, read a bit of it en route and leave it on your seat for the next occupant. *Comme ils sont beaux, les trains manqués!* If the audience for a serious novel is no more than fifteen thousand, then rejoice; it will soon be smaller. Hardly anybody knows how to read, and the universities are full of dimwits doing other dimwits an uncritical favor. One book to read in this prickly interim is Julien Benda's *La Trahison des clercs.* The outstanding thing is that, as the century comes to an end in decadence, as centuries do, fiction is still being judged by incongruous standards: it should confront us with "lovable" characters; its prose had best be clipped and lean and clean, like Himmler's greyhounds; and whodunits have to be scrutinized with almost philatelical seriousness (thrillers too) while the outstanding fiction of the century gathers dust.

Almost nobody has any taste, and those who pretend to inform the public have no hope of teaching anybody anything. We will soon be surrounded by so much electronic mediocrity we'll go blind. People like to be on their best behavior on TV, whereas I don't believe it's an occasion to groom oneself for, as, say, the writing of an unforgettable sentence is. Books will continue to pour out, and the shlock-purveyors will go on being advanced fortunes.

I believe in defiance, criticism, craft and, in the end, loyalty to language, our real author, in whose throat we die. Words are the *hapax legomenon*—the only known instance of a thing's occurring—in the human parade. To do them less than justice is to betray the ancestors alive in them; but I know only a small platoon who can tell good from bad and call trash trash. Idiots with charitably bestowed B minuses have already taken over: a stunning, stupefying majority, more than we could ever kill off. I keep a revenge diary, though, for posthumous publication, a kind of *Devil's Non-Jest Book,* in which I honor master-spirits and flay dolts, hoping to interest successors and survivors. Or I might squeak it in at the very end, so as not to miss the ensuing noise.

[1994]

Literary Lions
at the Public Library

B UFFETED BY AN UNSEASONABLE early-November wind, those to
be honored as Literary Lions slopped from melting snow into
the lion-guarded Public Library of New York at Fifth Avenue
and Forty-Second Street. Inside the plastic-swathed porte cochère, cold
photographers huddled and peered. The lobby was an avalanche of
light, a press of helpers and groomers, patrons and escorts. As each
Lion-to-be arrived and was identified, he or she received a gold-plated
lion's head medallion, hung around the neck on a scarlet ribbon, surely
one of the evening's starkest effects as the males at least were wearing
black bow ties and tuxedoes, the perfect contrast. That slash of red,
going all the way around, then dipping to the cummerbund, suggested
one of the more recherché forms of decapitation: a red line for a tiro
headsman to follow, or the job done and the severed head left cun-
ningly in place. Then the lugubrious moment was over, as gone as the
winter wind that caused it.

With the lion pendant came tiny envelopes from Tiffany and Co.
inscribed in italic, telling in which of the rooms housing famous col-
lections you would be taking dinner in an hour's time. Ours said
"Arents Table 2," and others said "Berg" or "AP&P," which stood for
Art, Prints, and Photographs. A useful typed, photo-copied list handed
out just before dinner, like an improvisation, revealed the game plan;
but few of the new Lions knew who the other twenty-five were going
to be until he or she hit the third-floor rotunda for cocktails after first
checking in and receiving the medallion. Oh well, if the Public Library

wanted to be mysterious, let it. In fact, Judy Blume, Antonia Fraser, and Robert Stone, among others, were going to be in Berg; Ronald Sanders, Otto Friedrich, Peter Gay, Wilfrid Sheed, Stanley Elkin, and Clark Blaise, among others, in AP&P; and another bunch of us in Arents. This was not going to be a spectator sport anyway, except for those at each table, given one author to watch. I thought of an old crack about the eighteenth-century British aristocracy (one went to hear them eat and watch them talk), but I set it aside as ungrateful. Ensconced at a table of patrons and trustees and lovers of books, who had paid the library for their places, was one also going to be at a table of people who loved one's *own* books? Were they fans?

I pondered all this while promenading along the rotunda between walls of marble resembling buffed brown ice. "What," some wag asked, "do they use the rotunda for?" "Mainly," came the answer, "for a rotunda." Tonight they were using it for a sparkling party some three hundred strong while, in just about every alcove, a flautist played airs vigorous and mellow, evoking what lay off in the recesses of the library: an almost unimaginable realm of paginal vitality and readerly ease, all clamped tight between the covers of nine million books. We had never seen gladsome festivity in such a bookish place, certainly not one as majestic as this. Something sacrilegious was going on under the high ceiling of the McGraw Rotunda, but it was book writers who were making the racket, released all at the same time from their craft or sullen art into little rigmaroles of mutual congratulation, people-spotting, and something like mercenary awe (an apparition to remember and use) as Candice Bergen swept in, a triumph of physiognomical delicacy, her walk fluent and rehearsed, her smile natural as honey, and Douglas Fairbanks Jr. stood his ground, all crisp and lean lines, like the salute of eugenics to minimalism.

There we were, we prose and verse fabricators, slap-bang in the midst of myth, which I take to be a publically sanctioned and nourished fantasy. It was as if all our books were not powerful enough in the presence of myth demystified, and the only comparable stunt open to us was somehow to bare our brains as lovers in medieval paintings bare their hearts. We too, on paper, cavorted and performed, trying to make people suspend their disbelief; but, confronting Ms. Bergen and Mr. Fairbanks, and then the familiar face of Estelle Parsons, there to read aloud to us after dinner, I wondered about people who came from a competing dream. We were lions, but they were unicorns. Their *faces,* not to mention portions of their shapes, were more recognizable than our *minds,* and even on paper this was true.

Could it just be, I wondered, that the burnished Ms. Bergen was there as a journalist and playwright, and the trim, swordless Mr. Fairbanks as a writer and an Oxford Master of Arts? Not any more than Harold Pinter was there for his prowess as a cricketer or Edna O'Brien for hers as an actress. No, the Bergens and the Fairbankses were there to salute books and libraries, of course, but also to bring glamour among us, and to keep the event from seeming too cerebral. The Library was fighting the traditional image of the library. This is not to disparage the movie stars present, but to intimate how nervous intellectuality gets in this culture, where people who have read reviews think they have read books and people who have read American books think there needn't be foreign ones.

The Library stands poised, almost in the manner of the American Academy and Institute of Arts and Letters, to engage in multiple acts of timely election. All it has to do is honor the deserving and remember it is a *library,* which means not leaving it to glitz hounds to report their ceremonies; it should issue a comprehensive press release, saying what is going on, and why (anyone reading the society column's account of the Lions evening would never know that among the writers honored were the poets Anthony Hecht and John Hollander, for instance).

High above the noise there came, like one of those Manhattan firetrucks, a bray of trumpets, telling us to stop talking and start walking. I wondered if the demure soloists in the alcoves had gone on playing through all the hubbub; if so, surely the trumpets told them it was time to quit. I have only three things against cocktail parties: I can never hear what people are saying to me (I pick up too much extraneous sound); I hate standing up; and I don't drink. I was glad to stroll off to Arents with my dinner companion. Our escort, Ms. Connie Buckley, propelled us along yet another gleaming marble corridor into the vast desirable silence of a reading room in which half a dozen tables shone with cutlery and china. On the chairs there were copies of my books, almost as if, in true library (or nursery) spirit, they had assembled to fête my absence, under the table complaining about me, their maker, in a long roll call of my wicked despotic ways and my godlike callousness in deserting them, one after another, to go on to some wholly untried newcomer, with whom I always became infatuated, for a few years at least. I saw Raymond Carver staring at his own books too, maybe wondering similar thoughts; then he and I swapped signed copies and someone said "That's a combo I never expected to see." Good: my ears were working again, after the decibels of the rotunda.

In the center of our table, white as the Cliffs of Dover, was a model of the Library, maybe twenty inches long and half as many high, with all of tonight's Lions' names lettered around it in gold and rough-coated plaster of Paris lions guarding it. Atop the whole thing was a maroon pennant bearing my name. So this round table was my oracular coracle, and the affable folk seating themselves alongside my hosts, Mr. and Mrs. Daniel Rose, were going to be my crew: patient, but full of questions. I realized over the "Smoked Salmon with Golden Caviar in Tiny Potato" that it is easier to write novels than to explain why or how you do it.

From this moment on, the photographers never seemed to go away, asking us (or me) to look up or this or that way, the better to record the look of unbridled agony I get when trying to answer questions. My fellow diners quizzed me about Oxford (where, it turned out, Mrs. Rose and I had been contemporaries), Columbia (where Mr. Rose is in charge of the Lionel Trilling Seminars), rats, Nazi atrocities, the Hopi language, the movie *Shoah* (which I told them had intellectually disemboweled me), the Warsaw underground in World War II, the Finger Lakes, my writing habits, the books I was teaching in Comparative Literature 570, and a dozen other things. Some distance away, at their own tables (*separate* tables, I thought), Edna O'Brien, A.R. Gurney, William Meredith, D. Keith Mano, and Raymond Carver were doing much the same gustatory seminar. As the food and wine went down, so did the voices, and the gracious gathering developed a surreptitious air: we were cells of literary plotters getting our acts together before the final plenary session and our storming assault on the castles of philistinism. What a wonderful room to work in, I thought, and for a second the atmosphere of the pure, quiet,

unassailable, dormant library reached me; I wanted, not out of rude-
ness but out of reverence for the place, to open a book and read, or
pore over a priceless manuscript right there in the dim light, a com-
municant, a secret sharer. Let it be tribute enough to the arrangers of
this delicious dinner to say that the whole mood and manner of it
harmonized with the spirit of the place: we were dining in a reading
room, which was akin perhaps to snoozing in a throne-room; you
could dine only one way, and this was it, and in a throne room you
might snooze only one way or you would be expelled, and in an
armory you made love standing up among the erect rifles out of sheer
suggestibility.

One of the lovely touches, to me at least, was that I got to keep
that model of the Library, our centerpiece. It was really, my gracious
hosts told me, a birdhouse, and I thanked my stars that, on this night
of lions, it had not been a cage. A ratman I knew would have revelled
to see his smallest rats coming and going through that little round hole
in the Library's forehead. I also got to keep the golden soapstone lion
that had held my napkin. If you love toys, you will understand my
obsession with model, based maybe on some intuition that, although
we talk about macrocosm and microcosm, the latter never quite corresponds to the former because the macrocosm must surely include all
microcosms too, not least my own, and they all keep changing.

I signed the remaining copies of my books and then went down
to the basement for a group photograph, at which I arrived last. An
imperious aimer of the lens told the Lions how to stand and where, but
by now we were a lazy lot, yawning and stretching, tossing our manes,
yearning to nap in the shade while the flash bulbs popped at an empty
set of stairs. Someone asked us to smile. Asked to roar, we would
have done better, knowing that there was still a poetry reading to
come. Then they coaxed us into another room, where we sat at the
front in two halves flanking the lectern, joined at the last by Isaac
Bashevis Singer, gracious and looking frail, his lion pendant and red
ribbon neatly in place. Quite a stand-in for Mary McCarthy, unable to
come tonight to be lionized, as was George Garrett.

The room we sat in glowed. Not quite. The room we sat in had
a ceiling of what looked like those concave surfaces astronomers use
to explain triangles the sum of whose angles comes to less than 180
degrees. When I told this to A.R. Gurney, he seemed to know what I

was driving at; he too had been admiring the ceiling's adventurous, challenging look. you had this feeling of rising up to the half-shell above you of glass and cast iron. Dr. Vartan Gregorian, the library's president, reported that the evening had netted the library some quarter of a million dollars and introduced us one by one in alphabetical order, asking the audience to reserve its applause until the end. Last to rise, I got a lifetime's applause and, so as not to appear churlish, rose again during it, trapped in a Jacques Tati pandemonium.

Estelle Parsons had brought with her some heavy old library books (a good sign), from which she began to read a series of golden oldies by Longfellow, Frost, and Wordsworth. The emphasis was on romanticism, and I, an old Byron buff, responded as I should, nonetheless wondering, *worrying,* if something more up to date might have been in order. Why not, since they were here being lionized, some Hecht, some Hollander, some Meredith, some Carolyn Kizer? Or something from *upstairs,* where the manuscript of *The Waste Land* nestled in one of the ad hoc dining rooms. What a waste indeed. Ms. Parson's thundering, euphoric iambs were an odd finale to this sybaritic, lavish evening, although I could see what somebody had had in mind: we were being romantic about books tonight, we were here to be heroically inspired by the opened and closed heart of the book in much the same mood as the Everyman Classics used to say, after Milton, inside the cover, "A good book is the precious life-blood of a master-spirit." Poetry, as Ms. Parsons told us, could be fun; but I am afraid I thought right then of all the serious work lying around us, above us and on all sides and maybe even beneath us too, done by fine minds in dismay or delight, living through words because there was very little else to live by, at least at the time they wrote what they did. I had seen one of the poets on the platform wince. I looked around and caught Mr. Pinter looking thunderstruck: a dumb waiter thrust on to the heath at the last moment instead of King Lear. Maybe we twenty-six should each have said aloud one treasured sentence from our own work. We would certainly have felt less tonguetied.

When Ms. Parsons ended her jubilant oration, someone behind me cried "Bravo." I wanted to catch the eye of some seasoned publisher out there in the audience; I caught the eye of a stranger and it was rolling. I wished we had been able to rise for a dignified three-minute silence in memory of Primo Levi, who died that year. It would have been an honorable, and grateful, way to end and take our leave.

As we left, too tired to rise to the proffered refreshments at the back of the lovely Celeste Bartos Forum, or go to Mrs. Henry John Heinz II's kindly devised post-prandial soirée, we found ourselves being handed a paperweight swaddled in soft tissue paper; a book of essays about a former curator of the Berg collection; and a letter from the chairman of the trustees thanking us for coming. The New York Public Library gives you the sense that, when you arrive at the pearly gates, Saint Peter will at least have skimmed your bibliography. "Libraries," says Dr. Gregorian, "make people forget." That must be why we skidded back out into the November snow with toys and souvenirs enough to keep us remembering the seventh night of the Forty Second Street Lions for ever.

In after-years you get invited back, for reunions and such; but you never get invited to read there from your work. That privilege they reserve for the Estelle Parsonses and other semi-literary personages adjudged, I guess, safe and bourgeois enough even for an audience of soi-disant booklovers.

[1988]

Tan Salaam
and the Aga Khan

JUST BACK FROM EUROPE in the searing August of 1973, I flopped myself on the chaise longue on the balcony and began to read my accumulated mail, too much of it bills. One of the smaller envelopes came from *The Paris Review,* and contained a handwritten letter from George Plimpton, telling me in a casual, off-hand way that my story "Tan Salaam" had won the Aga Khan Prize for Fiction. I froze: this was the first literary prize that had come my way, and I marveled at the distant esoteric machinery of *The Paris Review,* re-reading contributions for prizes and then, in reverse excitement, sending out a modest little envelope with the news. The award made me happy because I had pulled the story from an abandoned 600-page novel (which eventually yielded up several more stories). I knew the novel didn't work, but I was delighted to find portions of it doing well. In its Spanish incarnation, the story sits in color on the wall before me, illustrated by a photograph of an elephant fleeing from a huge pile of dung central to the plot. The title has changed too to "Otras Memorias de Africa."

My next encounter with George came about when he decided to publish my novel *Caliban's Filibuster* under the Paris Review Editions imprint. Off I went to the holy of holies on East 72nd Street, right next to the big dark swill of the river. George dealt with me as if he had known me from childhood, and his prophetic ability put me at ease while I relished the close-up view I got of his naked feet, propped on the table: not smelly at all, and huge, almost dinosauric.

Certainly we were relaxed. My agent at that time, Lynn Nesbit, had cautioned me not to let George talk me into anything cheap; but he wanted to *publish Caliban's Filibuster,* and who was I to resist? Indeed, he published a chunk of that word-intoxicated oblique novel in the *Review* itself as well. His brainwave of the afternoon was that we do a *Paris Review* Interview together and print it in the back of the book, lulling the nervous reader into an ex post facto dialogue that actually made the novel harder to follow than merely reading it did. Since then, with either George or Ronald Christ, I have resumed that Interview, in more general and expansive terms, heaping it up past one hundred pages to two, and maybe approaching even three. As yet, none of Interview II has yet appeared in the magazine, and maybe we should start afresh. The problem seems to be that we no sooner finish than I publish another book, and so on.

Our trial runs would fill an entire issue, so perhaps the way to go is a short, snappy interview (like some of the very first ones) done in Eternalese, the language that never wears out. I once taught a seminar based on the first five volumes of Interviews. The only requirement was that students read the interviews only and not go whoring off to read the authors' books. The resulting atmosphere was bizarre as we pored over just about every syllable uttered by George's victims. For an author to be judged, mainly, by his or her spoken words is an excruciating trousers press of a limitation, but it can be fun, most of all when the author rises to the occasion with wit and almost total inability to remember his/her own books.

At some point in our discussions, George told me about the novel he had never been able to write: about a photographer who (if I recall aright) chased around the world in pursuit of spectacular photographic coups, but was always too late, an absentee in spite of himself. I thought such a personage would eventually develop a keen sense of the unmediated texture of diurnal life, looking for seasonal or meaningful time but finding only mere chronicity. That's what I would have done, I said; but George was groping for some philosopher's stone, some catalytic knob of chalk, some way of parading a series of timely shots, with always, I thought, the cliché looming of the well-timed photographer, paparazzo as perfectionist who starts with Werther and supplies the visual equivalent of Goethe's "The ball has almost reached the brain." How about a book of famous literary suicides revisited? From Crane to Woolf to Levi to Pavese. In the right mood, I might undertake it myself.

When George visited Penn State to lecture, he defied midwinter by wearing an open jacket. he took over my writing workshop and won over even my most captious students, who had thought he was better known for sports than for his superb magazine. The person who sat and confabbed with them that snowy Pennsylvania afternoon was very much the Editor of the PR, as they wanted, a paper lion with a literary mane. I don't think any of those MFA students placed work with the magazine, but it did them good to rub shoulders with the Cambridge man who read the fiction, anyway, and sometimes called up to praise it in that bizarrely projected voice he uses on the phone, as if speaking from Antarctica. Whenever I finish something I find I like, I send it to either George or Brad Morrow, two magazine editors I really trust. More often, they ask me what I am working on and if I have a piece to show, which is how I prefer it. There is much to be said for the editor who is also an author and has done his own end-runs over the slashing broken glass.

[1993]

Enemy Coast Ahead

S EVERAL TIMES A YEAR I scoot forth into what might be considered
enemy terrain and read from my fiction to academic audi-
ences. Invited in, I think my invitation comparable to the ones
I used to get from scientists—as when, invited by NASA, I visited the
inner sancta of the Jet Propulsion Laboratory, Pasadena, to watch
receipt of images from Voyager spacecraft. The savants there were
eager to show us their mystery, which they did in a humble, altruistic
way, whereas academics, for better or for worse, assume that visiting
novelists are already familiar with theirs and have come in partly to
ogle it.

My standard opening line (I don't always use it—I sample the
atmosphere) has become: A creative man among scholars feels like a
sodomite at a convention of proctologists. And then I get on with my
reading, never thinking of the categories they fit me into (expression-
ist-voluptuary?), but aware that, although I too teach in English and
Comparative Literature departments, I am among a different tribe, like
T.E. Lawrence in Feisal's (or Alec Guinness's) tent, where Feisal has
an aide read from "The Brightness" to soothe everyone a bit and
reaffirm the spiritual tenor of the meet. I never get the sense that I am
among the enemy, though it is usually the youngest faculty who seem
to get the most from my stuff, as indeed at my own university.

My response to lit-critters as they sometimes call themselves is
that, in part, I too used to be one of them, though the jargon I evolved
and stole, toward a twentieth-century *Poetics* of fiction, came from De

Quincey, Artaud, Beckett, Gide, Malraux, and Breton: practitioners of high art rather than arcane theorists, nonetheless needing to conceptualize the demands and drives of their creativity, and perhaps, like the critics, adrift in a world of science and medicine, hoping to pass muster with their own discipline among those blithely and supremely talking about black holes and cannibal galaxies or sinus rhythm and transient ischemia. I have a fondness for secret societies. I think I know why doctors took to using Latin, Cockneys to rhyming slang, T.S. Eliot to the objective correlative, and deconstructionists to you know what. Isn't this why we had erector sets when smaller? The jargon comes from some ingrown distortion of creativity, some impulse both to hide the mystery and flaunt it, perhaps because all of us, as we create more and discover more, find out how much remains to be known.

So I more or less willingly take part in the charade of knowledge, in the courts of miracles often staged by academics and doctors, less often by scientists (whose mystery seems to them supreme even if it's only a different kind of poetry). I arrive in a mood of ecumenical euphoria. I read things I am happy with, that sound all right aloud. And I depart thinking myself a bit more a theorist, a clinician, at least until I next run into a paragraph about polyverse illative modalities of the zero text (I fudge the jargon, not knowing the dialect of the tribe) or, as in a recent issue of a glossy magazine, "multiinfarct dementia" and "coccioioidomycosis" used as if they were terms familiar as tonsillitis and scarlet fever. These savants are not aborigines, concocting aseptic abstraction and neo-Greek (or Latin) as they do, but would-be Origines, eager to pin down the human condition while actually leaving it, hoping to end up in some elysium of the understood, some paradise of mastered. They know, as all poets and novelists do, that we are still occupied with Adam's chore: naming, and the concomitant problem: Are there more words than things to pin them on? I'll say this, though: doctors twitch when they find out you know some Greek.

[1994]

Borrowed Time

TEN YEARS AGO, several bad things happened to me, all cardiac, and it seemed for a while I had no future at all, not beyond a few weeks. As it panned out, I didn't go rustling off the gurney down the chute, like some of my fellow-patients in Intensive Care. So my future shrank to this instant, this day, this week (if I was feeling sound and bold). Looking back on that time, having had the future I never thought I would have, I still have the sense of living on borrowed time and am reluctant even to ponder whatever future is left. Time for me has become concentric, really a matter of depth and simultaneity. Perhaps this is why numbers all look alike to me, and my way of reading a book is to fix on a phrase or a line and plunge away into and behind it, acknowledging time only in an etymological way. When I hear the phrase *cogito, ergo sum,* I worry that the *"o"* on *cogit* has no right to be there until *ergo sum* has taken place. M. Descartes has no right to presuppose his own conclusion, even if only to suffix a verb. Such my notion of futurity.

Thus handicapped, I shuffle the futurology cards and stop my mouth with clear answers. The hole in the ozone layer is already repairing itself. There will soon be altogether too much visually sharp television in the world. Already, few know how to read a serious book. Television, essentially a medium of redundant illustration (someone says menu of ideas and a groaning board of smorgasbord appears onscreen), has just about killed the initiative people used to put into metaphor. One side of me, very American, believes in progress: selfishly craving inhalable insulin and better cardiology; another side of me overestimates how much we belong to nature to begin with, and is appropriately fatalistic. I had my true future almost 10 years ago, lived symbolically in one month, and all else is trappings on that. I see my life swelling outward like a stain, or an algae patch in a pool, needing only sunlight. I reassure myself that the word future descended from the Indo-European base *bhau-, which gave us not only *fut* but also *fui,* the perfect tense of *esse:* to be. The future is only a matter of emphasis, a better equipped past.

How, then, do I communicate with people to whom the future is a *thing* to come? Like a thriller reader, I believe in the shapeliness of things to come, hoping we have really done our worst, plumbed our nadir, in the 20th century, and that, while cramming the planet with ourselves and our progeny (meaning it no harm), we will get less vicious. I say *hope;* the swarming cannibal of mice in the overpopulation experiments at Rockefeller University chasten me. The future is a repercussion, not a plan. The future is a novel that ends before you intend it to, or that goes on after you have lost interest. The future is a tesseract for babies to play with.

[1993]

II

Jean-Jacques Rousseau
Reveries of a Solitary Walker

B OUND IN BUFF PAPER by Manchester University Press and rein-
forced a dozen years ago by scotch tape that still holds fast, this
is the very book I took with me on my own solitary walks in Derbyshire.
It was a set book on which I would be, and was, examined, and I had
to know certain sections by heart. The text is in an old French that
uses "pourroit" for "pourrait," for example, and the margins are loaded
with schoolboy notes that mention Keats and *King Lear:* at best the
faint subterfuges of untutored eloquence, at worst exam fodder. In
those days, I read them wrongly, these recapitulations of dream walks,
as if Rousseau had written (or said) them while walking. I wanted
immediacy, but what does seventeen know? In fact, if anything,
Rousseau was using the memory of these promenades to detach him
from the world. He was writing his last book creating a final testament, installing himself in a glass house of memory.

Amazing, then, how much of the book's physical world comes
through, as at the opening of the fifth of the ten Promenades. The Isle
of Saint-Pierre, in Lake Bienne, was unknown to travelers, he said,
and just the place for a solitary who could relate the flow of his soul
to the cries of eagles and the thundering cataracts. The island is two
islands, really, one inhabited, the other derelict and fallow. From a
distance of twelve years he recalls the one house on the inhabited
island in a mood wholly Swiss: farmyard and aviary, fish tanks, vines
and lush pastures, Sunday dances. He stayed there two months, but
would have remained "two years, two centuries, and all eternity."
These he called the two happiest months of his life, and you begin to
wonder at his efficiency: managing to unearth the armature for paradise just like that, passing from what he calls a "precious *far niente*"
to an all-inclusive harmony. He succeeds because his mind is superlatively ready, ministers to itself without demur or fumble, as if he has
become an absolute, which is to say he is complete, needs nothing
further.

To the end, however, he analyzes the roller-coaster of his emotions, trotting about in his mind's eye with his Linnaeus and magnifying glass, identifying stamens and nettles while presiding over huge ovations of the soul. The difference, of course, is that, when he writes it all up, his soul is waning, but nonetheless insists on a vehement roll-call. Oddly enough, I now find him like Beckett's Watt, the mathematical maven always trying to tidy up the world, whereas Rousseau is the maven of exaltation, trying to tidy up his heart. At very least, this palpitant book reminds us that both walking and promenades are a series of recovered falls.

Jean Genet
Prisoner of Love

To HAVE BEEN DANGEROUS for a thousandth of a second," an old Palestinian woman said to Genet, "to have been handsome for a thousandth of a thousandth of a second, to have been that, or happy or something, and then to rest—what more can one want?"

This oddly nineteenth-century doctrine of the ravishing instant is much the mood of Genet's last book, written when he already knew he had throat cancer, and without pain-killing drugs. It's a document from within a grievous situation: hectic, dreamy, spastic, mellow, impenitent, and moving—in a prickly, didactic way. You have to respect it, even if you can't stomach Genet's fondness for the Black Panthers and the PLO, with both of whom he spent considerable time. It's a reverie-memoir about sitting in the penultimate middle of hurt, managing to get the next sentence down, the next transition done, the hankering to organize fended off again and again.

Written with pain's steel nib against a miasma of American and Arabian memories, it is a product of long incubation, tender and philosophical in an almost Proustian way, especially about the intermittences of Genet's own heart. We see him in the act of changing his mind, which means no mere alteration of opinion, but shuffling stances from atheist mystic to terrorist manqué, from keen observer to glazed nostalgist. Taken for the togetherness of its golden moments, it is a beautiful book, like the shower of brilliants a hard punch swats from a boxer's face, to vanish into the lights. One of the PLO fighters has never seen the sea, so Genet and others tell him it is blue, where the tinned sardines of their staple diet come from. They draw fish in the sand and he asks what sort of noise fish make. "No one," Genet notes, "felt equal to imitating the voice of a fish." Lest company discipline fail, a Palestinian officer bans card-playing, so through the book the *fedayeen* in their desert redoubt play cards without cards, gambling in their minds only. Hebrew, Genet says, has some letters with "a crane-like plume on top: three slim pistils bearing three stigmata and waiting for the bees who'd scatter their age-old, nay primeval, pollen all over the world. But the feathers—they belonged to a letter that sounded rather like *sh*—didn't add a touch of lightness." Cardplayers in Damascus fold the pack lengthwise "so that when a card [is] thrown down it [falls] on the crease in an unstable equilibrium.

Elsewhere he observes that "Nature plays hardly any part in Jewish history." In one Palestinian camp, women line up at the one tap with green, red or yellow buckets "each with a different picture of Mickey Mouse painted on the side." And he writes poignantly of "The hour when street lamps are lit in the city, and which children try to drag out so that they can go on playing, though their eyes, suddenly active, are closing in spite of themselves."

In his preface to a translation of Saint-John Perse's *Anabase,* T.S. Eliot spoke of a logic of images that Perse used to potent effect, and Genet uses a similar logic here, pressing on you his raw nerves, infiltrating into the mind of anyone who claims to have life summed up the incessant unfolding of Creation in countless unique phenomena. Genet was one of those foxes who know many things, not one of the hedgehogs who know one big thing. So it's no use looking to *Prisoner of Love* (the French is *Un Captif Amoureux,* which is humbler) for an account of how the Palestinians fared since being driven out of their homeland, almost two million of them, from 1948 on.

Yassar Arafat may have invited Genet to come see, and to write his book, but this is not history or politics he writes. It is voluptuous witness done, as Edmund White says in his tuned-in introduction, in a deliberately "boneless" style. Something limp-wristed and lackadaisical gets Genet from one thing to another so fast—events and images go swooshing by—that you go back and re-read, certain you've missed a connective, a copula. The method is elliptical graffiti done in the washrooms of recent history by a man whose childhood was spent in jail and who takes a vast embracing view of human emotions:

> . . . though I shall die, nothing else will. And I must make my meaning clear. Wonder at the sight of a cornflower, at a rock, at the touch of a rough hand—all the millions of emotions of which I'm made—they won't disappear even though I shall. Other men will experience them. . . . More and more I believe I exist in order to be the terrain and proof which show other men that life consists in the uninterrupted emotions flowing through all creation.

Such elaborated, visionary selflessness does scant justice to emotional originality, but makes a brave point akin to André Malraux's idea of "virile fraternity." When you feel anger, joy, disdain, or, say, mutinous reverence, you are at one with all who others who ever felt, feel, or will feel thus.

Perhaps this is what the old Palestinian woman intends when she views the human antic under the aspect of eternity—or, more fashionably, cosmological evolution. In a slewed image worthy of the old metaphysical poets, she goes on: "Did we stay for a few minutes in Oslo? Maybe. If we'd stayed there for sixteen years we'd have frozen the world." So through an intensity of presence made blatant in a sudden racial plural, the cold of Norway flows outward to chill the planet. It's a typical Genet formulation, cabalistic and raw; no wonder he picked it up, and a page later repeated it. He always went against the grain, doting on Hitler's SS and the Chicago police, construing prisons as courts of miracles, yearning to watch a naval battle from his window ("with drowned men floating"), arguing that only murderers can judge murderers ("The judges have never been to the places where the acts they have to judge were performed...").

Only those who as it were, fail to "understand" his book will get its desultory, cantankerous, romantic point: that almost nothing matters except on the level of diurnal novelty. Cynical he may have been, but he renewed an old point of Sartre and Camus, made it with a bellyful of much nastier experience, saying, as here, that the universe is not absurd, but humans are for wanting it to make sense to them. Only love and prose will please.

Some of the people burn through the haze of discrete particulars: Hamza the Palestinian soldier and his mother (who brings a cup of coffee to Genet's bedside and so becomes a permanent holy image in his mind); the candid and ultimately gagged poet, Khaled Abu Khaled, who broadcast on Radio Damascus; Mubarak, the Sandhurst-educated Sudanese lieutenant whose cheeks bear German-looking tribal scars, who reads Spinoza. But it is Genet the tireless observer and egalitarian rhapsodist who dominates, taking eight Nembutal nightly, noting that the Black Panthers eat fatty food and "wear a dense furry sex on their heads," envisioning Marx writing *Das Kapital* "on pink silk cushions," delighting in hairs lifted gently from a brow or a hummingbird flicked off a shoulder.

As he writes, he comments on the nature of his book, calling it "an upsurge in memory," confiding that he remembers "like an owl," wishing the book weren't so jerky. "Who is it for?" he asks. Sometimes he sounds fed up with it: "As I am writing this book in the form of 'Souvenirs,' I must cheerfully accept the rules of memoir writing and dredge up a few facts." Yet, identify as he might with peoples in revolt, it is God's (or humankind's) minutiae that attract him most, spellbinding him: cigarette lighters "no bigger than an apple pip... leather-bound imitations of Korans the size of a big toe-nail but hollow, with the name of God carved inside the Arabic." This lover of detail sees himself dwindling into a grain of sand and lets us hear it for the small, the minor: whatever archangels overlook.

Alain Robbe-Grillet
Ghosts in the Mirror

RECENTLY, "live" on Parisian television, I saw a French novelist
pluck out his earpiece and toss it across the set at me, missing;
of course, being tethered, the earpiece rebounded. Such antics seemed
a long way from my no doubt severe notion of a French novelist, at
least of the twentieth century. Alain Robbe-Grillet, for instance, the
epitome of rational poise and calibrational steadiness, would never
have tried such a stunt; instead, a voluminously described raspberry
would have arrived in the mail, inviting one to word it with even more
relentless philatelical finality, as if truth were a feat of exhaustion.
Scrupulously impersonal, in his novels at least, Robbe-Grillet won this
kind of reputation by cultivating sheer indefatigability of the eye, as
if to imply that fiction cannot be based upon, cannot *be,* anything
slovenly or vague.

That first impression remains: of meticulous, patient accuracy
achieved by a writer who maintains that the novelist has nothing to
say and might as well make a good job of describing the world instead. He sees the novelist as a top-notch phenomenologist, untouched
by the egotistical sublime.

Here, however, comes Robbe-Grillet baring his heart, exposing
the lyrical and rather lilting soul we knew was there all along behind
those solemn and strict *nouveaux romans* of his, revealed most of all
in the prose manner he adopts for this new book: controlled, of course,
but almost voluptuous and, throughout, lush, ripe, and luminously
intuitive. He still disdains metaphor, but he revels in sensuous describing, as if the people of his own life had conferred upon him licence
to plumb and guess, to sample their interior lives with eclectic fondness, not as copiously as Nathalie Sarraute does in her novels of "sub-
conversation," yet much more than is usual with him.

He still mistrusts "adjectivity," as he calls it, after Roland Barthes,
and the thick prose of Zola, but he does allow one phobia into view:
"I couldn't listen to Pelléas or *Tristan* without feeling instantly up-
lifted by the insidious, perilous surge of the sea, then sucked reluc-

tantly into the heart of an unknown, unstable, irrational liquid universe ready to engulf me." Look at the adjectives there. Without laboring it, he makes the point on every page that good prose must be at least as detailed as the world it seeks to evince or supplant, whether the writer is guessing or just reporting. Take this, for example—mauve if not purple, and essentially celebrational: "Caiques sailing up the Golden Horn through the lengthening rays of the setting sun; the main street of Pera already lit signs for dancing girls in the soft twilight and the floods of men in dark robes; the Galatasaray lycée where sugary, nostalgic melodies *alla turca* throbbed, lulling us to sleep in the big white marble dormitories." If writing is specific enough, it needn't be lyrical or heavily adjectival. Robbe-Grillet remains the researcher who began by working at a biology laboratory, "taking vaginal smears every eight hours from hundreds of sterile rats injected with urine from mares in foal." But he seems to be mellowing his effects, ushering in sentence after sentence that resembles a conga of gorgeous animals.

The most vivid and moving writing in this relaxed, well-tempered book is about his parents, to whom he pays devout attention, most of all to his mother, who once kept an ailing bat for several weeks under her blouse "in what she called her pouch," to the horror of visitors, who watched it emerge from her white collar and spread its wings over her breast and neck. Myopic, big-nosed, she doted on tiny things (Japanese figurines made from grains of rice, for instance) and so loved all forms of animal life that, when washing watercress, she became completely sidetracked by aquatic insects she found among the stems. She had no sense of time and, like her husband, was an anti-Semitic anglophobe. Without knowing a word of German, "Papa" translated Schiller's plays with gusto, resoled the family's shoes, worked in a cardboard box factory, had a passion for making porridge, and, like his wife, subscribed to "an almost visceral atheism." The book evolves by sentimental convection as Robbe-Grillet drops themes only to pick them up later, creating a wafty, haphazard atmosphere. With so many good things to get to, he sometimes tries to do them all at the same time, and the effect is of a book long resisted and then allowed to burst forth, ebullient and chiming.

As well as plenty of crackling gunfire about the stodginess of the twentieth-century novel ("a last-ditch attempt to forget the disinte-grated state we were left in when God withdrew from our souls"), Robbe-Grillet offers commentary on Barthes, Camus and Sartre; memo-ries of starting out as a fiction writer; and a dispersed portrait of Henri de Corinthe: a nebulous, mythic family visitant, a Wagnerian Nazi, sometimes a mummy stripped of its wrappings, sometimes a Breton horseman out of legend who lived alone in an old gun emplacement and bore a double puncture on the back of his neck. This is all solid material, required reading for Robbe-Grillet buffs, but the non-special-ist reader is going to remember the family, the sea-going forebears, Robbe-Grillet and his father renting a wheelbarrow to bring back across wartime Paris a sack of coal, the affectionate sketch of his child-wife Catherine who along with the author survived the crash of an Air France 707, and the days of forced labor in Germany, where in Nuremberg he worked as a lathe operator and began to turn a steel chess set.

Several times Robbe-Grillet reminds us that language, uniquely human, is subjective to begin with and can never with utter authority reveal the nature of anything. There is fiction among these facts, as he admits. Breast-fed until two, playing with china dolls bound hand and foot for sexual rituals, he comes across as a gifted dreamer, a conjurer, an uncontriving eccentric. His latest book has all the amenity of *For A New Novel,* and some other qualities too, once latent and implicit but now in the open for amazement and study. When *La Maison de Rendez-vous* appeared in 1966, the *Times Literary Supplement* of London observed that Robbe-Grillet had become a gifted pornogra-pher; *Ghosts in the Mirror* also shows him in a new role, that of gifted rhapsodist, akin to the Albert Camus of the North African essays. Jo Levy's translation is winning and artistic.

André Gorz
The Traitor

A NDRÉ GORZ WAS BORN in Austria of a Jewish father and an Aryan, Catholic mother. To the Nazis he was a defective person, a hybrid apt for Switzerland, where his mother eventually sent him, and from where he made his way to France. A fervent disciple of Sartre (who appears in the narrative as "Morel"), he shows in this novel how Existentialism helped him solve his personal problems. *The Traitor,* published in France in 1959, shows how Gorz gradually became not just a name but the name of a definite person who, under the combined pressure of inherited ambivalence, Nazi pogrom family break-up and acute neurosis, had to pull a self together or go under. This is a document of self-therapy, and a moving one at that.

The reader has to work hard to follow the course of events, for the main character's every action (a petty theft, a bicycle ride, getting a passport renewed) is encrusted with monstrously articulate speculations that result from the effort to "understand how you arrived at your condition, how you have chosen yourself starting from there, how you have let yourself be infected by it, half victim, half accomplice, how it has been possible that you have agreed to live it." *Homo existentialis* indeed.

Gorz's quest, therefore, for both him and the reader, has been an agony of revision in a sea of possibility. Naturally enough, being an intellectual, he advances by theorizing; and the identity that emerges is the result of his constant and meticulous use of philosophical language. Of the pitfalls he knows all he needs to know: "Parasites, then, or pariahs, always nonintegrated, oppressed by society or family, they are inclined by their theoretic equipment, having no grasp of reality, to judge the world in the abstract." The novel includes specimens of Gorz emergent (writing "to recover his existence transmuted into literary material") with commentaries by Gorz defined. The first section he calls "We," the next "They," and the one after that "You" with "I" bringing up the rear. Neat and almost natty.

Gorz occasionally lapses into facile paradoxes and forced-looking digressions. But then, his subject hardly exists until he gets it into words, and words of any kind help exteriorize the interior muddle. A young man, giddy from looking into the abyss of possibility, steadies himself by stern praxis and an occasional laugh at himself. It is odd to see the doctrines of *Being and Nothingness* put rigorously and effectively into action. No wonder Sartre's long and enthusiastic preface becomes a hymn of sympathy to the "accidental" man who, through soliloquizing, gets a grip on his destiny. It's almost like a dry run for the later tome on Genet, saint, comedian, and martyr.

From groping phrases that merely prove to "him" he is there, we are led through the more confident stage at which he tries to systematize ("The only valid philosophy is the one which demonstrates its own impossibility and abolishes itself in silence") and then, all sophistries exposed for what they are, into a phase of fruitful paradox that produces such observations as this (on Marxism): "This is the most difficult point—to be on the side of those one criticizes and to be separated from them by the very hope one places in them." That suggests he's getting somewhere, not asking too much ("I shall never be through beginning again") and coming to terms ("my world is this white paper, my life the activity of covering it"). Suddenly this unheroic hero comes to earth, recognizes his vocation and the treachery of all in a society that "measures an individual's success by the number and the power of the means he acquires to hold the community at a distance." His final point is sensible and brave: "My reality," he says, "is not within my power alone, it is also what you will make of me." His idea of betrayal is to be led farther than he can go by himself: in other words, to find a provocative affinity. To this admirable though not original conclusion *The Traitor* takes the toughest route possible; the journey is nerve-wracking, and written in French. I end up recalling Lord Salisbury's quip that, when big men get ideas, small men get the headache.

Samuel Beckett

C AN THERE BE, somewhere, someone who has not longed for oblivion, even if wanting only a novelty? The bitter thing about oblivion, though, if you come back from it, is that it has no texture to recall, remaining a space in a sequence. You may indeed, to use Beckett's phrase, have faded into the mighty never, but you can refer to the experience (or the phase, the transit) only in terms of ensuing relief, cathexis, calm faith. Beckett is the expert on this promotion of *idée fixe:* you have to think of nothing as though it were something, he says, and (complementary *de*motion) you have to think of God as of a man. The mind, Beckett schools us, can minister to itself in a thousand ways, but it cannot think itself to a halt. It can do the impossible only through the pretty sleight-of-hand of metaphor.

After you have read Beckett's fiction for long enough, you become a bit blasé about the voluptuous eschatology he peddles. Students in my seminar on him used to ask why, since he found life so appalling, he did not kill himself. They wrote to him and he sent them inscribed books in return; always in French, to get them working. The answer, I sensed, was that to find life appalling is in some way a tribute to mind, whereas the oblivion of suicide is a tribute to nothing. There was always in him something obtuse that wanted to stay alive fractionally more than it didn't: something ornery, cussed, keeping the flame of intellect guttering in the hope that, even in extremis, it might come up with the unprecedented, an aperçu that would bring a bleached smile to the lips of other curmudgeons—the absurd smile, the laugh laughing at the laugh. As I said, there is a temptation to get blasé, to think you understand him, even to the point of saying he grew to hate art because it did not render him godlike, because it fraternized with the ceaseless brain that has to go on, always going on when it *can't* go on, dribbling ahead beyond ostensible self-control. Of all modern eschatologists he turned enigma into style: Watt's funambulistic stagger, for instance, or the group of things he found of great formal beauty but indeterminable purport.

Rumor was, he lived in a furnitureless room because chairs and tables would sully the purity of space. That was a Platonic or Platonicized Beckett, an apocryphal vignette. He did not deal in such absolutes (an absolute needs nothing: Mr. Knott needs nothing, yet needs that recognized), but in dwindlings, deteriorations, declines, defungings, deponencies. He was really the muse of entropy, of systems running down, which is one of the main subjects of literature. Systems run down and do not perk up unless interfered with. I don't think any author has recognized this aspect of the human condition as much as Beckett, but his taste for terminal makes him hard to read. A prickly companion, he sends Christopher Ricks *(Beckett's Dying Words,* 1993) looking for quotes while grappling in his first chapter with death (48 pages, 25 authors, from Berryman and Empson to Clough and F.H. Bradley, from Spenser and Beddoes to Dante and Milton), brought up to testify in a more companionable way than Sam's, almost as if Mr. Ricks, having emigrated from England to America, were marching a pensum in the manner of the Italian Claudio Magris walking with friends from one end of the Danube to the other.

Ricks quotes liberally from both Beckett and his chosen two dozen, but the extraordinary thing, and most laudable, is the way he keeps Beckett the Frenchman and Beckett the Irishman level-pegging, checking the French against the English all the time. So there are two Becketts here, each a *Doppelgänger* to the other while Ricks makes a ghostly third right out of *The Waste Land,* slouching alongside with magnifying glass and Larousse dictionary. Not only that: most of the pages in his little book have plentiful, complex, fascinating footnotes, like shoals of contending maggots beneath, succubi of the sub-text, often giving the lie to what's above: heroic exegesis undermined as often as not by further, finer exegesis, or by mistakes pointed out (Beckett's "Grave's disease" for Graves's disease or his softsoaping a bit of *Hamlet*—"the fat weed that rots itself in *death* on Lethe wharf" from "the fat weede/That rots it selfe in *ease* on Lethe Wharfe ..." (italics mine).

What we have here, actually, is the Clarendon Lectures given at Oxford in 1990, and I wonder how Rick's pithy short paragraphs, in which he picks apart Beckett at his most curt and apophthegmical, must have sounded even as he beckoned to the sad ghost of Coleridge in the shadows, and all the other shades summoned there to make a chorus. Can scholarship be sung? Ricks almost makes you think so as he amasses tightly woven teasers toward an almost fearful recitative not geared to the slack or skimming ear:

> For by something which itself partakes of the oxymoron the antithetical sense is at once fully an oxymoron and yet not one at all (rather as *rime riche* may be poverty-stricken).

Take that. He has come to this perception by way of "I shall soon be quite dead in spite of all," the first words of *Malone Dies,* but his mind is full of trouvailles, such equivocal words as "quite," a word used as "maximizer, compromiser, and diminisher." Not only does Ricks pore over Beckett's French; he peers into the glottal mists in Beckett's mordant English, almost always with triumphant finds. To best someone and to worst someone, he writes (or chants) "may come to the same thing, or ... to say something *roundly* may amount to saying it *squarely.*" This is how Beckett's mind worked too, declining a *Paris Review* Interview with "I have no views to inter." Ricks reads Beckett, and all literature, etymologically, as one should; not to do so is like appraising silk without honoring its worm.

Those poring over his book (there is no other way to read it than, like Virginia Woolf in Kew Gardens, get down on your knees to see what's stirring in the grass) will find miscellaneous delight starkly rendered: Beckett sorrowing that Joyce believed in words ("they would express what you wanted"); Robert Louis Stevenson sharing with Beckett the distinction of having composed a work called "Not I"; the pudendal, scrotal and bandy-legged quality of *lunulae* or parentheses (these little curved moons); a meditation on *spayed* in spade; a piece of pure Beckettian prose in Dickens's *Our Mutual Friend* ("He is struggling to come back. Now he is almost here, now he is far away again. Now he is struggling harder to get back"—a fore-echo of The Unnameable's "He's backing away again, or, He's stopped to scratch himself...." "Are obituaries still viable?" asks Ricks. "Well, viduity exists." On he goes, quixotic don that he is, but only to think hard about Beckett's translations of Mexican poetry ("This translation remains an idea of the thing, not the thing itself") and his famous supposed answer (*"Au contraire"*) to the question, Was he an Englishman? The answer seems to mean, No he was not. Ricks links *Malone Dies* with Morte d'Arthur and cites W.H. Mallock's recipe for an epic poem like Tennyson's: take a blameless prig, wound him in the head, and keep him in a cool barge for future use. Then he laments, as do some others of us, that many critics of Beckett *"make nothing* of his art,"* without going on to say the obvious: that such critics have no brains whereas Beckett is perhaps the brainiest agonist we know, the one twentieth-century prose author who needs his texts as heavily annotated as, say, in the old days, *Beowulf.* In Beckett there is a crux in almost every line, and that's no Christian pun.

Ricks spends much time on the Irish love of contradictions, omitting from his list of Beckettian ones the one I cherish most: the hussar getting up on a chair the better to adjust the plume of his busby. Perhaps the most complex of Beckett's Irish contradictions—"Speak up, said Mercier, I'm not deaf"—"posits a world in which if they think you are deaf, they deliberately lower their voices so as to frustrate you, drive you mad." Ending with a personal postscript in which he charts his few dealings with Beckett the man, Mr. Ricks allows us to relax from his exegetical labors of love. His is surely the way to read Beckett, with fine tooth comb, dictionary, and either James Stevens Curl's book on funerary architecture, *A Celebration of Death* (1980) or Karen Grandstand Gervais's *Redefining Death* (1986).

You need something beside you if, as Arnold said, you are not so much going to prevail as keep alive a needed attitude. A musical friend told me his baseball-addicted fourteen-year-old son has discovered Rap and now calls classical repertory "geezer music." Beckett's is geezer music too, and Christopher Ricks handles it with rompy tenderness.

Beckett and Giacometti

A THOROUGH STUDY of Beckett's works, such as we still do not have, will have an awful lot of explaining to do, at least in the absence of an annotated *Complete:* the work is replete with allusions and unfamiliar words, all of which get the student working hard on sometimes marginal things. This done, the study would have to introduce and explore some of his favorite concepts, such as pseudo-couple, quaqua, Belacqua bliss, asylum, microcosm, text, and nothing, with special attention to his little monograph of Proust, repudiated by Beckett (it has never appeared in French), but useful as an index to a state of mind which, although set aside, was seminal, and helps the reader to traffic with the Beckettian use of enigma in such books as *Watt* and *How It Is.*

Matti Megged *(Dialogue in the Void)* does little of this, intent as he is on one of those affinities brought out, in art, by André Malraux's *The Voices of Silence.* Beckett is as tough a nut to crack in seventy pages as Proust was for Beckett himself, and even tougher when half of the envisioned space goes to Giacometti, himself a taxing subject. All that would justify such a tight braiding of topics would be a keen, chronic understanding of both men's work and the revelation that they have much in common. Well, Megged has, and, as he reveals, the affinity is nothing forced; you wonder why no one has pointed it out before.

In a sense, this makes his job even harder: there is something solid to mine here, and he has to do it deftly, almost like a miniaturist—without getting too aphoristic, without squeezing things to death. He has, at the same time, to cite and explain, to compare and contrast, without putting off the reader who has plenty of Beckett but little Giacometti, or vice versa. Remarkably, he pulls it off, fusing hemmed-in exposition with sophisticated commentary, making throughout the crucial point that, for both Beckett and Giacometti, style is what maximizes art's virtual incapacity to copy. For both, style is "more realistic than so-called naturalism," or, to use Giacometti's own words, "A realistic picture is a picture too unreal to become 'stylish.' The trouble with it is that it doesn't look like anything." So too, Beckett, noting in his Proust essay "The copiable he does not see," which Megged does not quote, though he might have. Early on, Beckett saw that art is not a brand of photography, but an irresistible emanation from within, distorting and deforming and, quite naturally, leading every artist to the brink of expressionism, a mental and emotional mode that too many American literary critics either overlook altogether or confuse with surrealism. Megged is good on these things, steering his way by implication rather than by outright textbook lessons; he writes for those already a little versed in stylistics, and he even manages to do justice to Beckett's plays, revealing their sculptural qualities, linking their visual spareness to Giacometti's own.

It is no surprise, then, to find on the first page the two of them, in 1961, trying to devise the right set for the revival of *Waiting For Godot* at the Odéon in Paris. They *built* the set together, juggling a bare stage, a tree, and a moon. Years later, Giacometti said: "We experimented the whole night long with that plaster tree, making it bigger, making it smaller, making the branches finer. It never seemed right to us. And each of us said to the other: maybe." As Megged makes clear, both men develop lifelong an intense sense of failure, feeling, as Beckett would put it, a compulsion to express together with the absence of anything expressible, but they part company inasmuch as Giacometti said a great deal about it whereas Beckett was tight-mouthed except for sibilant utterances in occasional interview. It was not that they wanted the tree to be perfect, they just wanted it to be as useful as possible, as commanding as the right word, the right contour, in the right place.

As it is, this so-called tree has always looked to me like some ricochet from Kirlian photography: a sprayed-out root system electrocuted where it stands—even a human nerve-ending blown up and made to stand every one of its fibers on end. I would have said it was successful, and provocative, beyond their wildest dreams; perhaps they looked at it too hard, unable to recognize the moment at which it settled down into something utterly appropriate because it could not be pinned down as tree or whatever. They both, as Megged shows, try too hard not to try too hard, and the fatigue conducts them into laconic misery, with Giacometti sounding like a Beckett character and Beckett seeming all the time to head for the denudedness, the strippedness, of sculpture, and its silence too.

I would not have expected it, but, maybe because Beckett is so sparing with comment on his art, I found that Giacometti elucidates Beckett better than any commentator I have read, with Megged coming in behind to touch in some of the finer points with worthwhile assists from Dore Ashton and Maurice Blanchot. For instance, all these Beckettisms come from Giacometti, who sometimes seems the latest recruit to what Beckett calls his troop or platoon of fools, his "vice-existers":

> I do not know whether I work in order to make something or in order to know why I cannot make what I would like to make.

> Why this compulsion to record what one sees? ... It's the modern form of adventure for men who are left on their own.

> I have always failed.—If only I could draw!—I can't. That's why I keep on drawing. (He couldn't get more Beckettian than that.)

> ... you copy the *residue of a vision* ....

And, where Giacometti doesn't quite come out with it, Megged fills deftly in: "the unlimited possibilities of non-representational art are even more frightening than the impossibility of representing reality." One might sometimes push the thought of either man, or their presenter, a bit further, as when Megged notes that Giacometti "believe he really saw living beings only through their gaze"; yes, maybe the creatures of both these artists are trying to gaze at themselves only, and all else is extraneous.

Significantly, there is more to quote in this book from Giacometti, whose explanations always go beyond himself, telling us about not only Beckett but modern literature in general, and especially about the American fiction writers I have come to dub The Lost Tribe, who, without ever adding up to a movement or a school, have actually picked up where Joyce and Beckett left off, and have formed organic links with the nouveau roman, magical realism, and abstract expressionism, not to mention Schoenberg, Messiaen, and Cage. What they do, in a dozen different ways, takes something from Beckett's *Texts for Nothing* which Megged (rightly, I think) finds Beckett's most moving work, in which the words are "spoken just for their own sake." One thinks of Novalis's view that talking for the sake of talking is the sincerest things we do, which in Beckett becomes a recitative of hereness: spoor, snailtrack, heartprints. And, of course, explaining that sort of thing to editors of glossies, to reactionary editors in publishing houses, or even to students reared on the copiable and the minimal in tandem, is wretched work. One of the moving things about this diligent, wise, and moving book is that Megged sees, in Beckett, literary art at last catching up with visual art, coming to the same problems and the same impasses, without ever quitting. There is something profoundly gladdening in the news that Giacometti "lived his life almost like one of Beckett's heroes," even at one point usefully trekking around on crutches like Malone himself. The sculpture named *No More Play* surely does evoke Beckett's endgames, and the one named *Life Goes* On embodies that classic Beckettian *possum quia impossibile* (Beckett once said that the animal he'd like to be is the opossum).

Matti Megged, himself a novelist *(The Last Day of Danny, Mem)*, has done us all a favor, with self-effacing cogency doing a book that goes beyond itself into the generative core of all the arts. All the same, I wish it had been longer, with more quotation from Beckett (which would of course enable him to quote Beckett on himself in toto!). The print is too small. The prose here and there is a bit too monofilamental for me. The past tense of *strive* is *strove* not *strived* (page 54) and one sentence on page 30 is quite misleading: "The atmosphere of Beckett's first stories in French, 'Texts for Nothing,' and his novels is that of a dim twilight.... "The first stories in French were the *Nouvelles,* translated as the *Stories* in the volume *Stories and Texts for Nothing* (plus one other, "First Love"). A second edition should tidy these things up, especially if the book has come to stay.

Frederic Prokosch
The Missolonghi Manuscript

As a CULT-FIGURE Byron has been displaced by such curiosities as Beardsley, Spies and Hobbits; but he has served millions of people of all sorts of conditions as a vicarious means of fulfilling the rake side of their natures. Or, as a lone wolf of charismatic nobility who nevertheless ended profoundly committed to the cause of Greek liberation, he has provided a rallying point for reformers and spiritual outlaws. Even now, thanks to gossipy oral tradition and a host of biographies, everybody has heard of him. His crammed, poetically short life still interests us; but, in the last decade or so, it is his writings which have won belated attention, some of it pedantic, much of it enlightened and lively.

Of course, the writings lead back to the man: they are meant to, especially *Childe Harold* and *Don Juan,* in which Byron disguises himself only to make us look at him more closely. Something of a gagster-prankster, he wears a nylon stocking over his head—not to elude identification but to make certain of it. He wanted to be unique and, except for a few lapses into stale taste and trim domesticity, he was. And Don Juan, that prolonged anthem to the deliciousness of cynicism, is unique too.

Yet most of those who revel in his life find his best writing too hard-boiled and insufficiently solemn, while most of those who delight in his best writing find his life a bit of a drag. *Don Juan,* in fact, is a rebuke to uncynical wallowers in Byronism, and the hectic life was in many ways a means of dredging up material for that "aurora borealis" of a poem. I mention the contrast because Frederic Prokosch, himself a cosmopolitan, a lover of the exotic and a prolific writer (15 novels) as well as a lavish stylist, has now fabricated for Byron an intimate, retrospective journal to remedy the absence (as he says in an ironic foreword) of "earlier 'intimate' journals . . . burned in the home of the publisher John Murray as a sop to the sensibilities of Lady Byron, Hobhouse, *et al.*" Alternating between the sick, haunted Byron dying at Missolonghi in Greece and the recollected exploits of the poet who became famous overnight, the *Manuscript* is meant to fill some kind of gullibility gap. Ostensibly presented by one T.H. Applebee of Bryn Mawr College, Pa., who wrote a dissertation on Byron at the University of Kansas, it doesn't quite square with Byron's habitual ways of spelling and punctuating. T.H. Applebee concedes this ("The thing, of course, may be a forgery"), preferring, however, the notion that "the tight and almost 'modern' phraseology of some of these passages is not so much in conflict with the poet's earlier style as in a subtle and self-developing harmony."

Feeble as the spoof is, it enables Prokosch to vent his embarrassment at having undertaken such a feat of mnemonic possession. Yet need he, after all, be embarrassed or coy at sentencing himself to such an arduous impersonation? The answer has to be, yes: unless he does the one thing we have every right to expect *The Missolonghi Manuscript* to do better than all the biographies, psychoanalytical and critical studies, rolled into one; better, even, than Byron himself does in the brilliant erratic letters and journals we do have. And that is to make Byron—given this chance—explain himself Byronically, see himself whole; or, maybe even more bewitchingly, to show him in the act of trying to do so but failing. Either way, a definitive self-scrutiny by Byron in the first dismal months of 1824, the 36th and last year of his life, would be useful. We could then, on no matter how hypothetical a basis, give up guessing and settle down to read his writings with a new sense of illumination.

But alas, unwilling to stretch his presumption to the limit, Prokosch gives us mostly a repeat of what anyone who's read a biography or two, and dipped into the letters and journals, knows already. I'm not saying he should have concocted "new" data (e.g., Byron suffered lifelong with shingles, Byron ate the clippings from his own toenails, Byron was really Shelley). Prokosch is too scrupulous for that. I'm asking who, if he's got Byron, needs Prokosch? For example, here is Byron's description of an execution:

> the *masqued* priests; the half-naked executioners; the bandaged criminals; the black Christ and his banner; the scaffold; the soldiery; the slow procession, and the quick rattle and fall of the axe; the splash of blood, and the ghastliness of the exposed heads....

And here is what Prokosch makes of the same scene:

> a row of masked priests, who were followed by a pair of
> half-naked executioners. Then came the trio of manacled
> criminals, followed by the effigy of the Christ of Death.
> Some soldiers surrounded the scaffold and the thieves ap-
> proached the block....

It would have been better simply to quote, especially when the Prokosch deadens the sense of paralysis conveyed by Byron's version. True, as Byron himself perhaps did, Prokosch is recalling something already written down; but he doesn't tell us that, and the only good reason for thus revamping the Byron would be to show how Byron saw the incident in a new light. In fact, though, this Prokosch Byron makes much the same comment as the real Byron; but "how dreadfully soon things grown indifferent" becomes elegantly varied into "an indifference which bordered on boredom."

Here and there, it is only fair to say, Prokosch does amplify and extend, retrench and imagine. I just feel that, after reading this insufficiently bold exercise, I've not found out about Byron much that I didn't know, whereas I have found a suave, earthy prose virtuoso imposing on Byron an erotic witness which is vividly his own. For the book abounds in curiosa phallic, vaginal, labial, spermatical, pederastical, sodomitical, menstrual, masturbational, fetishistical, fellational, gonococcal, but never—unless I've misread the bit about the cheetah—bestial. In short, it's an unashamedly fun book in which Prokosch enjoys his obsession with Byron's obsession. "If a stranger were to happen," he makes Byron say, "upon these parts (which Heaven forbid!) he might feel that I am obsessed with the lower anatomical intimacies. This is true and yet not true. All mortal men are thus obsessed." What, I wonder, would T.H. Applebee think of Prokosch? He doesn't get the chance to say.

Apart from Byron in pre-rut, rut, and repining in the sulk of post-rut, Prokosch-Byron gives us a thorough look at Byron as cripple, talker, swimmer, host, dieter, father, connoisseur of curious customs, proprietor of a menagerie, military commander and crypto-Christian. His mind teems with exotic people both ordinary and eminent; but, transcending both the recollected circus of British, European and Near

Eastern society and the anti-climactic muddles of Missolonghi, there come numbing hallucinations in which specks in paper turn into tiny orangutangs and heaps of laundry into huge hairy toads. Stark and utterly congruous, these hallucinations—and the distress of mind they evince and aggravate—should have dominated the book. As it is, they appear as mere phantasmagorical items almost lost among the routine recollections. How odd that Prokosch, who has Byron confess a preference for " the strange, the enigmatic, the bizarre, even the repulsive," should have so relentlessly trapped him in the familiar and the commonplace. Even odder, the book tells us less of the processes of Byron's imagination than do things as incidental and as little read as Byron's notes to his own poems. Prokosch has missed his chance here, I'm afraid; and that's a double pity because he is one of the few writers who could have done concise justice to Byron's last delirium.

Walter Abish
Eclipse Fever

ALTHOUGH NOT ONE OF OUR MOST PROLIFIC novelists, Walter Abish is one of the more noticed; he has more prizes to his name than he has books, and seems to have made almost a fetish of minimum output (he's a minimalist in nothing else, however). Call him an ostentatious parsimonist of himself. Some have described him as an avant-garde writer,mostly on the strength of the entertaining *Alphabetical Africa,* but, truth told, Abish excels because he is a stylist, often executing delirious parabolas above the basic bottom line.

Mixed in a box with specimens of other writers, Abish's prose is readily recognizable: a touch mincing, but also sardonic and austerely fastidious, his is not an American style (his rhythms are those of British English, or indeed of Chinese), and his fondness for interpolated bits of other languages is plain. He is more a cosmopolitan than he is anything, and he needs, as some of us do, a purview wider and more erudite than that of the frontier or the suburban gabfest.

Something sleek and taunting emerges when Abish writes; he's a fondler and a juggler, a savorer of surfaces and explicit finitudes, one who can see the American in the German and the Mexican in the American. Painting from an ecumenical palate, Abish loves ideas as if they were gazelles, and this gives him a distinctive flavor. He thinks while ogling.

For instance, in *Eclipse Fever* we find numerous examples of Abish the well-read man of letters imposing himself on the American reader, as if to say, well I can figure things out; so should my characters, so should the reader. Alejandro the literary critic, tormenting himself about his estranged wife Mercedes and her behavior in Manhattan, wondering "Would she finally, inveigled by Jurud's desire, relax her guard, that innate rigidity, that formidable inflexibility?" With Alejandro she has been "passionless" and "diagrammatic," but what is she going to do now she's pelvically in harm's way? What will she do? With whom? In fact Alejandro has no proof of anything; he reminds you of Bertrand Russell's phrase, "positive opinions in the absence of evidence." He is like the narrator behind the venetian blinds in Robbe-Grillet's novel *La Jalousie.* "Proof? Why, the proof available to anyone capable of reading between the lines of Cervantes, Proust, Flaubert." *There:* you know what kind of novelist you're dealing with—one who sedulously attends to the guesswork in life, to the rampant imagination, implying that, just as novelists imagine, so do characters and actual people. So few American novelists give imagination its due, however, reluctant to have the minds on show speculate, hypothesize, pursue in full the agony of jealous or vengeful dubiety. In a sense, Abish restores soliloquy to its rightful place in the fiction of our time.

On another page of this miasmal, ratiocinative, silky novel, Abish's first in eleven years, we find a rather startling sentence about Jurud, the American novelist with whom Mexican Mercedes is having an affair. "Was it that Jurud, an outsider, a non-WASP, had the temerity to introduce into that indefectible WASP existence an element of *Verneinung* and repression?" Here is the perfect portrait of the worldly American novelist making no concession to his audience; you no sooner reach "indefectible"—a word I have never heard used in speech— than you cannon into *Verneinung,* little heard in the subway and the Century Club. Impenitent Abish is not writing for children, or dodos

either; *Eclipse Fever* is mature, intellectual work hunting intelligent
readers who, though they may not have reared themselves on Cervantes,
Proust, and Flaubert, recognize the novel as the pagoda of mind, nothing
to do with Zane Grey, James Jones, or Hemingway. This is. the literature of the salon, the fiction of the subtle scrutineer, the voyeur with
the monocle. Abish has courage, always loyal to his sentences, to their
march and tympany; he goes where their cadence takes him, into
never-never land, the lost archive of bewildered motives, the magnetic
field of contumely. He comes out of Henry James through Proust,
making himself nervous here and there, using Alejandro the critic to
namedrop as if depositing soothing pheromone to quiet the restive
American reader.

But there is more to Alejandro than careeristic namedropping.
He suffers sexually: "I still love Mercedes, Alejandro admitted to the
old critic. I dream of her.... I still make love to her in my dreams.
Passionate love." Even as he confides such things, she begins translat-
ing one of Jurud's earlier novels, then moves on to his most recent
one, *Intimacy,* still preening herself in the bedroom, naked in front of
a man in a suit, who stares "Dry-mouthed ... at her pubic mound."
Gioconda-chinganda, she attracts Abish more than his other characters do, perhaps because, of them all, Jurud included, she melds the
literary and the lustful, much better than Alejandro ever did. And so
it is that we hear much about Alejandro, not only cuckolded but sur-
passed in the literary world, left high and dry, become a pendant to his
wife, a man increasingly to be thought of as former teacher rather than
as a commanding literary figure. Abish studies Alejandro's torment
with suave meticulousness, drawing on his grasp of how older people
see things:

> The problem, his mother concluded, was clear-cut: In her
> opinion, Mercedes was too striking in appearance, too self-
> reliant, too self-absorbed, too independent, and far too rich
> for him. You'll be at a decided disadvantage—she comes
> from old money. Her "blanco" family will disparage your
> values, your manners, and your mestizo background.

Still, Alejandro plunges ahead and marries dangerously, soon to become the tuning fork of the book's misery and sadism. The epigraph to Part Two comes from Kafka, ending with the perhaps unverifiable assertion that "women faint easily, the world has no time to notice all their doings." What you get here is a psychological novel inside a picaresque one: Alejandro and Mercedes mutually and distantly involved while all the others rattle around on their way to Mexico and an eclipse. Alejandro is an expert on Mexico, Mercedes on copulative positions. Together with Anadelle Partridge, a former female American consul who has donated her pre-Columbian collection to Mexico, they compose an elitist ghost, making the other characters seem coarse and crass: a vulgar background out of which now and then pops an anonymous face whispering "She's left him!" And Alejandro quails, drawing from Abish his most insightful and disturbing passages:

> Suddenly, for no particular reason, he'd read into the most innocuous occurrences—a woman's bare arm reaching out to close a window, a woman's taciturn face in a passing bus, the sight of an empty parked car, its motor running, a man glancing up at a window—a meaning not unrelated to his present quandary. The *abandoned* husband? In a country where the transmission of this deadly pestilence had been perfected to an art, poisonous rumors spawn paranoia and ill will. She'd gone. She? Who? What precisely was she to him? His *love?* Didn't she also denote his preferential station as a critic, his dignity, his manhood! Each day another blemish. Feverishly he scratched until he drew blood on his forearm. The cuckold adapts himself to the vilest misrepresentation....

One can hardly blame Abish for favoring the sea-changes involved in jealousy over the crass and violent antics of those who wish to install a high-speed elevator in a ziggurat. He is more interested in wondering if Mexican novelists are confined to "loathsome celebration of death" or are free to write any novel they choose. He would rather explore the finer repercussions of Bunuel's *That Obscure Object of Desire,* at least as far as it illumines the predicament of Alejandro, than ponder the biggest shopping mall in Mexico or what truly lies behind Preston the American industrialist and his shady Eden Enterprises. To some extent, in order to create ambience, Abish is a camera, but by preference he is a discriminator of ideas. Certainly he will, at least in this novel, contrive to present sperm—"the first of several spurts reaching as far as her uncovered breasts"—and Mayan reliefs, Aztec pendants, skulls inlaid with turquoise, polychrome pottery and effigy jars. We get the full fatuity of Bonny, Jurud's daughter, a runaway to Mexico, observing the eclipse in her motel on CNN; but our minds linger on Alejandro the emancipated Mexican wondering about the Americanization of Mercedes—and this in the context of a mental spectrum that includes restrictions put upon Mexican novelists and the freedoms to which American novelists are heir.

It is as if, all through, we find a *sotto voce* novel in which whatever American things Mercedes does don't matter, and whatever Mexican things Preston and Jurud and Bonny get up to don't matter either. Anyone getting more than a whiff in this of *A Passage to India* may be on the ball. Americans will never fathom Mexico, and Mexicans will never fathom America. Clearly Abish's violent climax corresponds to Forster's own, looming up toward the end of the narrative like a prophetic telos, and twisting a psychological novel into a portrait of two incompatible cultures jinxed by proximity into believing they can communicate with each other. The fact that Abish, liberally mentioning the names of Mexican writers, nowhere mentions Elizondo's *Farabeuf,* one of the most Abishian Mexican novels, just about proves the point.

I am delighted to welcome this ingenious, poignant psychological novel, for which some of us have been waiting so long. Cast within the expectations of the reading public, it transcends them all the time, showing what an agile mind Abish has, giving us Forster when he truly intends Husserl, and Husserl when his mind throughout slides home to Proust. Abish made his first trip to Mexico after finishing this novel, and that is how strong imaginations behave.

Joanna Scott
The Marvelous Sauce

S ERVING UP *guillotin au jus,* Joanna Scott resorts to a creative device or procedure used by few, mainly because few know about it and, in any event, don't deploy their fiction on such a level because to do so is rather French, insolently European. Call it the layer cake of motivation. Its essence is to divine the route of a story or novel from the fleeting introversions of the people: not that old canard, letting the characters dictate the plot, but tuning in to the barrage of the mind as it chatters to itself. In other words, there are different levels to be tuned in to, some crude and basic, some lively and burly, some so metaphysical they can be expressed in only the most extraordinary combinations of words, only through style.

At the very outset of "The Marvelous Sauce," we read the words "I didn't recognize it, my poor girl's desperation, the panic in her gray eyes, and she was gone, as lifeless as our great ancestor Corneille, like him leaving behind only hollow words." Joanna Scott, of course, does recognize the salient states of mind, the panic in the gray matter, the goneness like a tinkle in the attic of literary history (as when you walk the rue Corneille, where my French agent pitches her tent). Scott excels at these modulations, knowing that bald recitals of plot have little to do with the mental armature of fiction, and she really weaves in and out, not so much listing events as capturing the terraced pre-liminary to them, the mental obbligato that fans out during the act.

How cleverly the author's mind transcends the mind of the narrator, making the narration both evince the author and peel the teller. The author's attitude to her narrator becomes a figure in the story's weave, perhaps using the story as a metaphor for the act of telling it. Or cooking it. Cooking it up. So the work is covered with Scott's fingerprints, present despite the ostensible hyper-control exercised by the narrator. Scott insinuates herself past this personage, proffering her in calipers. Style is the manager here. The story is made of prose as much as of events, people, or historical re-enactment or modification.

It is an impenitently daring piece, owing little to Christophe's history of the Sanson family, but much, I think, to Virginia Woolf's railway compartment full of Wells, Galsworthy, Bennett, and Mrs Brown—full of Brownian motion, to be sure. Scott deals in supernal ambience, like Woolf, and we may well conclude that this is a tale about *consuming:* the world chews us up, the guillotine consumes us, we go on eating. Marat has to thrive as an image in the zone of what he eats: clay, calf, Peace. We read about him not where he eats, but where is is eaten. My students at Brown teased me for citing T.S. Eliot so often, but he understood the creative process with extraordinary grasp, and could explain it as only a top-flight critic can. He spoke of there being several levels in Elizabethan drama, much no doubt as there are in butchery, origami, and soccer. Scott's fiction, certainly this monologue and her novels, has these levels too, or comparable ones; she knows, and studies, how vacillation flogs itself into a froth, even while the done thing begins. Dubious motives and insufficiently pondered brainwaves precede action without necessarily provoking it. In a character's head, especially one doing the telling, a maze of impulsive thought often defines the person as much as whatever he or she does next.

When the peacock shriek comes "unexpectedly" from the narrator's own throat, we are in De Quincey land, newly knocking at the gate in *Macbeth,* a sound he made much of, seeming to find voodoo in enigma. That shriek is the true external emblem of the state the narrator has tried to pin down, unravel, construe. When she eventually eats peacock, she will have consumed her own response, made it as domestic a thing as that "blush of sound" the crowd gives out. Joanna's story works so well because "the plump woman wearing black" Ancient-Mariners us with the detritus of her own mind.

John Barth
Chimera

I N ONE OF THE DEFINITIVE EVASIONS that enliven and underpin *Chimera,* John Barth offers this thought:

> To the objection that classical mythology, like the Bible, is
> no longer a staple of the average reader's education, and
> that, consequently, the old agonies of Oedipus or Antigone
> are without effect on contemporary sensibility, I reply, hum,
> I forget what. . . .

Just so. I've heard the objection (which itself belongs to mythology, like the inability to remember the reply) and felt it pawnbroked the truth. The fact is, we think myth even in the act of claiming we've forgotten it, and, profoundly, in all sorts of ways, relive the patterns identified by Joseph Campbell in "The Hero with a Thousand Faces." Or a thousand heroes with the same one. No one's exempt. So hooray for myth—except that Barth, instead of composing realistic fictions that insinuate mythic archetypes, chooses to address archetypes head-on.

He isn't updating myth so much as pushing his own present backward; and this makes *Chimera* demanding reading—demands the brain is grateful for.

I applaud Barth's astuteness in calling his book *Chimera,* which is Greek for she-goat, thus providing Giles Goatboy with a fitting mate. The word also, however, means a creation of the imagination, or an impossible and maybe fond fancy, and the book is all of that. But besides being wry homage to verbal art, *Chimera* (predictably) is an organism containing tissues from at least two genetically distinct parents: for openers, try Scheherazade and Melpomene (the Muse of tragedy), or the Muse of "The Thousand and One Nights" coupled with the "Hero with a Thousand Faces."

The spare night surely belongs to J.B., the instigator, the prestidigitator, the ostentatiously self-effacing, devoutly blasphemous Factor of this Neo-Arabian Sot-Goat-Road-Funhouse Urpera, first berthed in Dorchester County, Md. Even after the Destroyer of Delights has brought J.B. low, Barth's works will still be there, voluminous witness to a fabulator who, among contemporary Americans, has one of the most developed senses of the edifice of his imagination and works with inclusive sureness of grasp.

Barth's previous book, *Lost in the Funhouse,* was his best; my own favorite, at any rate, because therein he heeded, and did something about the fact that American fiction lags well behind European.

Barth, it was clear, was Upsilon Sigma Alpha's most literate novelist of ideas, who might have arrived sooner at his cosmopolitan epiphany had he been less rooted in American soil. And now, *Chimera,* crammed with intellection and resonant cross-references, a sly tenderness and a hankering after the sciences.

I hazard a guess, predicated on this book's prankish eidetic games, that immersion in myth might work for Barth as a rehearsal for confronting tenderness in the context of science. There is scientific fiction, but not much, little of it American. The problem of scientifiction, however, is universal; it's that of making abstract scientific principles interesting without sentimentalizing them.

No cinch. Yet as one of Barth's speakers in *Chimera* has it, "the empire of the novel, vaster once than those combined of France and England, is shrunk now to a Luxembourg, a San Marino. Its popular base ursurped, fiction has become a pleasure for special tastes, like poetry, archery, churchgoing.

Well if writing is on the walls, it's up to novelists to make it do things which the movies and music can't. Barth has. Style, often thought the key to the treasure, is the treasure itself. For style, offering no explanations, can't be right or wrong, only good or bad.

Witness, in "Dunyazadiad," the first of the book's three units, Scheherazade (Sherry) is telling her kid sister, Doony. "It's in words that the magic is—Abracadabra, Open Sesame, and the rest—but the magic words in one story aren't magical in the next." A lovely piece of weaving, this tale introduces us to "a genie . . . a light-skinned fellow of forty or so, smooth-shaven and bald as a roc's egg," from "a land on the other side of the world," who, freshly arrived at an impasse in his own career, supplies Sherry with the stories of "The

Thousand and One Nights" (none of which she knows!) in return for stories that'll see him through his bind.

It's an inevitable piece of Barthian ingenuity and as well, a captivating example of the framed-tale, in this case the second part abruptly modifying how we read the first, the third, the second and even the second's modification of the first. The whole thing is worth several readings and seems more vernal with each.

The second piece, "Perseid," about Perseus but evoking meteor showers, begins with a pregnantly affable "Good evening," and wheels into an increasingly dense recapitulation, and recomplication, of the mind of the man who despatched the Gorgon Medusa. With his marriage to Andromeda on the rocks, Perseus becomes convinced he's petrifying ("late effects of radiation from Medusa"), only to have his doctor tell him to give up ouzo and get more exercise. Diddling his mistress Calyxa while telling how a demigod feels at 40, he just ends up covering too much ground. It's as if a gifted teacher were being stifled by the syllabus. Maybe with more anachronisms and more astronomy, and a less dutiful calling of the myth-roll, this enterprising tale would have seduced me.

Third, "Bellerophoniad," is 170 pages long. An abundant, feisty, kaleidoscopic intervention on Bellerophon's behalf, it's one of the best things Barth has done. Daunted by reading the "Perseid" (by Perseus's exploits, not the classical allusions), he bewails his lack of heroic status, but, as if for the first time even in myth, rides "the heroic cycle"{ and is "recycled." "Mythopoeia interruptus" has rarely been so winning; Barth seems relaxed, yet in absolute control, and builds his third iad into a love-hate choric hymn in which Bellerophon, Perseus's cousin, deals double death to "the three-art freak Chimera" while Barth himself brings back into currency the preceding pages, then his entire writing career, as well as all he's cared about and all he's likely still to do.

The resulting artifact may seem to some a mash of "visions of an order complex unto madness," but it's more like a witch hunt with sundry obbligatos made to come via contrary pastiche from Beckett via long quotation from Robert Graves via chutzpah from Napoleon, Hamlet and Colonel Fosset of Vermont and via Polyeidus the seer. Colorful, open-boweled, and eminently of the school of writing whose hallmark is mirrors, it's an inexhaustible work, funny and funambulistic, spawned by Barth's drive to "open (his) life's closed circuit into an ascending spiral." Everything goes right, even to the extent that the "Perseid" gets assimilated through irony. The book adds up insidiously in one's head and is far from the self-destructing "acte gratuit" that Bellerophon's presence might imply. Which is head or tail, I don't know. Sufficient that the whole is stylish-maned, tragically songful and serpentinely elegant.

William T. Vollmann
Thirteen Stories and Thirteen Epitaphs

IF VOLLMANN'S SURNAME were to generate the adjective "Vollmanian" or "Vollmanic," what would his adjective mean? Ambitious, erudite, innovative, sarcastic, impenitently prosaic? *Whores for Gloria, The Ice-Shirt,* and *An Afghanistan Picture Show,* to name only three of his half-dozen works, would establish at least that; I myself heard him on the radio saying he regarded himself as raw material for things to happen to: an ideal companion for the riff-raff he prefers to write about, almost as if he were redoing Kerouac. Just get on the road and see what comes of it.

We used to call that attitude existentialist, intending a philosophical version of what's impromptu, and impromptu Vollmann certainly is, appearing to pull these thirteen stories together at the last minute from only distantly prospected materials. The result is a flavor or intonation that implies a feeling about people and phenomena: the random handful is best, and the less studied the writing the better. Certainly, if you were doing an imitation of Vollmann's prose, you would have to include some of his favorite devices—gaps in typography, asterisks, a sudden drop in letter size, transliterated onomatopoeia ("spoingg!" and urrrrrrrrrrrrrrrrrrrrrrrrrrreeeeeeech!"), and heaps of run-on sentences.

Something callow in this mode of writing suggests that prose should resemble what it describes and not be worked-at, lovingly honed, loaded with a *mot juste* here and a Nabokovian verbal felicity there. For him, writing seems impetuous and reflex-like, set down with informal casualness, just so long as there's a lot of it, something so stock it looks like mere typewriting done with a straight face. It reminds me, sometimes, of the work writing students do in their persuasion that fine prose is for others, for wimps and exquisites.

Vollmann has his moments, however, from his opening sentence ("Before I had even gone away, I started polishing San Francisco as if it were a pair of glasses to look through and every *new* thing dust and dandruff . . .") to the "malignant boom" at the end of the collection. You are suddenly drawn into the world of the story: no preamble, no fanfare. Suddenly what was not going on around you is. Chubby Monique and narrow-faced, serene Vera are feeding each other in a restaurant with the same spoon, and the narrator feels excluded, wanting to see more of them

> at home, where among the plump hard pillows of their futon, or condensing on the dark-lobed underleaves of their many houseplants, their innermost tendernesses must live, freshened by a thousand kisses, guarded and protected by the horned ram-skulls that hung on the walls. . . .

Vollmann excels at telling how it feels to *be* someone, how it feels to want to feel the same as someone; and he does so with ebullient density, seeming to have at hand far more than he needs, endowed with a big helping of the world's contents, as if Balzac were redoing Rousseau or Jules Verne William Burroughs. When someone or something takes his fancy, he goes all the way, ignoring the existence of the paragraph and flowing on into undeniable plenty. If you need him to pause or break his pages up into small assimilable units, you are crying for the moon while he assembles a spate in which Ken pees in a juice jar, Ben jerks off on to a hundred dollar bill, Ken's van reeks of pussy, and the narrator just yearns and yearns for "weatherbeaten blonde Megan, who had once been the beauty queen of Georgia." Spell-breaking trivia, these, blown into the haphazard story by some feckless wind, so you learn that a transsexual's pussy "kinda caves in," that the narrator has a book made for him with "a twenty-pound steel cover," that he goes away from his friends and it is as if some "wide throat of sunlight . . . had swallowed us."

Vollmann excels at babble and lyrical, sharp-edged interruptions of it. You are glad of "the idiotic self-confidence of the flamingo" on one page because on the next there is a shower of ands and clause structure breaks down. Vollmann tends to repeat himself rather than pin something down in a sparkling epitome. So, instead of narrative moving forward into causation and momentum, you get people swirling around in an affable dither, running into one another again and again in Vegas, Belize, Thailand or Gun City—Elaine Suicide and Abraham Yesterday, dickering about handcuffs, or Abraham and a shrink ("Just as eggnog drips off a blender-blade like mucus from a tonsil, so the shrink's words went *pingggg-gaplopppp!* inside Abraham's mind"). Mr. Yesterday sends his eldest son off to join the Special Forces, where, if he is lucky, he will get to study with Doctor Bacteria, an expert on reducing the enemy intelligentsia to sulphate. Vollmann writes strongly about the godlike pretensions of those who bribe girls with crack; napalm falling and burning; and jungle hunters who arrange a collar of leaves around the cut throat of an animal.

What an acrid, scapegrace world he conjures up, in which nothing matters very much: only a kind of dispirited hedonism as lax in Omaha as in India, practiced by a cosmopolitan clique whose enervate lives he sometimes graces with cerebration. Mostly not, though. His people, as he says, "really *are* rather rubbery and NEED handcuffs." Or they need watering to make them bloom. Vollmann has an original mind, an intermittent gift for phrasings on which you want to linger, and a massive, awed sense of flux.

Zulfikar Ghose
The Incredible Brazilian

ACCORDING TO THE BLURB, this is the first volume of a projected trilogy which, credibly enough, will track Gregorio the hero through a series of incarnations beginning with the seventeenth century and ending in present-day Brazil. It's a splendid idea thus to raid and exploit a nation's history for purposes of long-distance picaresque, but a better idea would be to vary the narrative mode over a thousand pages, shifting from the roustabout episodic to, say, voluminous Proustian excursus or an avalanche of epitomistic fragments. Born in Pakistan and now resident in Texas, Ghose has lived in Brazil as well and, this book shows, knows enough about it and isn't reluctant to draw with a bold, often caricatural hand. Whether he *will* vary his narrative strategies, I don't know; I just wonder if we now need, or can stand, a trilogy that's all (as the blurb puts it) "brawling, bawdy, and picaresque." I'm just hoping something standardized and inflexible won't ultimately afflict even this frisky hop-step-and-jump with sameness.

Son of a well-to-do planter, Gregorio at fourteen is effete, virginal, and corrigibly vain, and, as you might expect, chutzpahs through the novel shedding disqualifications while compiling and losing one fortune after another. Picaro here, picaro there, he's an everyman on greased skids, and his vicissitudes, his bounces-back prefigure his incarnations to come. Follow him, if you will, sexually attempting a hen and a cow, perfecting his marksmanship on puppies and kittens, playing voyeur to a lecherous priest, and thrusting his way through all manner of jungle flora and fauna and the thighs of lubricious women only to re-encounter more of the same. It's as if he's trapped in a Brazilian Klein bottle (which has neither inside nor outside, and which to exit from is to enter), and this rotational semi-delirium of marking-time while time marks him sets him apart from picaresque forebears. Like light travelling at its own peculiar speed, he doesn't seem to move at all.

Especially to the sexual episodes here, Ghose brings a juicy voracity for saliences: the nipples of the servant Aurelia, on whom Gregorio's father has fathered a bastard, get snipped off by the betrayed wife and served, it's rumored, in father's meat; a young wife straddles a supine statue of Jesus in an empty church *(caritas interrupta?);* and menstrual blood goes into the stew. To boot, Gregorio is subjected to homosexual rape, a Lawrence of Arabian Brazil, and then sold into slavery; but eventually, like a bubble in a sump, he surfaces. Becomes a leader. Discovers gold. Fetching up in Rio, he's there during its bombardment by the French, and suffers a heart attack when the Françoise he's in bed with turns out to be a François. As it happens, that mutation only confirms the Byronic mood of the whole; the novel's last word is penis.

Turbulent, atavistic Brazil is as rich a presence here as our non-stop Gregorio, and I particularly enjoyed Ghose's Janus-faced portrait of atavistic colonials copy-catting the urbane ways of the Old World. Ghose writes with momentum and verve and, in his chosen old-fashioned belly-thumping way has made quite a meal on Brazil the luscious. But as yet only breakfast.

Leslie Marmon Silko
Almanac of the Dead

The longer my own novels get, the more I sympathize with novelists writing blockbusters, and I do so because the massive novel models itself not on the vast universe, our huge planet, our big continents, but on the grandiose behavior of the Creator of all things. There is surely something godlike in concocting *Remembrance of Things Past* or *Finnegans Wake* that you might feel in only a minor way if concocting *Death in Venice* or *Candide*. E.M. Forster must have felt this when he spoke of some enormous thing looming down the road, "a solid mass ahead," though he himself never attempted the mega-novel.

Leslie Marmon Silko attempts it, hauling together tectonic plates called America, Mexico, Africa, "The Fifth World," concluding with a home-made synthesis entitled "One World, Many Tribes." She creates with a free, impassioned hand, keenly aware of terrain, history, and that bedevilling paradox known as the past in the present. Her personages, of course, are American Indians, loaded down with legend that affects them much more than the common-sense mercantile wisdom of so-called Western civilization. Ancient and modern jostle together in minds continually at risk, indeed doomed, like the character, Menardo, proud owner of a new bullet-proof vest, whose manual is his bedside book. The President of universal Insurance, Menardo gets helpful marksmen to test the vest and dies of a flaw in the weave. As flies to wanton boys are they to themselves, always wondering how far a modern magic—a Mercedes, a skyscraper, an electric chair, a Tucson vacation home—can be pushed, but just as ready to listen to "macaw beings" and to heed a dream about a rattler on an asphalt highway in the moonlight. Silko makes her novel a spirited mix of boundless primitive feeling and sophisticated urban sloth.

My problem with it, as she gradually fans out the action from initial scenes of Seese, a one-time drug dealer now nurse-companion to old Lecha, a witch-seer whose own notebook of the dead runs through the book like a vein in rock, is that Silko deals more graphically with myth than with folks. Her myth remains unforgettable whereas her characters, apart from a few, remain invisible and forgettable: too many, introduced too soon and then abandoned for long stretches. There are five on the first page, and they keep on coming at a fast clip for the rest of the book, almost as if the point were their expendability, their virtual interchangeability contrasted with the personae, gargoyles, incubuses, demons, and revenants of another dimension altogether in which a pain is "a jaguar that devoured a human live from the inside out. It left behind only the skin and bones and hair."

I found myself peering back, wondering who was who, only to remember something that, while vivid and energetic, didn't help me in my belated quest for a family tree: Hitler's borrowings from the sadistic De Guzman, ancient invader of Sonora, making lamp shades from human skin and seating Indian women on pointed sticks, then weighing them down with silver. I even remembered, from a page close by, Maximilian and Charlotte, emperor and empress of Mexico, he collecting insects and servant girls, she "ridding castles of spiders and vermin." These legendary or fabulous beings have more bite, more impact, more staying power, than Silko's imaginary "real" characters, perhaps because at heart she's more attuned to myth and ceremony, things not so much diurnal and ephemeral as hallowed, ripe.

Candidly, I am happy with it this way because here is an excellent work of myth and a second-rate novel full of lacunae because there are just too many people in it. As it is, the most powerful and magical material in the novel is what happens to Lecha's own almanac of the dead, inscribed on sheets made from horse stomachs ("the little half-moon marks were places the stomach worms had chewed"). Three young girls and a boy take the almanac north, little knowing that the tale of their march is already included in the almanac itself. After many weeks, lest they starve they suck and nibble at the edges of the horse-gut pages, eventually enriching a stew with a whole page as the letters fly away like small birds. Of course, this has more in common with Indian myth than with down-town Tucson or indeed with what we later learn, apropos of the bullet-proof vest, were "Microscopic imperfections in the fabric's quilting; a bare millimeter's difference and the bullet would have been stopped." Both are hair's-breadth situations: the edge of the pages vis-à-vis the edge of the hole, the former the gist of life, the latter the peephole of death. If only more of *Almanac of the Dead* were thematically linked in this way; one might remember events and faces better, have more the sense of reading a myth-fuelled novel than a novelized myth.

Silko's own sensibility is to blame. It prefers to amass magical contortions while the more humdrum part of her stacks up simple declarative sentences modeled on the rough-hewn part of the Hemingway canon. The whole book could have been done with half a dozen characters, each endowed with enough heft and depth to balance the myth. As it is, Silko does not interest herself much in psychology, in the unsaid words, the thought uncompleted, the murmur lost. Death and disrespect come moving through the brutal, narcotized world she likes to deal with, and I begin to wonder if the disjointed, non-cumulative nature of her enormous book represents the shattered mind of an atavist or comes about because, here, half a dozen disparate novellas have been rammed together. Of all the characters who appear and vanish, Sterling, Seese's hired man, lingers in the memory. Fired from his old job as "a film commissioner," which meant keeping Hollywood film crews away from sacred sites and holy land, he reads "The Police Gazette" and tries to figure out the proper clothes to wear in restaurants.

For the rest, there is an infinite variety of greasy detritus, from sex malls to abortion movies, from organ transplants to cocaine shipments made by balloon, from a federal judge merrily swyving his basset hounds to Serlo who makes love to stainless steel cylinders intended for cattle. Silko's desert wasteland aches with pain and deprivation, and her sufferers hate all others who suffer. What keeps you reading is the hum of magic within the arid pasacaglia.

Anne Rice
Lasher

WITH A PROMISSORY THUMP, bound proofs of this novel land on the doorstep bearing two bits of news: Rice finished it at 10 p.m. on August 5 1992 (so the last page tells us), and, say the publishers, the first printing totals 700,000 copies. One wonders how to construe that big number: as a bit of bullying (why bother reviewing the book except to make aesthetic points nobody cares about?), or as a challenge to explain the hold Rice exerts on nearly a million souls. One thing is clear: if you have read *The Witching Hour,* you will understand who's who among the horde of names the book unleashes. Reading *Lasher* is often like hearing someone mumble on in a monotone about famous cricketers of the nineteenth century, and you, the reader, a baseball fan or a fan of nothing at all.

This novel about the branches and generations of a witch-matriarchy called Mayfair evokes a part of London once given over to a hospital for leprous women. In their complex comings and goings, the Mayfair witches wangle themselves into the fabric of society with experienced ease, a subversive class that has risen and prospered over the centuries without always doing what it was best at: sorcery with malign intent, traffic with the devil, and the exercise of supernatural powers. Rice's female witches are not broomstick riders with brooms dipped in genital mucosa, as in the old days, but Mafia wives encased in brainwashed daintiness. Witches' craft is the savviest science, the keenest smarts, at least for them, and irresistible power is the book's focus: power passed on and made new, power grafted from nature and upturned against it. A powerful theme, to be sure, but here tacked on to a silly vehicle.

Qua writer, Rice evokes a type of person we have all met: the ectoplasmic orator who says aloud everything he/she thinks—in this case writes it down. That's why this is a six-hundred page novel instead of one half that length. I could take all the commonplace, monotone rambling about this or that branch of the family tree, and every witchbird roosted in it, if we were getting Jamesian amplification, or (as in the novels of C.P. Snow, even) new doors opening on familiar personages, or Proustian superplus created because humans are inexhaustible subjects of study. But Rice repeats herself, never for stylistic felicity, only to confirm some kind of ritual, to tell readers they have been here before, sucking on the same fustian, and isn't it wonderful to be going in circles? As it is, most well-educated readers will not get beyond the first chapter, done with a faux-naif folklorish touch: "Father was waiting for her. She had to grow fast and grow strong for Father. When the time came, Mother had to help her. She had to drink Mother's milk." It goes on: "Mother slept. Mother cried. Mother dreamed. Mother was sick. And when Father and Mother quarreled, the world trembled. Emaleth knew dread." Well, so did I after the first page; the prose picks up and does a better job or recording the detail of phenomena, though there are no sentences (or clauses, even) so beautiful they dare you to go past them without savoring them several times.

The book has several ideas deployed in it, the most powerful and arresting one of which is the brilliant neurosurgeon witch-mother who gives birth to an extraordinary not quite human being who comes out of the womb with an erection and rapes her on the spot. More or less, anyway. He impregnates her with a being similar to himself. Potentially this is vigorous stuff, limning a Mother Courage of obstetrics, otherwise known as Rowan Mayfair, queen of the coven. Unfortunately, though dramatically mentioned and suggestively evoked, she does not appear in the first two hundred pages, no doubt because familiar to devotees. Once she at last turns up, thinking "Have I done this to myself? Is this how it ends for me, because of my own selfishness, my own vanity?", the novel convulses into an almost orgasmic pageant of miscegenation—its horrors, its marvels, its sheer biological hubris, and we have to make our own way through the thicket of implication, wondering exactly how *we* stand with mutants, how we would cope with them, where human self-interest leaves off and enlightened interest in cosmic variety begins.

Ms Rice seems much more at home with such a tornado of ideas than with traditional witchcraft. Indeed, she is more a writer of science-or speculative fiction than she is a purveyor of gothic or whimsy. Amid the blather of names, few of whom surge up as characters, and the roughhouse sexual coupling, the poignant image begins to form of Rowan Mayfair breastfeeding her mutant, getting into X-ray departments to run a brain-scan on him, hemorrhaging time and again and scraping up the "tiny gelatinous mass at the core of her hemorrhage . . . . There was something here, and it had limbs!" She asks him what he knows of pre-human history and notes that his sexual organ is thick and slightly curved (Peyronie's disease, perhaps?). Rice tells all this in plodding prose, but she does tell it as if it interested her, as does literature, at least if we heed the roll-call of authors grafted onto Julien, who tells a story within this story, citing Terence, Ovid, Chapman and others.

Eponymous Lasher, six feet six inches, blue-eyed with luxuriant black hair, sometimes resembling "An acolyte of the rock music star David Bowie," can speak Latin and Gaelic, sings menus aloud and brings to mind the Jesus of Albrecht Dürer. As far as he goes, he's an imposing energumen; but Rice sometimes calls him "The creature," gently stereotyping until he almost becomes a prop. This creature does not collect birds' eggs, for instance, does not memorize the Indian railroad timetable, and does not smoke cinnamon in secret. He has little private life, and little interior, at least until toward the book's end when Rice, perhaps recognizing his abeyance, hands the book over to him: a good idea, calling into question the omniscient narrator; but

Lasher's prose is the same as everyone else's in the novel. He becomes just another droning I, rising to dutiful perfunctoriness when he might have become a belatedly revisionist voice both stylish and cantankerous. Scotland and Assisi occupy his memory, but only in the woodenest way, and his spell as narrator gives Rice a chance to begin even more paragraphs with "I."

Unusual smells pervade this novel, and Rice records them with care, tracing one from butterscotch to caramel, chocolate, cherry cordial and hot tar. A mysterious, dust-caked Victrola sounds throughout and, off in cosmopolitan society, a foundation—the Talamasca—devoted to historical research, addresses itself to the hypothesis that Lasher possesses a unique genome, is desperate to reproduce, and needs witches with whom to do it. This is a more dignified image of the alien than we get from the three movies titularly dedicated to that concept, and Lasher, bearing a double set of chromosomes, nags at the mind. More's the pity that Rice cannot delve into him as Nathalie Sarraute might have done, probing with deviant finesse yet another man unknown. When we read the following stock vignette, we are being cheated and denied by a Nosferatu clone: "A slight figure, but the perfect incarnation of menace with its blue eyes fixed on him intently, mouth vivid beneath the black gleam of the mustache, white fingers long and bony and almost twined around the bedpost. Monstrous."

A simple addiction to building balsawood airplanes from kits would have given depth and poignancy to that stock image of the monster. Some flecks of balsa cement stuck to his fingers, emanating an aroma of nail polish, might have given him a counterpoint dimension such as Rice brings to Rowan Mayfair, that other Eve, having a Christmas all her own.

Richard Price
Clockers

Clockers arrives with a press kit, a cardboard folder that might have held silk stockings, and, appropriately enough, raises on its first page a certain literary agent's legs, "the best," says Liz Smith, "in the literary business." Then you learn how much Price likes toughness, writing, for the movies, how much Martin Scorsese paid him for the screen rights. Get it straight: this is a self-consciously hard-driving guy who nonetheless, in an earlier novel, could write something as awkwardly delicate as "Everything still had that post-rain placental shimmer to it, enhanced by the deepening slant of the late afternoon sun."

Price is not averse to purple patch, even in *Clockers,* a long novel in which he seeks to probe the soft core of certain tough guys; it figures that, sooner or later, he's going to need pathos, poignancy, the distortions of ingrown tenderness, and an appropriate language that lets him do the probing the revealing, without sentimentality. In other words, to do the job without such clichés as the drug dealer who goes straight and the disaffected cop who comes back to life. Because his touch is didactic, Price doesn't pull it off—he's too simplistic an explainer—but he does provide in full the data of his milieu, in this case a futureless dump called Dempsy, N.J.

Someone once asked me, as people do, where to go for material to write about, and I answered "Go to those who have no hope." Price did that, much as he has done it before in *The Wanderers* (1974), plunging himself, nay immolating himself in New Jersey crack dens (whereas for *The Wanderers* he had to do no such research; he had come from the Bronx housing project he wrote about). *Clockers* evinces his courage and his slithering empathy, and anyone requiring an in-depth vision of America Narcotica need look no farther. Price knows both his dealers and his cops, although he tends to look at them with an almost morality-play fervor; he knows what they stand for more than he understands them, and he rarely, as an articulate novelist should, sweeps us in the best language into the dankest, most miserable crannies of people, grandly ushering us into a rumination that speaks for those who cannot speak for themselves. In other words, he takes no chances and so achieves a middling realism rather than a devastating vision.

His two main characters, Strike Dunham, a black nineteen-year-old crack dealer with an ulcer,and Rocco Klein, an almost burnt-out case of a homicide cop, suck a lot of energy from Price and between them create a force-field in which the lives of almost everyone can plausibly go awry. Strike's boss is a niggling psychotic millionaire. Someone bumps off one of the boss's people and Victor, Strike's good-guy brother, confesses to the crime. At this point Rocco Klein begins to take a developed interest in Strike, convinced that Victor is covering for him; so he frames him as a stoolie and hangs him out to dry. In the end, when Klein's baby vanishes and the hitman after Strike dwindles away with AIDS, Strike turns to the now thoroughly animated cop for help. It's a neat enough contraption, one third misery, one third bristling dialogue, one third homily. In his bald, movie-oriented way, Price is as dogmatic as E.M. Forster. Strike thrives on power and status, Klein on risk and glamour. My problem with them is that, without an Al Pacino and a Paul Newman to flesh them out, I wonder if I will remember them. Already they are fading and I begin to suspect they are only temporary, proxy types occupying space for another art form whose lights blaze brighter than fiction's. Written words are not this fable's final resting place in spite of its streamlined teacherly fiber, the density of its research, the street-smart twitch that never quits.

In one of its least humdrum efforts the television channel C-SPAN recently set up cameras next to a line of outdoor barbers in a Hanoi street and filmed whatever happened: a kind of hands-off mass reportage that made the idea of Hanoi solid and casual. They did the same for a backwater street in a Hanoi suburb, allowing whole minutes of no action, no movement at all. Price does something similar for Dempsy, reminding us that his skill is not literary at all, but optical, clerical, anecdotal. He's more like Frank Norris with a degree in labor relations. What he really needs is a TV show.

Mary Butts
The Taverner Novels

S TYLISTS GET OVERLOOKED whereas experimenters don't. Stylists modulate voice, tone, rhythm and pace whereas experimenters just keep on asking for attention. Stylists work on you like radioactivity or radon where experimenters do it with a bang. Asked if he experimented, the composer Edgard Varèse said yes he did: first, he said, he experimented, then he composed.

Mary Butts rarely bids for attention, but she hones and shines her prose with self-absorbed joy. One can see why she vanished into jet-vortices left by Woolf and Pound; a great deal of what she most wanted to say had no public visage, no exoteric face to be called up by. After all, a woman obsessed with "visible Pan" is probably not going to tout it too well on the Rialto. For Butts, the finding and rendering of this Pan was enough. She knew that a good thing would out and did not require commercials; indeed, she thought it better to leave a thing to find its own way, gently propelled in roughly the right direction by style, then left to float into others' lives like a baptized butterfly. You can see what she is by reading *Scenes from the Life of Cleopatra,* her lushest last novel. She was a Sitwell of the Grail, but in many ways she was a European author, on one occasion talking pure Valéry when she said what interested her above all: "Nothing but spiritual development, the soul living at its fullest capacity." In other words, *implexe*.

Her prose is startling without being ostentatious. Perhaps some of the most elliptical prose in English, it reveals the space between things, inciting the reader to fill the space or begin to commune with what is there already, in between. That is why her prose seems so sliced, sometimes devoid of cumulative rhythm. She writes staccato anthems, training the reader to apprehend autonomies she then puts side by side, saying these, ladies and gentlemen, are the collocations of a universe. Where nothing is, is most. Perhaps she is a metaphysical writer, one who believes in jumps and bridges, stiles and leaps. While the rest of the world that is going to be famous busies itself with transitions and causative euphony, Butts points to the gap, which is really the portion of the figure's ground that happens to be between two salient figures. She's looking at saliences, yes, but much more at the big buzzing blooming fusion that lies behind things, around them. She is the celebrant of context. An unfortunate role, this; it makes you an usher rather than a soloist, attuning the reader to your Pan-mindedness of course, but hardly making you a lordly delineator. Woolf derided her first novel, *Ashe of Rings,* perhaps because she felt she'd been scooped, much as Nathalie Sarraute in *The Age of Suspicion* derided Woolf, and for similar reasons. Butts, on the outside socially, and always diffident, went her own way esthetically, knowing she was right, and that her punchy, trenchant, almost jactitatory English proved her so.

Her most conspicuous originality consisted in her resolve to depict worst things, or things at their worst, with a view to transforming them, which means assimilating into one's being a sense of Creation's massive, impersonal onslaught. Try to steal its thunder by feeling a little godlike, by getting proprietorial with the tornado that swipes you, as if it were your own. I link this *deinosis** to certain primitive rituals that enhance the human being with the chills of grandiosity. Her paragraphs contain a great deal of isolation, almost as if she is trying to stunt the mind's ability to connect one thing with another. Take this, picked at random from *Armed with Madness:*

> They went in. Pine-needles are not easy to walk on, like a floor of red glass. It is not cool under them, a black scented life, full of ants, who work furiously and make no sound. Something ached in Cárston, a regret for the cool brilliance of the wood they had left, the other side of the hills, on the edge of the sea. This one was full of harp-noises from a wind when there was none outside.

See how she uses the annotative disjointedness of the clinician or the lab assistant, striving not for euphony, but for carefully built dis-location. She does it all the time, not to be staccato or telegraphic, but because things that look isolated are not. Butts conveys holism through short breaths and a host of long, similar pauses.

---

* See page 41

I see two things: her inclination not to be gracious or polite, and her love of outlandish things—themes that others might find fey, daffy, far-fetched. She may have modeled herself on Charles Williams and M.R. James, but she often seems to have more in common with such novelists as Nelida Piñon and Clarice Lispector, Brazilians both. Whether she is addressing her prose to the Holy Grail, Bradbury Rings, or whatever drove Alexander the Great, Butts finds the style that suits her matter, not her reader. There is a reportorial pertness to her prose, not quite genteel or considerate, and you have to get used to it. Some would think her rather dotty, even on the strength of this peremptoriness joined to her weirdo subject-matter; but she was only trying to get across to us her private sense of the universe, an enterprise that hardly conducted Blake, Messiaen, and Ensor to extremes of amenity or what tends now to be called reader-friendliness. *Il faut avoir un aigle,* said Gide, or your work will be just a gentle pit-a-pat. Well, Butts has her eagle or her demon plucking at her and drawing her away from the hallowed bows and scrapes we associate with more circumspect authors. She's a bit of a redneck in fact; she's something of a Djuna Barnes, minus the addictive wordplay.

There is an instructional tone in what she writes, a touch of what in the military we called Station Standing Orders. She shows the ecstatic, suppositious mind reeling itself out into the arcana of life along a rubber band that eventually snaps it back into the company of all those crisply registered finitudes. Trenchant she is, with a penchant for gossip overheard from people who take part in an atavism they are not aware of. I do not see her laboring among movers and shakers to make her career a success; rather, her vision sustains her, revealing what she needn't do. She has this uncanny sense of something's always being slightly wrong with the universe, almost like an early intimation of the absurd—or at least of the finding that the universe is not absurd, whereas we are. Everywhere, she says, "there was a sense of broken continuity, a dis-ease. The end of an age, the beginning of another. Revaluation of values. Phrases that meant something if you could mean them. ...She wished the earth would not suddenly look fragile, as if it was going to start shifting about. Every single piece of appearance. She knew it was only the sun, polishing what it had dried." This is bracing stuff for 1928. Her prose becomes more fluent, more protracted, but she never loses her addiction to the thing *per se,* to the phenomenon considered in its own right. She is the hummingbird of English prose.

The best account of her, with critical aperçus shining through his gentle kaleidoscope of her image, is by Virgil Thomson. One expects a composer to tune into her daimon, for a while at least. Thomson extolls Butts the gentle-born roisterer who wore a single dollar-sized white jade earring under a man's felt hat tipped-up, who "toddled" because one of her knees came easily out of joint, and who revelled in the pub-crawl. Socially, her act was to lead people on until they shot the works. Literarily, as Virgil Thomson says, she preferred revealing people caught up in something overpowering, "so irresistible that their higher powers and all their lowest conditionings are exposed ... an ultimate clarification arrived at through ecstasy." Glowing at the center of a cyclone she created, she eventually proved too much for Thomson. I would like to think her time has come again, though she is essentially a Parisian author, similar in some ways to Auden, as in this:

> O Lord, call off the curse on great names,
> On the "tall, tight boys,"
> Write off their debt,
> The sea-paced, wave curled,
> Achilles' set.

She envisioned some perpetual good husbandry of the planet that could be learned through opium or emotional upheaval. Was it the storm goddess, as Thomson dubbed her, or the seemly earth-ecstatic who wrote these lines?

> Curl horns and fleeces, straighten trees,
> Multiply lobsters, assemble bees.

Lawrence Norfolk
Lemprière's Dictionary

IF YOU LOOK IN A DICTIONARY to see what a dictionary is, you run into the word *diction*. A dictionary is an orderly book of the said; of the thought, the sayable, indeed the unsaid. It also brings our ancestors to life (especially a dictionary that includes Indo-European roots). Reading the dictionary is an act of anthropology, and it may well get you reading in an etymological way, scanting modern denotation and connotation for the slow, uncouth parabola of the word through the throats of all who went before.

First novelist Lawrence Norfolk doesn't go quite that far, but he does have a brilliant premise: a hero, John Lemprière, who composes a dictionary of classical myth, celebrated now as the predecessor to *Bullfinch's Mythology*. Lemprière decides to do it, inscribes the letter A on a blank sheet, and he is off. Soon he has arrived at D, marvelling at the growing linguistic prism through which he sees all human doings, keenly aware of himself as a driven eclectic, one who, longing for completeness, finds even rowdies in a tavern beyond his scope, their horseplay infinitely unfathomable. He finds that, the more you set down, the more you need to know. So he goes on, creating an indelible abstract, haunted by taxonomy and the recondite, increasingly aware that what he's making is a spoor, a trace, a little regimented poem to humanity.

At one point, he looks at his heap of pages, and muses on the first one's "competent 'A'":

> "Aaras'sus, a city of Pisidia" It was difficult, sometimes, to imagine anyone even interested in such facts, let alone making them laugh or cry. "It is probably the Ariasis of Ptolemy," he had added. So it was. Who cared? The answer to that was that he cared. It was all whirling around inside him, he had to care. He wrote his name carefully beneath the entry and dated it, "twenty-first day of December, 1787."

His is very much the mood of Milton writing *Paradise Lost,* envisioning characters through a Greek mist, sometimes almost seeming to translate his ongoing English into a thick compost of classical allusion. Only two weeks after beginning, Lemprière, whose dictionary seems to want to be written at night, wonders at the thing he's saddled himself with:

> What began, only a fortnight ago, as a simple list of persons, places, and events had since grown strangely, with odd nodules and tendrils sprouting in all directions and linking up with each other to form loops and lattices, the whole thing wriggling under his nib like a mess of worms on a pin. It looked in all directions, spoke scrambled languages, and made wild faces at him, an Argus-eyes, Babel-tongued, Chimera-headed catalog of all the true things that had turned to dreams and the men who had turned to their dreamers.

What fun. The *Dictionary* wobbles throughout the text of the novel, an outrageous Durrellian Interlinear constantly reminding Lemprière (and us) how esoteric and fatiguing the exhaustive is—and how far from the rough and tumble of everyday. In our own century, a man such as Lemprière, wrestling with over twenty people called Dionysius, is likely to walk under a bus; or, in his own time, as in the novel, almost into a pile of dung: a man voluminously distracted by an engrossing and quite factitious mental problem. The novel is a wonderful epitome of mind's inwardness, the mind that absently hearing does not heed, but communes with imaginary beings become more real than buses or piles of dung.

It is here that I, as novelist, begin to worry. Norfolk had a difficult choice, between letting Lemprière take over the whole book, transmogrifying all he sees, and setting Lemprière among hundreds of folk to whom dictionaries matter not at all. You either inflate Lemprière's mind like an enormous balloon or you counterpoint his almost autistic ramblings with realistic knockabout. Lawrence Norfolk chose the latter way, involving Lemprière with the 1628 massacre at La Rochelle—thirty thousand massacred when the siege is lifted—and the honorable Company of Merchants, venturing from England to the

East Indies. The novel leans back two hundred years away from Lemprière's own time and so becomes a more conventional, orthodox artifact, swollen with names rather than characters (indeed, a bit like a dictionary) and pitched on a different plane as if to give Lemprière both an historical and sociological context when both might have been implied, leaking through rather than pouring.

You toiled too hard, Mr. Norfolk, to make a poetic masterpiece into something picaresque, like somebody turning *The Death of Virgil* into *Tom Jones*. It's a figure-ground problem, with Lemprière getting rather swamped by a host of loudmouths, tarts, dons, crooks, drunkards, crackpots, footpads, magistrates, aristos and pirates, when, as a conjuring and omnipotent imaginer, he might have prevailed through swift allusion. A more commonplace novel has resulted than you'd expect from the premise: a novel that teems with characters, subplots, and hearty action. As a serious exercise in mind-delving, or emotion-plumbing, it slides away from us into noise and froth.

To be sure, it is of more than passing interest that an ancestor of Lemprière's involved himself in a deal between the Huguenots of La Rochelle and the bold, prospecting burghers of the Honorable Company of Merchants, whose ship comes back from the Indies full of pepper, with which the Dutch have already glutted the market. Documents surface, making Lemprière the heir to one ninth of the Company. There is much evocative writing about sailing ships of the early seventeenth century, but, like most of the writing in this novel, it's matter-of-fact stuff, neither graceful nor winning. Quite often, Norfolk does the minimum and moves on, a tourist in haste; and his set-pieces, about mashed potato, an automaton gone wrong, a woman executed by being filled with molten gold, are the exception. The real drama is in Lemprière's opening up all his books and arranging them on the floor "in a sort of bookcarpet. Gaps were left for his feet. . . ."

For those who care to burrow, an adroit, poignant novella about masterful introversion lies buried among the dusty uneconomical subplots of this unusual novel. Off on the right foot, Norfolk took a step back, making Lemprière's mind only a part of the book when it could have been the whole.

Michael Ayrton
The Maze Maker

I AM PRIMARILY A VISUAL ARTIST," says Michael Ayrton, the British painter and sculptor, "and I write as one. I write to complete the concept originally conceived in bronze or paint." Having already published a book of essays and written scripts for documentary films on Leonardo da Vinci and Greek sculpture, he gives us next a fictional "autobiography" of Daedalus, maker of the maze at Knossos and author of other marvels, including wings for himself and his son Icarus, and the fake cow inside which Pasiphaë crouched to be mounted by Poseidon in the form of a bull. For ten years, Ayrton says, this legendary figure obsessed him as one "from whom I depended" and whose meaning he had to define in order to discover himself.

The result—Ayrton calls it "a text derived from images which I had finished making before I began to write it"—is an exercise in intermedia. The painter-sculptor gives the writer things to say that writers usually do not know about, and the book abounds in fascinating accounts of what it means to design in minerals, to melt and pour bronze. Sometimes, however, design takes over, and Ayrton-Daedalus strays away from the dramatic alchemy of art into lengthy recitals of who is related to whom in Greek mythology, and the book becomes tame and monotonously dutiful. In between these extremes there are some captivating, fluent and often funny set-pieces in which Daedalus ironically watches himself fussing, conniving, racking his brains, astounding laymen and kings and gods, and getting touchier and more sceptical as his reputation grows. Disdainful of ancients and moderns alike, he admonishes the reader with a mixture of pedantic forbearance and tart sincerity.

After flying he says: "I saw the seal-backed shapes of islands sleeping under me. There will be nothing remarkable in this to you, but it was new to me." He continually corrects the record: "It has been said that I saw him [Icarus] fall into the sea, but I did not." And he sums himself up with magistral irritability: "I am involved in matters which I do not wish disturbed nor interrupted by eloquent activities, the facile assumption of power, speculation on immeasurable phenomena, nor any apotheosis. What I make exists." It is a daring, subtle portrait of an anti-heroic, bibulous, baffled, cantankerous, sexually ambivalent genius. Noting but never quite accepting the ordinances of all the powers-that-be, Daedalus comes tetchily and unquenchably alive without losing his place in the brutal-beautiful delirium of mythology. Ayrton informs him but does not over-inform him, keeping him from the woodenness that afflicts the *Imaginary Portraits* of Walter Pater, but stopping short of turning him into a mouthpiece for a London-born painter who knows his Greece.

So far so good; but Michael Ayrton isn't interested in anyone but Daedalus, and Daedalus is interested only in himself. Therefore, if Ayrton intends a rebuke to his subject's self-centredness, he achieves it only through a parade of names—Minos, Tauros, Naucrate, Talos, Endoios, Laerces, Dactylos, Perdix *et* many *cetera*—that remain names only. The effect is of Orson Welles reciting zip-codes: the timbre of the voice and the panache of the delivery almost make the numbers interesting, but not quite. They remain ciphers; indications and proofs of nonentity.

This would not have been so if Ayrton the writer hadn't just a little failed Ayrton the daedalian artist. This is a "pretend" autobiography—not that of Michael Ayrton, nor that of Daedalus, but a piece of sleight-of-hand as deliberately confected as it is passionately conceived. Either it should have been confected to the full and taken out of the mouth of Daedalus, or it should have been executed utterly as what it basically is: a study in temperament by an impersonator. In other words, Ayrton should have identified less or identified only.

If he had done the former, he would have been able to realize the Minotaur as something more than a gross prop and take us into the lewd paranoia of Pasiphaë, its mother, not to mention the mental processes of Icarus, whom Daedalus cannot fathom. Even for the Greeks, to whom they signified much more than they do to us, these creatures and men and gods had more *personality* than Ayrton-Daedalus allows them: quirks, crankinesses and kinks.

If, however, he had done the latter—locking us without outlet into Daedalus' true self-absorption, so that the nonentities are what Daedalus creates through disdain rather Ayrton by default—he would have been able, I think, to shift the most brilliant and the most Beckett-like of his conceptions into a dominant role. I mean the double image of the ant which Daedalus has inhaled into the labyrinth of his head and his own inhalation, by Gaia, into the labyrinth of mother earth. This multiplication of the double theme—the imprisoning prisoner, the invented inventor—seems to me the core of the book. "In all my life," says Daedalus at the outset, "I never learned from one experience how to encounter its reflected twin." At the end, having come full labyrinthine circle, he can only add: "Toy, trial and torment, the topology of my labyrinth remains ambiguous." The walls of the maze, as he tells us, are polished and reflect each other continually.

Flawed, I'm afraid, but extraordinary, both profoundly and poignantly ruminative, The *Maze Maker* is a parable about the precarious nobility available to man during his few "insect minutes" in the amazing macrocosm; and as such, whatever its shortcomings, it makes a great deal of contemporary British fiction look banal and trivial. This is Minotaur, not mini-tour.

Doris Lessing
Briefing For A Descent into Hell

DORIS LESSING'S NINTH NOVEL is briefer than *The Golden Notebook* or any component of The Children of Violence. Lugubriously invited by the title, with its promise of sulphurous guidance, I turn to the publisher's blurb and find she "defines" *Briefing* as "innerspace fiction." I'm not sure what that means, and I think "dub" would be a more appropriate word than "define," but it seems she intends an excursion into private consciousness, and excursion beginning with everyday mentality and ending up in the darkest reaches of the unconscious at its most primitive—as if Dostoevsky were to redo Conrad under the auspices of, if not Jung, at least R.D. Laing.

It's an exciting idea, especially in the light of one comment in her "Afterword, or End-Paper" to the effect that "extra sensitivity and perception must be a handicap in a society organized, as ours is, to favor the conforming, the average, the obedient." In thus addressing herself to interiority as both a gift and a handicap, Lessing may find her most receptive audience among the alienated young (the only thing against that being the middle age of her protagonist); she has staged a bold and fervent experiment, directing the novel where it has to go or perish—into the ineluctable isolation in which we all live and are ultimately destroyed—and undeludedly evaluating the clutter with which we hope to distract ourselves from that state.

The book's occasion is Professor Charles Watkins's losing his memory and being received by the Central Intake Hospital, where patient although disagreeing physicians ply him with drugs in successive attempts to restore him to his customary self. In the end they prevail, and there is something chilling in his restoration to Classics at Cambridge (England) and the evening-lecture circuit; for in the interim he has opened up from within and, in a whole series of extravagant and contrasting mental sorties, has met chaos, cosmos, prehistory, world geography and world history on his own involuntary terms. In so doing, he flexes and extends his being beyond all conventional (and even imaginable) limits, so much so that he becomes the protagonist of an anthropological trance, moving from freak-out to a status almost mythic and enriching the mental life of the reader to an almost incalculable extent.

Readers will not find this a soothing trip, but Lessing is not trying to soothe; her intention, as I see it, is to reveal the elastic inventiveness at the heart of our being, its lawless and "uncivilizable" fecundity, its role—both intoxicating and terrifying—as the creative faculty with which we dare defy the Creator. In a word, here is a ringside seat in Adam's head, the contest being that between man's profoundest intimacy and the society that would "normalize" him. It is not surprising to find that Lessing believes society's treatment of the "broken-down"—the folk who crack or fall apart—is monolithically fatuous; she believes society needs the recognitions that such people experience and, instead of excommunicating the "mad," should authorize them as—well, if not prophets quite, at least as sayers of what is sooth. Common sense if I ever heard it, and, if I'm not mistaken, fairly close to what Hemingway was trying to get across in his fascinated explorations of men on the verge of breaking. (Charles Watkins's home, it is worth noting is in a place called Brink.)

Obviously, Lessing takes upon herself a damning liberty: Whatever she cares to write she can assign to the mind of Charles Watkins and, in view of his condition, need not make either cogent or logical, either well-written or per se interesting. His tabula rasa, at least as far as his Western identity goes, is a carte blanche for her, and this raises the fascinating problem of how much literary skill to show where all that really counts is the specimen-quality of a man's thoughts. Indivisible from him as she fabricates him, Lessing has to discipline her own imagination to an extraordinary extent and the reader has to trust in her judgment—has to believe that, when the writing seems flabby or tame, it is the fault of Watkins's condition and not authorial fatigue, and, when it is crisp and vital, that this isn't just Lessing deciding to show us a thing or two.

All in all, the exercise works. For example, one conversation runs as follows: "I have a wife? / Yes. Her name is Felicity . . . is that funny? / Ha, ha, ha, I have absented myself from Felicity. Ha, ha, ha." I know Lessing is better than that, is deliberately limping along at the ha-ha minimum; but when I read the following passage, for instance, I'm not so sure if the generality of the "Brazil" references is her fault or his:

> . . . you must not let my cycle South too far, dragging in the Brazil current of my mind, no, but let me gently step off your slippery back on to the silver sand of the Brazilian coast where, lifting your eyes, rise the blue and green heights of the Brazilian Highlands.

Brazil, as even a classics professor at Cambridge would know, is where John Donne said the sun dines, and, granted Lessing's initial license, that could have given the prose a greater specificity. I gave Lessing the benefit of the doubt; the problems and temptations of this mode are enormous, and for the most part she makes Watkins stand and congruously deliver as only an adept prose highwaywoman can.

In fact, there are some engrossing, vivid passages that, merely through being together in the same book, bring more of space, time and Nature into enigmatic mental collision than we have seen outside of Italo Calvino's cosmicomical fables or Gabriel García Márquez's jungle panoramas. Thanks to Watkins's mind's being the way it is, we hear Minerva and Hermes flashily conversing not long after a mating orgy of an indeterminate species called the Rat-Dogs, and, in a long written account, Watkins himself describing his imaginary wartime affair with a Yugoslav partisan called Konstantina, who gives her life to save him from a charging deer (which then gives birth). The book's convention not only sanctions such incongruities, it insists upon them as a procedural principle; and all credit to Lessing for launching out in this un-British way.

The vision-by-proxy quality of *Briefing* I can best exemplify by juxtaposing three passages which, opening and relaxing our minds as they do, help us to receive the novel as a whole. Very early there is this:

> Round and round and round I go, the Diamond Coast, the Canary Isles, a dip across the Tropic of Cancer and up and across with a shout at the West Indies to port, where Nancy waits for her poor Charlie, and around, giving the Sargasso Sea a miss to starboard, with Florida puissant to port, and around and around, in the swing of the Gulf Stream, and around, with the Azores just outside the turn of my elbow, and down, past the coasts of Portugal where my Concita waits for me, passing Madeira, passing the Canaries, always *en passant. . . .*

A bit mechanical, yes, but it gets the eye rolling. Then, halfway, there is this:

> Moon spinning closer in to Earth makes animals and plants such and such a size and Moon lost or disintegrated or wandering further away changes animals, plants, the heights of tides and probably the movement of land masses and ice masses, changes life as draconically as a sudden shower in a desert. . . .

Not exactly news, it nonetheless makes the horizon into a headline (and that adverb, "draconically," makes what is familiar there seem new). Finally, towards the end, there is this, about the deer's fawn:

> . . . on its hide lay some dried threads of the birth liquor, and on its creamy stomach lolled the fat red birth cord, fresh and glistening. Three or four days later, the cord would be withered and gone, the faun's coat licked and clean, the faun, like a human child, or like the maize plants I had seen that morning. . . .

Observation here lifts into reverence with those maize plants.

Not all the writing in *Briefing* is as enterprising as in those three samples, but enough of it is. The book isn't quite dynamic enough, but it's a long way from being sedate. Lessing has written herself quite beyond the novel-of-manners tradition and yet, oddly enough, her occasion—that of a life which cracks under some indefinable strain and then re-seals itself around an emotional death—evokes Henry James. In view of her evident aims I wish it had been Jesse.

Michael Moorcock
Byzantium Endures

WHEN YOU OPEN *Byzantium Endures,* a bulge forms down the middle of the two-page frontispiece map, all the way from St. Petersburg in the north to Constantinople in the south. A handy fluke, because it's along the time-line of this vertical bulge that Michael Moorcock's anti-hero whizzes up and down, from Kiev in the dead center of the map to Odessa, due south, then up to St. Petersburg, after which he goes to Constantinople, which is old Byzantium. Like mercury in a fine tube, he measures the revolutionary climate in the first decades of our century; a twisted H.M. Stanley looking for the source of Russia's pain.

But he's more than that: self-engrossed and self-serving, he is an accomplished liar and an anti-Semitic Jew whose emotional life is a series of agonized twists. Determined not to be what life has made him, Maxim Arturovitch Pyatnitski only becomes more so: for supposedly hygienic reasons his father had him circumcised, and this obsesses "Pyat." In fact he is nothing but obsession, although some of the things that haunt him are more interesting than remembrance of a prepuce past: his love of aeronautics, for instance, comes bewitchingly through. As a mere boy, he devised a manned flying machine and, partly to impress Esmé his childhood sweetheart, jumped into the Babi Yar ravine, thus attaining premature fame as the Icarus of Kiev.

If you believe him, that is. A first-person narrative, *Byzantium Endures* has all the usual traps: no corroboration by witnesses, no interventions by an all-knowing authority whose mind is the novel's locus. Moorcock supplies an introduction which explains how Pyat's papers came into his hands, eventually to obsess him and drive him "half-mad." There is even a "A facsimile page from Pyat's manuscript" to thicken up the illusion, and Moorcock makes a tempting job of the preview, offering the image of old Pyat in London, his final retreat, tippling in favorite pubs with his mysterious mistress, a Mrs. Cornelius, who wafts through the book proper like some Cockney angel of mercy, rescuing him from trigger-happy Bolsheviks and spiriting him across the Black Sea in a double cabin aboard the *Rio Cruz*.

A game of mirrors is going on here, a game whose rules extend beyond the immediate concerns of *Byzantium Endures*. As Moorcock says, Pyat "knew that I had already . . . 'exploited' [Mrs. Cornelius] in some books," and there are several Jerry Cornelius novels to prove it, as well as *The Adventures of Una Persson and Catherine Cornelius in the Twentieth Century*. And, if you jump ahead to the last page of Moorcock's fantasy novel, *The War Hound and the World's Pain,* you find a note saying that he "is working on an ambitious four-volume novel *Some Reminiscences of Mrs. Cornelius Between the Wars,* the first volume of which, *Byzantium Endures,* has already appeared."

Hence some of the huffing and puffing in the introduction, which is essentially a portrait of the artist as an inheritor of materials. He resists the opportunistic Pyat's demand that he write the life of Mrs.

Cornelius but, eventually succumbing to Pyat's spell, ploughs through 11 shoeboxes of papers and ends up with the present text (1900 to 1920) whereas the papers go all the way to 1940, with Pyat in a concentration camp. The reader has to work out whether or not, granted the constraint of editing, the entire novel should have been cast in the mode of the preface, with Pyat given not raw and unmediated, but planted in the living tissue of authorial speculation. I wonder, because Moorcock as himself, or impersonating himself, is a subtler teller than Moorcock impersonating Pyat, who limps and drones and fumbles, enlarging what an expert novelist would have trimmed, and vice versa. If the gain is a greater realism, the loss is in technique; a loss which perhaps the other three volumes will justify.

As it is, some of the book foams along. The disastrous parabola of Pyat's cocaine-heightened private life is undeniably vivid, and it survives the log-jams of data allowed by the putative editor. An odd mix of picaro, Cartesian diver, and thwarted pilot who flies all the time in his mind's eye, Pyat is someone to remember: a warthog of the Ukraine, a flunked Prometheus convinced he never had the life he deserved; a fake, a snob, a lover of machinery ("the sight of a simple English bicycle" ravishes him), and a misfit who says to Winston Churchill "How are you, you old bugger?" He runs errands for wealthy women and watches the world go to hell while he acquires a special engineering diploma, dallies with homosexuals, invents a death-ray that fails, and ponders "A Thousand Books That Bored the World."

Rasputin stalks through these pages while Pyat lurches from high to high in white suit, boater, walking with his silver-headed cane into and out of aliases, leaving only the "liquid steel" of his sperm behind him. He struts along the rim of history and topples off, a man who might have ruled the world (or so he thinks), an H.G. Wells figment who ends up in real Wells-land, living over a second-hand clothes shop in Notting Hill, surrounded by bits of old bicycle "petrol engines, old spark plugs, electrical bric-à-brac." A new New Machiavelli in a white golfing hat, he has in his day been flogged by a commissar, crashed into the ocean in an obsolete seaplane, and remembered always that Odessa was named for Odysseus. Something gritty and nasty about him keeps him at a slight distance, at exactly the distance where personification thrives; so he easily becomes what he thinks himself—

the spirit of the age, an Ancient Mariner who's read Nietzsche.

A memorable though greasy creation, he puzzles me only if I try to figure out when he wrote things down. The blurb says "told . . . during the Russian Revolution," but it all feels as if set down much later, in the later '30s, perhaps. It will be uncanny to have him presented by yet another first-person narrator: Mrs. Cornelius, to be sure.

Miguel Angel Asturias
The Eyes of the Interred

WE KNOW WHAT TO EXPECT HERE. The novels of Miguel Angel Asturias, Guatemalan winner of the Nobel Prize for Literature (1967), spill over with characters, evoke continually the feral presence of the jungle, and into a lavish tapestry of myth and folklore weave anticapitalistic propaganda which can make for some tedious reading, especially so because Asturias likes to spread himself. The present volume, the final one of his Banana Republic trilogy, is no exception: there's a whole army of dynamic, closely-observed, bulging characters; the jungle comes through graphically and excitingly, never a mere backdrop; and the onslaught on gringo capital—this again personified in banana king George Maker Thompson—renews itself in the form of a successful, although untidy, general strike. In other words, this is committed, doctrinaire fiction, light-years behind Borges, reminding us that during the 1950s Asturias was exiled for eight years on account of his political convictions. An unpolitical reader must take the ideological rough with the atavistic smooth.

What's surprising in the long run (and it is) is how much of the smooth he gives. The writing combines relentless observation with pliant, instant mythology, heraldic dream sequences with resonating and witty talkfests (in which Asturias, who often forgoes narrative, stages ventriloquistic *tours de* force that supplement the loud jungle with a human obbligato). One character has "rings under her eyes like two rotten lettuce leaves." Another dreams he is a small calf, "son of a pinto cow," that gets colic and is given a purgative of cane juice and fat, all this from going to sleep with a dry milk froth on his lips from his bedtime drink. And another character, to make his one pair of good shoes last forever, goes barefoot, marking how bird droppings on the tops of his feet "would cool off, stiff and toasted." From such modulated vignettes, to eaters of sun-orange mushrooms and "The black cactus from the center of the earth" and bearers of ocote fire "taken from moonstruck pines, drunk with turpentine" it's not far, nor to tall stories about tiger-petting and Yancor the ashman, who is also the striker's messenger, "breaking up pieces of lace, needles, towers, bridges, castles and other fantasies among the accumulated ashes."

What Asturias excels at here, though, is trains very closely watched indeed. Reptilian in motion and claustrophobic in effect, they force speakers on top of one another, keep the scene changing, build suspense, and go charmed through the furnace of "green fire," the inextinguishable vegetation. In the military section of one train, a general on his way to a conference laps cold champagne "off breasts, thighs, sexual organs" while watching his soldiers shoot the rebels in the nearby countryside; later, the women are pitched off the platform while the train is going full speed. Then there is Blinky, "the cruelest agent in the secret police," who in the train's toilet relieves himself without dropping his pants and so feels "the weight of something like a saddle" affixed to his buttocks. The trains encapsulate, have the effect of installing humans in microscope slides.

Meaty, earthy, yet sometimes impulsively lyrical, *The Eyes of the Interred* tells also a delicate, wry love story, that of Malena the school teacher and Juan Pablo the revolutionary, which becomes a vernal plateau in the text, at once dreamlike and unhistrionic. Just as vivid a character as these two, however, is the oldest of the green popes (banana kings), choking with throat cancer and having a platinum tube hammered into his trachea; obsessed with the safety of his grandson, he wants him to remain Stateside, but the youth goes off to the banana republic and the strike and gets killed. The time of all this is the Allied invasion of Europe, a mere transmarine mirage unnoticed by the local radio stations, which play military marches hour after hour, or by those hell-bent on dynamiting reservoirs, bridges, oil tanks and electric plants, or by the parakeets, parrots, monkeys, macaws, herons, jaguars, or the tail of a comet that is really the river with the setting sun on it.

As the book itself says, "one [has] the feeling of moving through a forest of dream reflected at his feet and a living forest on his shoulders"; no chip, to be sure. It's a forest of beggars, soldiers, priests, urchins, whores, agents provocateurs, slum-dwellers and peasant visionaries. *The Eyes of the Interred,* in fact, is a novel complex and lush enough almost (although by accident, I'm sure) to bury its politics in overgrowth; where that doesn't happen, especially toward the end, it becomes earnest and two-dimensional and the "volcanic vehemence" cited by the Nobel Committee dwindles into mousy pietism. The "eyes" are those of "the interred . . . waiting for the day of justice." The translation couldn't be bettered, although Márquez and Cortázar seem to give Gregory Rabassa more scope.

Hermann Hesse

AT ONE SALIENT POINT in his not uncritical but, in the main, celebratory book, *Hermann Hesse: Pilgrim of Crisis,* Ralph Freedman shows us Hermann Hesse, his wife, and a few friends, themselves in an act of celebration. They sit down to trout, roast chicken, and unusual wines. It is December 10, 1946, and Hesse, unable to go to Stockholm to receive the Nobel Prize for Literature, is being given a quiet party at his doctor's home. When a servant enters with a tray of telegrams, all bogus, from such sources as heaven, Mount Sinai, and Noah's Ark, Hesse briefly forgets the chronic pain in his legs. Nearly 70, he has latent leukemia, but he will last until 1962 and have a tremendous vogue among the young of the counterculture: an afterlife among acolytes.

Those telegrams, fudged up by the doctor's wife, catch the mental temper of Hesse the German who became a Swiss, the teacherly Peter Pan who hankered after things Asian and what he called "a space within ourselves in which God's voice can be heard." Grousing his way through incessant headaches and a whole series of breakdowns and marital disasters, Hesse was much more than the first well-known writer to be psychoanalyzed; as Ralph Freedman demonstrates, he quite openly used his fiction to defuse mental crises and let them fix its themes and patterns. He came, Freedman wisely reminds us, from the German tradition that uses the novel "to make music," but he updated that tradition by borrowing the tropes of his own analysts, Josef Lang and C.G. Jung.

The results were not always happy. "Your heartbeat is the hammering of my arms that long to be freed," Lang wrote to him in 1917; but Lang wasn't a professional writer, whereas Hesse was, and so could be charged, by readers less affably loyal than Freedman, with being thin, vapid, sentimental, and more concerned to let off steam than to mold the egotistical sublime into flawless prose. Afraid that analysis might end his creativity, he nonetheless seemed to think that what worked in the clinic must work in art as well, which is no doubt why much of his fiction defers to the mental events that spawned it: a by-product, a blotter, a spoor.

Align the fiction with the copiously recorded life of a Mann, a Proust, a Faulkner, and the work still dominates the life because each of the three has the gift of voluminous transposition. While the interior life waxes and wanes, a big structure begins to grow within it. Most novelists' heads are full of folk, but Hesse's wasn't and not even the stepped-up vogue for reflexive fiction can rescue him, as it rescues Beckett, who baldly makes the pain of having a mind into his main subject-matter, and to hell with character, scenery, the rest. In the end, Hesse's parade of posed aliases only tells us that, like Kilroy, he was once there, fuming and hurting, and always wanting the opposite of what he had. For such an "antithetical mind," in Freedman's summary phrase, biography amounts to release and vindication, and this biography has him in exact focus.

The consolidated image that emerges is astonishing: that of the hero in a novel Hesse didn't write, although his magnum opus, *The Glass Bead Game,* that glacial continuum of futuristic repose, could have contained him whole, and should have. Given to violent temper tantrums, he seems incorrigible, and is obsessed with sin even as a small boy. After trying to shoot himself at 14, he ends up in a home for retarded and epileptic children. An egg without a shell, he longs for another revolver, but learns to repair clocks instead and goes on to work for a bookseller while grooming his neurasthenia. Insomnia frays him. He keeps aloof from his dying mother. His eyes begin to fail. Dreading ties, he marries, and fathers children. Taking a draconian cure, he sleeps on the earthen floor of a mountain hut, under a thin blanket. His Eden is the spa, where he is no longer responsible for himself. When he eventually heads for Asia, he travels first class. In a Malayan cinema he falls asleep and, when he wakes, is beating his head rhythmically on the rail in front of him. In 1914 he both supports and deplores the war.

On he wavers, massaged, given electrotherapy, beginning to paint, remarrying, living on rice, milk, macaroni, and chestnuts, psychoanalyzing his friends, churning out book reviews, absorbing and using racist jargon though married to a Jew, taking on Radio Basel, asserting his status as a Swiss citizen, rebutting postwar vilifications by Hans Habe. There was a tumult here, a marathon of paradoxes, and it's no surprise to find him saying in 1950, "How good that our life has its limits, that one is certain of the end. It is the only security in a human life which in other respects the existentialists don't understand very well."

Freedman nods occasionally ("The missionary spirit of Johannes Hesse's tracts were not to prove useful to his son") and leaves unquestioned Hesse's assertion that, for the Catholics and the Socialists opposed to Hitler, "There had been no camaraderie, not even a community of sufferers." There was, as Annedore Leber's *Conscience in Revolt* and Peter Hoffman's *The History of the German Resistance 1933-1945* make abundantly clear. And his reading of some faces in the book's photographs is sometimes perverse, but not his reading of the long, grievous, relentlessly productive improvisation that Hesse's life was.

Milan Kundera
The Unbearable Lightness of Being

W HOEVER THIS BOOK'S NARRATOR IS—not Kundera exactly, yet of course no one else—he refers to himself as "I" and to The Unbearable Lightness of Being as a novel. In fact, he is as much a self-regarding essayist interested in chance, erotomania and frailty (all three dealt with as abstract ideas) as in the dismal but busy quadrille of Tomas the womanizing surgeon; Tereza his seemingly *complaisante* wife; Sabina, Tomas's painter mistress; and Franz, Sabina's lover.

The result is less a treatise than a testament interrupted with erotic eavesdropping, but less that than a discursive portrait of a Czech intellectual's mind in the act of weaving parables. The book is not diagrammatic, however, or psychological, at least as far as the characters go, but symptomatic. Terse, dry, and acute, it gets almost out of control, and thank goodness it does.

Here, for once, in this time of the minimalist vogue—self-righteous plainness masquerading as austerity—we have a plot inferior to the author's mind. And the narrator knows this, for long hitches losing interest in Tomas and the others, and wandering off into Descartes, Duns Scotus, Parmenides, Nietzsche, and Sophocles. You might call it a novel of ideas with tongue in Czech. The allusions bear on the character, but only because the allusions are to life and the characters look alive, frustrated and hounded as they are by their Russian overlords, as by Czech boorocrats, in Prague of the late 1960s and after.

What Kundera's latest novel is about, thinly disguised or lightly, is disgust with life in general. It used to be called *Angst* or nausea, caused by the Absurd which Camus defined as the gap between the mind that desires and the world that disappoints. You find here no specialized aversion to totalitarianism, which you might expect from Kundera, sacked from his Prague professorship (at the Institute for Advanced Cinematographic Studies), his books banned, and since 1975 in exile in Paris. You do find, however, an almost enraptured aversion to things human.

Kundera blunders into the raw grossness of being like someone who has been watching on TV the sitcom antics of Tomas and Sabina, but then moves about and somehow gets his body in between the antenna and the signal's source, at once amplifying what he messes up. That buzzing blurt reminds him of the invisible signal coming through all the time, pouring through us, who are flimsy, fleeting, and faint. We might waft away. We ultimately do. If being alive is such a momentous thing, runs Kundera's complaint, it should feel more solid, more imposing, leaving nothing to be desired. All we have is an ephemeral fleshliness which Tomas, as a surgeon, wants to probe, in both his patients and his women yarning to "take possession of something deep inside them," not for pleasure but "for possession of the world (slitting open the outstretched body of the world . . .)." In this he has something in common with the gourmand, who briefly dominates a portion of the things around him by devouring it, or the dictator, who dominates life by taking lives.

Yet Tomas, like so many seekers after what is not there at all, ends up with the fruits of surgery and lust lying heavy on his hands. Eager to be rid of the flesh, which never explains itself, he goes from one undignified position to another, eventually demoted to the post of window washer, roaming Prague with brush and pole, lustful and clinical as ever, akin to Webster who, as Eliot pointed out, saw the skull beneath the skin. Tomas sees the mouth as the nozzle of the hose supplying oxygen to the lungs, and the human animal in general as an alimentary tract in disguise. In one of his last sexual encounters he and his partner (a woman like a giraffe and a stork combined) stand with their fingers up each other's backsides, in almost heraldic parody of the desire to know: stymied, cloned, frozen in a pseudo-proctological tableau. All through, Kundera amasses comparable images of indignity, toward the end having his narrator—in that relaxed, urbane manner he adopts throughout—dismiss the notion of a "divine intestine." God is pure because He has no guts.

Most interesting of all in this wry, spasmodic, idea-haunted book is the way the narrator reports, on page 122, the deaths of Tomas and Tereza, and then goes on filling out the details of their lives, both in the same past tense: "He informed her of the deaths of Tomas and Tereza" precedes by several pages Tereza's noticing that Tomas's hair smells of women's groins. Kundera thus creates within this book a dimension of non-temporal time, artificial maybe, but justly so because, as the narrator claims, life is as artificial as fiction: people improvise their lives just as much as novelists improvise their novels. All is arbitrary, so why bother about the ought-to-be, in fiction or in life?

A patient reader will find felicities to savor while moving back and forth between the book's narrative and its essayettes (such as "A Short Dictionary of Misunderstood Words," actually titled whereas several of the divagations are not). The image of Prague, with all the street names changed to Russian ones, is eerie and moving, as is the ritual injection of the pet dog Karenin at the end—Tereza throws a handful of chocolate into the grave. Tereza has at least two fascinating nightmares about execution, one on a lawn and the other on an airport ramp. What I find most memorable, perhaps, is the way in which the book confronts us with enigmatic phenomena which, when you try them against the book's abundance of theories, end up unexplained. The theories cannot explain even themselves. The flesh is chalk, the idea is cheese. And closely watched trains of thought never arrive at the station.

On the next to last page we find Tereza and Tomas "at the last station" out in the country on a collective farm from which there is no return. It is a mental metaphor, of course, an end not so much dead as moribund, as loaded with spry melancholia as with political outrage. The translation is readable, but the translator several times ignores the grammatical function of commas paired, giving "And lulled by that blissful imaginary uproar, he fell asleep" instead of "And, lulled" *et cetera*. And on page 205 he writes "precipitous" when he surely means "precipitate"; it's the suddenness of Tomas's move, and not its steepness, that knocks the woman over on her back.

Tom Wolfe
The Pump House Gang &
The Electric Kool-Aid Acid Test

FOR A LONG TIME NOW, this nearly visionary journalist has been remedying an omission perpetuated by Ernest Hemingway, who chose not to write about American popular culture and so deprived himself of abundant materials as well as denying intelligent American readers something they very much needed and needed, it is now clear, not in the form of fiction. The something is How It Feels To Be this or that contemporary type; not just observation of but penetration into the type's distinctive performances and even into its head. Eyeball invasiveness; the metamorphoses of an inquisitively adaptable personality; the wire-tapping of a thousand individual psyches—call Wolfe's own freewheeling performance what we will—it tells Americans what is going on in such a way that, even at two removes, they feel part of the scene.

Not only that: Wolfe's own dizzy-making pyrotechnical prose style—curt and lissom, sopped up and contemplative—somehow tells them, even as they are reading him, *how it ought to feel* while they are reading him. Here comes the prose, ogling and cavorting and aflash with gorgeous virtuosity, and with it a built-in response-kit; Wolfe not only possesses his surfers, fine art tycoons and his London dollies, Carol Doda the tit-dancer and Hugh Hefner and Marshall McLuhan and Ken Kesey and the lumpen-dandies and the Mid-Atlantic Man; he dominates the reader too, so that you either go along with him in everything, letting him dictate the timbre and duration of even every buzz or whoop emitted (such is the acoustical insistence of his style), or you close the book at once, feeling like Mike Hammer after he inch-lifted the lid of that heavy box containing a nuclear reactor (or whatever it was). Slam shut or (what Wolfe wants) open up wide: woo death with Hemingway or go beyond acid with Ken Kesey. In motive at least, I keep thinking, Wolfe and Hemingway are pretty close.

They both seek to draw us out of ourselves (fitting us out with selves if we haven't any), Hemingway into delicious pastorals and exotic townscapes, Wolfe into the off-beat, the far-out, the extreme, the super, the It: faultless surfing, the biggest known bust, the Hardest Head in the West. They both—as well as specializing in deeds done and poses struck according to a code that is also a life-style—deal in ecstasy in the strict sense of that word, which is "displacement," always from where you are to where the weather is somehow more relishable, say the track at Auteil, or to where there is the most putrid-smelling red tide ever, off Manzanillo, say. Except that, really, the weather at Auteil and the red tide off Manzanillo aren't half as potent where they are as in prose reports which, in effect, mobilize us to appreciate any weather and any red tide and quicken us into a best awareness way short of milleniary ecstatics but coming under ecstatics all the same, one end manifest in "this *ecstatic* in Columbus, Tom Reiser—the stud who rides a motorcycle with an automobile engine in it—Liberation!" (Wolfe) or (Hemingway) "Linart, the great Belgian champion that they called 'the Sioux' for his profile, dropping his head to suck up cherry brandy . . . when he needed it toward the end as he increased his savage speed."

That's the secular end. At the other (less finite) there is what happens when Ken Kesey and his Merry Pranksters serve up a punch laced with LSD or when a man and a woman together under a blanket feel the earth move. Secular or mystagogical, this is the ecstatics of getting out of oneself, of maximizing each moment, of burning with a gem-or laser-like flame, of not being confined to (although starting from and maybe regaining) prosaic social rigmaroles, of realizing we have one life only, and without guarantees, and had therefore better do all we want while there is time. Neither Hemingway's tight-lipped sensuousness nor Wolfe's near-spastic intensity amounts to anything new; but what is a welcome change is Wolfe's scope over Hemingway's. The one is choosy, omitting most of the trash of living, whereas the other—well, he wolfs it and so achieves an ecumenical lyricism that never reads like a falsification of the world we live in. An open mind denies entry to nothing and can thus arrive at—what *The Kandy-Kolored Tangerine Flake Streamline Baby* (national), *The Pump House Gang* (international) and *The Electric Kool-Aid Acid Test* (supranational) add up to—the "Scene individable, or Poem unlimited" of which Polonius incongruously speaks to Hamlet.

Free to observe or ignore the rules (syntactical, punctuational, typographical), Wolfe might easily have gone wrong, manufacturing trendy-looking but tame portraits of orthodox and unorthodox status-seekers. But, as well as logging all the pertinent trivia and working hard his ear for goofy chatter and his lepidopterist's eye for any kandy-kolored tangerine-flake on the move, he also indulges in the gutsy, volcanic joy of writing to please himself. The fun he's had doing it comes through almost always. "What struck me throughout America and England," he writes in one of his less hectic moments, "was that so many people have found such novel ways of . . . *enjoying,* extending their egos way out on the best terms available, namely, their own." Tom Wolfe too, of course; and it's his own epicurean ego that gives all those other egos that extra patina. For what he does is meta-reporting, something creative and inventive which releases a lot of his own static into their ecstatics and demonstrates time and again that imagination (which he has in abundance) wasn't given us to make copies with but to help us masticate actuality (as if the universe were lazily at play with itself).

Of course, what is *is:* Tom Wolfe himself plainly reports that white Norway rats behave consistently under consistent experiment conditions, and there is no place for imagination in describing that behavior. But for what lies "beyond acid"—what Wolfe approaches via "the mental atmosphere or subjective reality" as distinct from the Pranksters' apparatus and paraphernalia, patois and garb—there is only imagination to use and only imagination to judge by (and judging here is guessing, for imaginations do not police other imaginations). So you just have to take or leave drug-induced encounters with "the Management" and Kesey's own discovery that "It's kind of hard, playing cello on a hypodermic needle and using a petrified bat as a bow." The individable scene that includes the convention of counting 1-2-3 also includes imagination the unknown "x", not to mention quasars and DNA, curved space and Leptis Magna, voodoo and LSD, dollars and dinars and drachmas, belly-dancers and computers, $6.95 semi-spread Pima-cotton shirts and No-Kloresto egg substitute and Telstar and *Queen* Magazine. . . . *Endless.* I don't know what "making sense of" it all could possibly mean, but I think there are many ways of marveling at it, among which Tom Wolfe's is one of the most exciting because, primarily, he knows how much of it there is, as well as knowing how little of it many of our most esteemed writers—novelists as well as essayists and playwrights and documentary men—confront. In addition to having that Huck Finn thing, the sense of adventure, he also has—never mind what the girl called Doris Delay said was missing from his appearance—the colors of the world in his coloratura poem unlimited.

Santa Claus of Middle Earth

ONLY INSOFAR AS IT RECOUNTS the long life of their conscripted magus is Humphrey Carpenter's life of Tolkien a book for Hobbitomanes (which verbal hybrid would have made Tolkien the professional philologist wince). It's the biography of an Oxford professor, an expert on the West Midland dialect of medieval England, who loved to invent esoteric languages and concoct new exploits for personages from Scandinavian sagas. As such, it winningly captures an historical period (Oxford 1910-1960), reveals the texture of a teaching scholar's life, and introduces us to a many-sided humanist whose mind was as keen and picturesque as his clothes were drab, except for a fancy vest.

That, on the side, this poetic pedant produced a new mythology for England was natural enough, and natural to him: it renewed for him the rural ethos of his boyhood and honored the pre-Renaissance pith of national life, as well as providing him with a zone in which to play, half-dreaming in damp sunlight while correcting the examination answers of grammar-school students to make extra cash. That Middle-earth had world-wide appeal both puzzled and re-energized him; he diligently answered much of the mail from fans but chose a life of sheltered celebrity and, as Humphrey Carpenter brings out, undevious humility. You like him at once, without effort, whereas C.S. Lewis, his career-long crony, emerges as an invertedly Byronic loudmouth, a taste for whom you assembled only over the years.

In the wrong hands, this could have been a tame recital indeed, a hagiography of exalted outlines and dogged blather. Instead, it's a panorama of vignettes done with poise and exhaustive command. A man emerges whole with his mind intact, gradually insinuating his ancient interests into the format of an almost-as-ancient university and, at the same time, making the characters in most campus novels seem empty and deficiently observed. Carpenter has an eye for the magic in what's pedestrian, and in his charge a "quiet life," such as Tolkien's, becomes an in-depth act of relish.

Tolkien was born in South Africa, where as a toddler he trod on a tarantula, which bit him; his nurse sucked out the poison. He grew up fatherless, in England, and, after his twelfth year, motherless too, although in the rural Worcestershire where his mother's family had lived for generations and where the local dialect ("gamgee" for cotton wool, "miskin" for trashcan) beguiled his imagination into a lifelong mania for obscure words. He loved trees and leaned on them to talk to them. He liked "Red Indian" tales and longed to shoot with bow and arrow. At seven he composed a story about a green dragon. His dreams included an engulfing wave which he later dubbed his "Atlantis complex." He first saw Welsh names on the coal-trucks in a railroad siding.

At school in Birmingham he discovered *Sir Gawain and the Green Knight,* of which he later prepared a famous edition, and in school debates held forth in Greek (Latin was too easy) or Gothic, to which he added neo-Gothicisms of his own. His guardian, a Catholic priest, kept him from seeing Edith Bratt, his sweetheart (whom he eventually married) until he won an exhibition to Exeter College, Oxford, where he later took a First in English. While a student he "captured" a bus during a "rag" and studied with Joseph Wright, the Professor of Comparative Philology, who had worked in a woolen mill from six to fifteen. For Tolkien, English Literature *ended* with Chaucer. A devout (though intermittently lazy) Catholic, he despised the Church of England as much as he despised Frenchmen, trains, allegory, and the Concorde. After surviving World War I, which claimed two of his dearest friends, he returned to Oxford as a researcher for the New English Dictionary, his first assignment being to the etymology of *warm, wasp, water, wick,* and *winter.*

Then he went to Leeds University for five years, returning to Oxford next in 1925, to a Chair of Anglo-Saxon. "And after this," writes Humphrey Carpenter, "you might say nothing else really happened. Tolkien became Merton Professor of English Language and Literature, "went to live in a conventional Oxford suburb where he spent the fist part of his retirement, moved to a nondescript seaside resort, came back to Oxford after his wife died, and himself died a peaceful death at the age of eighty-one." Unremarkable? Yes, except that "during these years when 'nothing happened' he wrote two books which have become world best-sellers." Carpenter adroitly tracks him through the years of academic eminence and lucrative authorship, neglecting neither his preference for male, Christian friends, nor Edith's lonely, misfit role in Oxford, neither his giving far more lectures than he had to, nor her somewhat tyrannical compensatory control of their successive homes. One chapter sketches a typical Tolkien day from reluctant getting-up to his return by bicycle to a house in darkness, where he stokes up the study fire, lights his pipe, and scrawls something creative on the back of an old examination answer.

What made him tick? "England . . . my country." Something superlatively rustic made his speech indistinct, his politics royalist right-wing, and the clown in him offer shopkeepers his false teeth in a handful of loose change or don an Icelandic sheepskin rug and paint his face white to impersonate a polar bear. He loved doing "Father Christmas letters" to his four children, and that side of him—the Santa Claus of Middle earth—fits well with his assertion: "I am in fact a hobbit, in all but size. I like gardens, trees, and unmechanized farmlands. . . ." To the last he kept meticulous accounts of his outlay for postage, razor blades, Steradent, and the like, but he never met deadlines, had a TV, or found publishers easy to deal with. Oxford gave him its honorary D. Litt. for his contributions to philology only. If one word describes him, it is one whose old meaning was "lay," "non-clergy," "of the ordinary people," and whose current force would have made him grin. The word is *lewd*.

Octavio Paz
On Poets and Others

THE MEXICAN PHILOSOPHER-POET Octavio Paz writes with winning informality, honoring the externals of life, its tone, its casual encounters, mocking the pomp with which many intellectuals handle ideas. His opening essay in this collection, about a visit to Robert Frost, begins like this: "After twenty minutes walking along the highway under a three o'clock sun, I came at last to the turning. I veered right and began to climb the slope." More than a dozen lines later he is writing the same kind of thing: "The wind began to blow; everything swayed, almost cheerfully. All the leaves sang." His anecdotal mood is hard to resist, and I don't think he works it just for variety's sake; it is more that he sees ideas in a narrative context and finds himself—as walker, caller, observer, friend, opponent—an interesting piece of the universe on the move.

Sometimes, however, this relaxed mood gets him into less engaging postures, not so much setting his emotions and ideas in the ferment of a life lived from day to day among meals, friends, weather, streets, as reminding us that he has emotions at all. One essay begins: "The death of Jean-Paul Sartre, after the initial shock this kind of news produces, aroused in me a feeling a resigned melancholy." Of course: it hardly needs saying, whereas sometimes what he says doesn't need saying at all. He ends the first of his two essays on Solzhenitsyn thus: "I say this with sadness, and humility." Anyone finishing *The Gulag Archipelago* will feel the same, at the very least. And, beginning his essay on Ortega y Gasset, he writes "I write these lines with enthusiasm and with fear." Why doesn't he just get on with it? It sounds to me like the small change of self-importance easily parodied ("I approach the theme of Hitler with hatred and revulsion"), and it puts this reader off because I know I can infer, pick up, tune in to, resigned melancholy, sadness and humility, enthusiasm and fear, in between the lines and along them, without having a placard shoved in my face.

That said, I hasten to assure the reader that Paz has much to say that is worth hearing, although I felt let down by his heavily political

pair of essays on Solzhenitsyn, whom I have been re-reading. I wish
this poet had heeded *The Gulag's* subtitle: "An Experiment in Literary
Investigation," or the literary quality, the involutedly elliptical strategies, of Solzhenitsyn's rhetoric. Paz rightly tells us that the Russian's
voice is "not modern but ancient" and that *The Gulag* is "a *witness-
ing*," but then gets off into villainous names—the Cheka, Mao, Fidel,
Lenin, Marx—until Solzhenitsyn gets lost in a prison camp of a new
kind: of abstract politicism, however right-minded.

The best of this book is concise, visionary stuff such as we find
in the essay on Whitman ("One ought rather to speak of the invention
of America than of its discovery") and that on the poet Charles
Tomlinson: "The world turns to air, temperature, sensation, thought;
and we become stone, window, orange peel, turf, oil stain, helix." This
is his way of fleshing out his point that in Tomlinson's poems "outer
reality . . . is a climate which involves us," and the same is true too
of Paz's best essays. He talks about Sartre's astounding lack of intellectual curiosity (Sartre's admiring a work's reputation without feeling
the desire to read it), something akin, I think, to what Paz finds, in his
essay on Dostoevsky, to be the crime of the ideologue: "He calls
others *comrades* but he never talks to them: he talks to *his idea*."

Paz is at his most refreshing and stimulating when he gets allusive and complex, when he takes a chance or two, as in "The great
invention of man is men" (though you could make a case for the
reverse too) and "thinking is an erection and I still think." On the point
he tends to harp, off it he lets his mind and memory unfurl, making
lively fusions of the trivial with the grand. As he himself says, the
essayist "must be diverse, penetrating, acute, fresh, and he must master the difficult art of using three dots." I wonder about those dots.
Sometimes the essayist must elide, of course, but must also expose
ideas to the wind, the noise of buses, the sound of children coughing,
even if only to evince thereby the huge, heterogeneous confusion that
the chastest, severest essays ignore in order to achieve inductive purity. Sometimes, Virginia, the essayist must use irrelevance.

Some of these essays have appeared in another book, most no-
tably the brilliant, ground-breaking one on Henri Michaux and mesca-
line, although it comes through less well in this translation. Compare
Helen R. Lane's version in *Alternating Current* ("Once I had fallen

into that panting maw, the universe seemed to me to be an immense, multiple fornication") with Michael Schmidt's "Fallen into the great panting mouth, the universe seemed to me an immense, multiple fornication," which is ambiguous to begin with. Mr. Schmidt's introductory essay is somewhat better than his translation, another sample of which is the phrase "confiding in my memory," something no one can do. He means "trusting my memory" or "trusting to memory." He does, however, draw attention to Paz's pluralism, his unideological radicalism, and his avowed debt to—of all poets—William Wordsworth, although Paz seems closer at times to Thomas De Quincey.

There is a lovely essay here on William Carlos Williams, whom Paz understands in the profoundest way, rightly drawing attention to Williams's doctrine that "art does not imitate nature: it imitates its creative processes." This is Paz's view too, and it is instructive as well as somewhat amusing to find him applying it tot he Spanish poets Jorge Guillen and Luis Cernuda, to Baudelaire and André Breton. Paz is hardly ever Procrustean, relishing instead the fluidity and mercuriality of the human mind. "Man does not speak," he writes, "because he thinks but thinks because he speaks." I find this emphasis on the helplessness of human brilliance both moving and timely, most of all when he says, apropos of André Breton, "The I does not save itself because it does not exist." Identity for him, whoever he is, is a process not a fixity.

All the more praise to him, then, for achieving so consistent a tone in these essays; you would never mistake him for anyone else, oddly enough. It is one of the predictable oddities of minds as open as his that they sometimes, like Paz when he shuffles around a bit before starting, behave as their own gatekeepers, nervous at being responsible for so vast a terrain. For him the Territory is cosmic, the Frontier is mental, while Art is "a bridge" alluding to something it never names, a something "which is identical with nothing." No wonder he seems like a thought with a thousand arms.

Geoffrey Moorhouse
Hell's Foundations

CROPPED OF STEM AND THORNS, a Minden rose lolls in a glass of champagne in front of each new subaltern or other uninitiated officer. At a special dining-in night in the Mess, the officers of the Lancashire Fusiliers are commemorating the day in August, 1759 when their predecessors, marching against a huge force of French cavalry, plucked and wore roses from the gardens along the River Weser. This was the day of the famous "Minden Yell," named for the nearest town. The Lancashiremen broke through three lines of cavalry and prevailed. Now, as on Minden Day ever since, officers who have not done it before stand on chairs, eat their roses and wash them down with wine.

Geoffrey Moorhouse's sensitive and vibrant tale seems conceived in a similar honorific and ritualistic mood. his book is a rose in memory of not only some two thousand officers and men of the Lancashire Fusiliers who died in the assault on Gallipoli that began on April 25, 1915, but also the town of Bury, the regiment's home base. This is social history of uncanny force and carefully judged figure-ground. now the smoky humdrum mill-town comes to the fore, now the battle for a peninsula not far from the site of Troy; now bury's fabrics—sackcloth, fustian, stammel and russet, yellow buffine and red durant; now the sharp spikes the Turks have embedded in fresh-dug pits on the Gallipoli beaches.

As attuned to myth as to life in the terrace houses of industrial Lancashire, Moorhouse tells all we need to know about Troy, the Hellespont (swum by Leander, whose feat Byron emulated in 1810), and copies of *The Iliad* carried to this campaign by young sailors "itching to see where Homer's epic was set." Winston Churchill, ever the poseur of strategy, and Lord Kitchener devised this plan to capture Constantinople, but commanders in the field were equipped with intelligence a dozen years old, and troops were landed much too long after the naval bombardment ended. The Turkish wire was hard to cut. Watches had not been synchronized. And the Turks were up above the beach, firing down at anything that moved.

Snafu is what we nowadays call such a shambles, but shambles
is a more vivid word. Peter Weir's film is about the heroism of Aus-
tralians in this assault; Moorhouse's book, like some keening, throb-
bing family album drawn in coal on skin of North-Country pallor,
addresses a regimental town suddenly empty, for a long time misinformed and uninformed, and then laid low by only too calculable
losses. Bury becomes a town castrated by military carelessness, its
only destiny that of creating Gallipoli Sunday.

No one who reads Moorhouse's description of the various beach
landings is going to forget it: first the calm, oily sea filled with sway-
ing replicas of mirrored land; no sound from the Turks on the heights;
then soldiers drowning under the weight of their packs; the shore red
with blood; some of the Lancashires lying dead halfway up the cliffs,
their rifles still in their hands; arms, legs, brains, skulls and lungs.
Only one of eight floating piers had arrived. Few guns or transport
animals had been unloaded. Product of muddle that it was, Gallipoli
appeared to be some perversely devised Draconian test. Steaming off
to Alexandria, two transports of Lancashire wounded came alongside
each other. "Are we downhearted?" came the cry from one.
"Nooooooh." Then came the answer from the other vessel: "But you
bloody soon will be."

Not so much of as with Bury, the Lancashiremen had come from
a barracks set in a countryside of uncemented dry-stone walls, coarse
tussocks and barren peat where the dominant sounds were those of
rushing water and "the bubbling trill of the curlew." Damp country,
where spun thread would not snap. Crude but gentle songs from the
cotton famine in the early 1860's came to their ears and wafted away,
not quite fathomed, one about a newborn child:

> Bless thee, lad.
> Th'art prettiest bird we have i' th' nest,
> So hutch up closer to mi breast;
> Aw'm thi dad.

Bury itself, which the Lancashires regarded as home or home
from home, had as many as fifty hovels in one terrace line, parallel to
fifty others, with between them a long narrow lane up which nightly

would come the night-cart to collect excrement form the outdoor priv-
ies or closets. During the day, housewives pegged out billowing sheets,
knowing that here in the tough North they were judged on clean linen
and the whiteness of the front doorstep, scoured and then whitened
with "donkeystone," named for the rag and bone man's donkey (which
pulled a cart filled with worn-out clothing swapped for sandstone
blocks). Moorhouse superbly delineates the dark satanic, and deafen-
ing, mills, revealing how the racket within turned workers into "mee-
mawers," who lip-read one another both in the weaving sheds and out.
Here the chimneys, some 250 feet, bore names in glazed and colored
letters: "Pilot, Egyptian, Eagle, India, California," a touch of myth for
laborers living on offal and black pudding, walking in clogs whose
irons struck sparks from the cobbles. Life here was so bleak that men
would readily take the Queen's shilling. Rather that than starve, or
slave in the bedlam of the mills. So there was osmosis: the men leaked
away into the Army, to the colors, and the Army leaked into the town,
both semi-loyally, in a tiny, drab transhumance that would eventually,
out of blood and soot, noise and Pennine silence, yield high holy days
of military disaster, celebrated because that was all the town had got.

Among those who responded to the British invitation to a military career in a pleasant climate were not only brothers but father-and-
son pairs, such as Jim Scotson and his father, who saw his son shot
dead by a Turkish sniper and was sent back to Egypt on a hospital ship
with nervous breakdown. This is a book of heartbreaking, awkward
letters, mostly from stranger to stranger, but some from surviving
brother to mother ("instantaneous and painless. He fell with his face
to the enemy. . . . "). Stances of almost heraldic nobility haunt the
stilted prose of dutiful report while Moorhouse diligently watches the
freeloaders, shirkers, jingoists, rabble-rousers, and political arrivistes
back home.

For a while, news of the disaster at Gallipoli is hard to come by,
The town marks time. The Mayor swears off alcohol; the main toyshop
touts patriotic brooches and war games; bullet-proof vests (36 ounces
in weight) go on sale, and proponents of crackpot diets—crows and
potato butter—sound off. Then news of the horror. Local women catch
new-made widows as they faint, telegram in hand. Curtains are drawn
all along the street. Moorhouse knows his Northerners and captures

the dourness with forthright emotion, the unassailable solidarity on which the rough-tongued, isolated-looking bereaved depend.

He has just as keen an eye for returning survivors, some of whom after a mellow interlude of repatriation cut their own throats, gas or shoot or drown or poison themselves as if a brush with death has unfitted them for life. Few bodies came back to Bury, but the Lancashire Fusiliers won six Victoria Crosses for extraordinary heroism. The social history of all this blood-letting begins to add up when small illuminated scrolls, "lavish with draped flags, and with a steadfast Britannia counterbalanced by a sorrowing maiden," reach the widows. Later comes the brass plaque, with more Britannia and an adjacent lion, and, still later, a scroll into which is tucked a slip of paper bearing a reproduction of King George V's signature. Within and around a town that isn't sure if it is being conned or not, there grows a mirage of righteous beatifics: buglers, firing parties, bonfires, trays of flags on sticks, Compassionate Funds, fog signals on the railroad tracks.

The bravest (and some of the not so brave) have gone over, creating behind them a legend Bury finds hard to swallow; all those soldiers becoming crosses is harder to believe than what happened to Bertha Collier, an unmarried munitions worker made pregnant by a soldier on furlough and self-aborted with pennyroyal and sweet niter, dead in Bury Infirmary from septic peritonitis. Another wartorn baby turns up in the sluice of a local bleachworks. So long as life is productive, runs the Calvinist adage, let it be bleak; but, for the men and women and children of Bury, Gallipoli revised it: No matter how bleak life is, it can get bleaker.

Moorhouse's analysis of myths and mores in post-war Bury develops into a startling, luminous and humane study of how propaganda—elegiac and mesmeric—goes to work on the cannon fodder of the future, asking or obliging it in ostensibly noble terms to abandon its wits in hope of cutting a final figure so illustrious that nothing else matters. Or, as one company commander expressed it in a letter to a dead man's family: "The moon, which was behind the clouds, appeared suddenly and exposed him to view. His death was instantaneous—not a murmur and not a pain." We begin to see why, after World War Two, the working classes of Great Britain began to get "bloody-minded" (obtusely uncooperative), and stayed that way, insisting on a place in the sun, both at home and on the Costa Brava. The sooner people cease volunteering to save their so-called betters, the braver the world will be, with or without a murmur or a pain. Moorhouse's grave and sage book reveals how glory can be something of a canker.

Charles Sprawson
Haunts of the Black Masseur

To EMBARRASS FRIENDS who urinated while swimming in his pool, Orson Welles procured a chemical that reacted visibly to uric acid and left offending guests "swimming around in raspberry-coloured clouds." Among the adobe bungalows of the Garden of Allah, where Scott Fitzgerald lived, the actress Alla Nazimova placed an oddly shaped pool the same shape as the Black Sea, to remind her of her Yalta childhood. According to some, Hart Crane did a swallow dive when he jumped to his death from the steamship *Orizaba* in 1932. John Cheever always made sure he was the last swimmer of the year in his Connecticut pool.

And so on. Charles Sprawson is that English marvel, the insatiable browser, a snapper-up of unconsidered trifles, just so long as they pertain to swimming; categorically speaking a mix of Isaac Walton and Sacheverell Sitwell. The Black Masseur of his title is he who "mangled the poor clerk in the [Tennessee] Williams short story and still haunts [the] recesses" of the New Orleans Athletic Club. Some might have thought this Black Masseur the soul of all dark waters, the osteopath of the deep, but Sprawson prefers to tease us with a literary, Boris Karloffian version while assimilating to his hero's cause all kinds of tales, vignettes, episodes, and, sometimes, personal memories. The result is a fascinating scrapbook loaded with lore, responsibly but not elegantly written, and suffused with the mystery of water.

Here and there throughout *Haunts of the Black Masseur* Mr.

Sprawson—a graduate of Trinity College, Dublin and presently a dealer in nineteenth-century paintings—gets quite personal and tells of his own swimming, although off-handedly implying joys and terrors you have to guess at. Deep water terrifies him, but he recently swam the Hellespont, like Byron. You never quite know what he's going to say next. Right after several fascinating pages about the Hellespont and those who swam it, he blurts "Four years ago I flew to Turkey to swim the Hellespont. I left it rather late." In that first sentence he doesn't italicize any of the words, though he might have done so to stress "I," "flew," or "swim." We get not so much an intonation, orchestrated and strategic, as the sense that he's just moving on to the next piece of business. And perhaps you have gleaned from the jacket that he's already polished off the Hellespont. His personal forays are brief and rather haphazardly distributed when they might have dominated the book and subordinated much of the gossip to a series of self-discoveries. As it is, we read with scattered fascination about his learning to swim in India "in the flooded subterranean vaults" of a palace, "among columns that disappeared mysteriously into black water."

That is how the book begins, and vividly so. The first dozen pages reveal him reading Pindar at a hot spring in Turkey, swimming in Portofino and Benghazi, answering in Latin a job advertisement also in Latin in the London *Times*, getting the job (lecturing on "classical culture" in an Arab university), and so able to quit his previous employ "as a swimming pool attendant in some old Victorian baths in Paddington, so dismal and dirty that no one ever came." He makes notes and lists, of famous swimmers and their feats, a very philatelist of plunges, anxious not to miss the trees for the wood. An arcane obsession begins that he says he could barely communicate. He fixes on Rose the Olympic gold medallist, an Australian reared on ancient Greek literature, seaweed, sesame and sunflower seeds, and eventually challenges him to a race.

This is fascinating stuff, especially to me, who wrote a book on learning-to-swim-rather-late-in-life. But then we are told what the remainder of the book will be about—"The peculiar psychology of the swimmer, and his 'feel for water'"—and we have to wait another hundred pages before the personal odyssey boldly reappears, as it does with Hellespont. Sprawson flashes into view, silvery and enigmatic,

but inviting and candid, and then slips away to become a mere con-
ductor, a guide, a bit of an aquatic motor-mouth. The scholarly, sensuous atavist shows up again only briefly discovering his dread of the
deep in a rowing-boat on the Red Sea, swimming on a dark February
evening with "joyous naked Germans," climbing over the fence of
Tennessee William's empty house on Duncan Street, Key West, "to
swim through the green slime of his pool."

What we are left with, then, instead of the personal analytical
and emotional triumph the book might have become, is a compendium
that will entertain water-people world-wide. Rose used Glenn Miller's
"In the Mood" to get his rhythm right. Swimmers shave their legs. If
you stay on a rival's hip, you can be borne along in his surge. Swimmers copied dogs, then frogs (kept in tubs poolside). George III swam
off Weymouth to the accompaniment of a chamber orchestra. Jane
Austen loved sea-bathing and, once, in 1804, stayed in too long.
Charlotte Brontë fainted when first in the ocean. W.B. Yeats's grand-
father jumped overboard into the Bay of Biscay after an old hat. The
Roman army had a regiment of swimming Germans, and divers who
dribbled oil from their mouths so as to see clearly. In the basements
of certain Hamburg hotels, nude sirens loll on velvet sofas and "offer
up their charms." As a boy, Matthew Arnold spent an entire vacation
imagining he was a corpse at the bottom of Lake Windermere. Both
Swinburne and Jack London let themselves be carried out to sea, miles
out, only to be rescued. London wrote of an "amazing peacock-blue
of a breaker, shot through with golden sunlight, overfalling in a mile-
long sweep and thundering into white ruin of foam on a crescent
beach of sand." Zelda Fitzgerald wrote from a mental home in 1935
to Scott, wishing "we could spend July by the sea, browning ourselves
and feeling water-weighted hair flow behind us in a dive."

Sprawson brings Shelley, Byron, and Swinburne—those golden
oldies of literary swim-lore—very much to life as water-ecstatics; but
inquisitive readers may prefer learning that Goethe had himself a life-
jacket made of cork, that Iris Murdoch is "one of the last of the
English river-swimmers," that Rupert Brooke swam naked with Virginia Woolf by the light of a bicycle lamp on river's edge, that Rose
Macaulay took "lone compulsive bathes from the fabled shores of
Spain and Portugal, naked whenever possible." Mary Kingsley dried
herself on her cumberbund. Walter Pater, when asked what he would

like to have been if not a man, answered "A carp swimming for ever in the green waters of some royal chateau." He would have loved the pools at Hearst's San Simeon, about which Sprawson writes rapturously, as he does about the finer touches of batting in cricket.

Half a dozen of his sentences, alas, have broken backs: "He managed to carry on swimming mechanically until, almost unconscious, a couple of Greek fishermen haled him over the side of their boat," or "Now, in the grip of the outgoing tide, their survival depends on Marston." Don't editors read manuscripts for such things any more? From Sprawson's chromatic extravaganza, I missed only F.T. Prince's poem, "Soldiers Bathing," Handel, Spenser, Stevie Smith, Richard Dehmel ("The Sinking Swimmer"), and Charles Tomlinson for his long poem, "On Swimming Chenango Lake." I too long to become a connoisseur of pearls and pools.

Art and the Double Life

S PECULATIVE READERS should have a field day with *Significant Others,* Whitney Chadwick's and Isabelle de Courtivron's collection of "artist and writer couples." Frida Kahlo and Diego Rivera, Clara and André Malraux, Camille Claudel and Auguste Rodin, to name three of the duos examined here, might have done better to stay apart. They might have fared better together if only one of them had been an artist, or neither. People compatible with each other may well mutate into mutual monsters; all it takes is an influx from the muse, or one to be a night person and the other a day person, or one to be a maximalist to the other's minimalism, or one to be successful and the other not. I say speculative because, half the time, we never know the salient intimacies of such relationships. As Anne Higgonet says of Claudel and Rodin, "The facts of their professional relationship have been almost completely obscured by the personal circumstances of their ten years together." Yet their ten years together were "the most innovative and the most productive of their careers." One lumbers about among masterpieces and flops, trying to fish the private life from the public one only to discover that biography does not leak from artifacts but vanishes into them to dry and wither.

We do not know how Claudel spent her time; there are no records, and her works are a diaspora of art, uncatalogued and often lost, whereas Rodin hoarded every scrap of stuff about himself and handed it over, as Ms. Higonnet says, to "a permanently staffed institution." Where we have not known, the guess has been king, as in the assumption current for years that one piece, *Brother and Sister* (1890), was his just because it echoed *Maternal Kiss* (1885) whereas it was hers, as external evidence proved. So, much of the time you cannot guess at the art, even though it survives, and the diurnal improvisations of life together have blown away. It begins to look as if probing significant others is a bad idea, undoable, best left to fiction. It is enlivening to ponder Claudel's limp, making her socially awkward, and Rodin's habit in his later years of hardly looking down at his work, "so rapidly," Ms. Higgonet says, "was his pencil moving in apparently automatic response to what he saw, and what he saw was usually the part of woman he identified as the origin of life." Can we elicit from her limp and his cunnal obsession the to and fro of their decade together? No, we end up, and surely this is destructive to biography, seeing the pair in mythic terms, with her playing not second but umpteenth fiddle to him. His women were not individuals, or even individuated, but vessels and organs, and certainly not minds or gifts. His bombastic sexuality was *grata,* but her urgent eroticism was taboo. Faced with her years of increasing relegation, from aide to patsy to reject, and from there to crackpot, obsessive, and victim, Claudel produced less and less, a piece of gyno-leftover eventually to be celebrated in a movie often sneered at for being overblown, shallow, and emotionally uninvolving. I always liked it as a fairly subtle attempt to break down the mythic trap Camille perished in: in other words, to acquaint us with useful particulars, to get her away from stereotype.

It is as if Simone Weil had lived with Teddy Roosevelt, or Mary Shelley with Hemingway. I linger on this pair because the discussion of it, coming first in the book, announces angers and indignations that recur elsewhere (Lillian Hellman and Dashiell Hammett, for instance). This is not a book about what the editors call "the endless complexities of partnership itself," though they do show up, but one about how throughout history gifted women have been shafted by creative men. It is not the book's whole theme, but when the contributors find evidence of it they make the most of it. And why not? One winces at Claudel's non-career, or Clara Malraux's belated one, or the way art histories have short-changed Sonia Delaunay—as Whitney Chadwick says in her elegant essay, "setting aside her own career as a painter and instead devoting herself to applying [Robert's] esthetic theories to the decorative arts." And to becoming a hostess. Sonia came into her own later. Certainly there is an agenda here, and why not? *Singular Others* could have been a raucous demand for justice, but instead it cites the offense and then amasses particulars about each life in the pair.

The right context of such portraits is the recent emancipation from the shadow of their "spouses, teachers, lovers, and mentors" of such marvels as Claudel and Kahlo, Berthe Morrisot and Anaïs Nin. Women keep on heaving into view, closely followed by their artifacts, peeled away at last from a male system of support (teachers, critics, journalists, publishers, curators, reviewers) and what the editors call "female systems of domestic support." What we have here is a book of rehabilitation fused with a well-tempered, generous overview that celebrates creativity as a human miracle no less imposing than love itself. The editors' introduction, full of ideas, reads like a genial Magna Carta, setting up the ground rules for what is sometimes a painful exploration of gifted women fobbed off as copycats, mere Others to the Significant male. Thus we are reminded that Lee Krasner, Kay Sage, and Leonora Carrington are just as Significant as their Others (Jackson Pollock, Yves Tanguy, and Max Ernst). I can only add that, after years of studying MFA students in fiction writing, I find it is the women by and large who have done best, who have subsequently published the most, who have been more open to life and the possibilities of prose. Derivative? Hardly: quite a few have hammered out their own prose styles, no doubt after soaking up Virginia or Nathalie, Djuna or Gertrude. The editors even glance disdainfully at the spent notion that creativity for woman means childbearing. They spell it out with resentful precision:

The hierarchy that is often assumed to be the "natural" order reinforces the notion that women do not do "serious" work, that they paint when they are "bored in bed," as in the case of Frida Kahlo (whose marriage portrait of the couple portrays Diego Rivera as the one who holds the paintbrushes) or Kay Sage (who always denied any formal artistic training and was vigorously rejected as an artist by the Surrealists until she endorsed the socially acceptable role of widow of Tanguy). Through the examples of couples like Kahlo and Rivera, or the Delaunays, we can begin to understand the opposition between those who do, *and* those who do and also create a theory about what they do, and in the process structure meaning.

I can pay tribute to the force and splendor of this book by recalling my mother, often the concert pianist but never enough for her, first hearing about feminism and gender studies. After having been thwarted by her parents and obliged to subordinate art to her needy brothers, she then found a way to transcend the commonplace and philistine by backing to the hilt her son's increasing gravitation to art. She taught me theory and harmony and, most of all, grammar. For art, almost any sacrifice was worthwhile. A tear would form, then be banished, as she heard about careers for women, and the proto-version of what Chadwick and Courtivron say in their preface. My mother saw the beginning of women's being freed from the penumbra of secondariness, subordinateness, derivativeness—ugly, clogged words for a clogged condition. She had three brothers, two of them brilliant in technology, but she was the one who heard and heeded the muse: not the muse of men only, but the sexful or sexless muse who comes to birth in Stravinsky's *Apollon Musagète* in which Apollo, newly born, bestows distinctive gifts on three muses: Calliope, Polyhymnia, and Terpsichore. I see this birth as a thing distinctly bi, with Apollo putting marvelous gifts into superior hands in exchange for white raiment and ambrosial gifts: poetry, mime, and dance. What a bargain! In the apotheosis Apollo guides the three Muses to Parnassus, their eternal home. Apollo's useful, but the muses know where their bread is buttered. Or so I think as I listen to this best of parturition music.

Lisa Tickner's essay on Vanessa Bell and Duncan Grant begins with three flashes of Vanessa's sister, Virginia Woolf, living her own life: being enthusiastic about Vanessa's paintings on show in 1926; saying of literary work "Children are nothing to this"; and admiring Vanessa's "handling of life as if it were a thing one could throw about." Then we get to it, reminded none too gently that Bell and Grant have both been overshadowed by *literary* Bloomsbury (the start of the essay itself symbolized that fate) and Vanessa, omitted from the second volume of John Rothenstein's *Modern English Painters* (1956), sometimes suffered the blight of having her work mistaken for Grant's. In the seventies this began to change, and Bell, insecure and submissive, has emerged, an earth mother with daring hands (see the picture Roger Fry owned of a woman after childbirth). Ms Tickner writes capably about "the androgynous integrity of a work of art," not a surprising concept in the context of Bell, who began a ménage à trois with David Garnett and Grant, by the second of whom she wanted a child. Most interesting of all is her discussion of Grant's insouciant bisexual charm and Vanessa's "masculine" traits. The work of them both abides, startling, emphatic, psychological. They helped each other, each fortifying the other's self-esteem. Who can ask for more?

Right after this essay comes Louise DeSalvo's valuable study of Virginia Woolf and Vita Sackville-West, whom Virginia seduced on a sofa on December 18, 1925 in what Vita later described as an "explosion." Vita took the place in Woolf's esteem of Katherine Mansfield, dead in 1923, impressing Woolf with her "supple ease" and aristocratic manner," yet also seeming (as Woolf put it) "florid, moustached, parakeet coloured." In their ten years together, Woolf and Sackville-West did an impressive amount of distinguished, lasting work (Woolf: *Orlando*, celebrating Vita, *Mrs Dalloway, To the Lighthouse, The Waves*, and *Flush*; Vita: *Seducers in Ecuador, The Land, Passenger to Teheran*, and *All Passion Spent*). Then Vita's lust turned to tenderness; Virginia was not sexual enough for Vita's "grenadier" appetite. As Ms De Salvo says, "Neither would ever again reach this peak of accomplishment. They wrote with each other in mind, and they learned from each other. Vita became more highly skilled, more concerned with style and form. Virginia became more playful in her prose, and could write more quickly and for a far wider audience." Not only that, "their correspondence is one of the great love duets of contemporary letters." Ms De Salvo amasses in a short space all sorts of sparkling details, from masturbated dogs to Leonard Woolf's ways with Virginia's money. When I took this book to my MFA class, one lively young student asked to look at it and went away mesmerized by so much concentrated, salient information. You come away from the reading as from an old-style three-decker novel, intimately aware of twenty-six lives and thirteen matches, aching to know more and almost headily persuaded that it is *better* for creative artists to live together—though eager for another book on these lines, revealing the lives of artists who live alone.

Noël Riley Fitch's essay on Anaïs Nin and Henry Miller elicits order from often confusing phenomena (both wanted to play Don Juan) and Jonathan Katz's on Jasper Johns and Robert Rauschenberg is quite astonishing: ". . . Jasper and I literally traded ideas," said Rauschenberg. "He would say, 'I've got a terrific idea for you,' and then I'd have to find one for him. Ours were two very different sensibilities, and being so close to each other's work kept any incident of similarity from occurring." Indeed, Johns was not even an artist until they met. After they parted company, they eschewed explicitly gay imagery while remaining the same as before: Johns shy, Rauschenberg ebullient. The only essay that troubled me was Ronnie Scharfman's on Simone and André Schwarz-Bart in which Ms Scharfman seems to have to grope for the minutiae of intimate togetherness, here citing André as "in a convent in Europe, trying to write" while Simone runs an antique shop in Pointe-à-Pitre in Guadeloupe. Here, for once, apartness is the catalyst, shedding a keen, generous light on the other portraits and their, as Ms Tickner puts it, "painful asymmetry." Fearful too.

Johann Wolfgang von Goethe

Q UITE BLACK" with asphyxia after a birth lasting three days, the
infant Goethe had to be shaken and then rubbed under the heart
with wine. Eighty-three years later, expecting the spring air would
make him well, he died in the armchair by his bed, crazed with fear
and pain but tracing on the coverlet about his knees a large W—for
Wolfgang or World. What happened in between—the world Wolfgang
made, the Wolfgang the world made, the Wolfgang that Wolfgang
built, all that "full, rich and very varied life"—we do not know as well
as we think we do, even after we have digested G.H. Lewes's work-
manlike biography, sampled the intimate inaccuracies of the *Conver-
sations with Eckermann,* skidded along the dawdling glacier of *Dichtung
und Wahrheit,* and (if we are brave) sampled some of those books
which, purporting to be lives, develop into critical interpretations,
uneasily mixing the works with the 30,000-odd days.

As Richard Friedenthal says, "No full and scholarly account of
Goethe's life exists, although the writing of a comprehensive biography was one of the tasks envisaged when the Goethe archives were
opened in 1885." The Goetheans, understandably anxious to relate
him to so much—from the history of science to the social structure of
Thuringia—have continually overshot the man. Goethe the Olympian
has increasingly obscured Goethe the earthy, a man of almost festive
paradoxicality, while Goethe the writer has dwindled into being the
least read of the masters. But now, Friedenthal, with a muted censo-
rious dryness that reads like Suetonius forestalling Lytton Strachey,
restores the man to us in the world of his times without either neglecting his mind or allowing it too separate an existence from his three
main selves: the gilt-and-gingerbread Apollo who at thirty paid cash
in order to have his first thorough look at a naked woman; the
polymathic, busy Weimar bee—both factotum and potentate—of the
middle years; and the cantankerous, terrified old sage, lucid in his
white woolen dressing gown at the still center of Goethe empire, or
out tapping rocks with his little hammer.

Thanks to Friedenthal's labors, *Goethe: His Life and Times,* we
can now hate or enjoy Goethe the man as well as realize why so much

of his writing is aloof and miscellaneous. This is better than a mutinous deference to the culture-hero whose forced optimism attracted
droves of visitors to Weimar. Instead of Goethe the Grand Cham of
exhaustive intellect we now have Goethe the grandiose chameleon of
repeated puberties. He lived many lives and in none of them quite
grew up. With each of his massive self-projections into love, science,
politics, travel, poetry, drama, fiction, there went an equally massive
neglect or cold storage of something else. Always trying to catch up
with himself, to make his various selves come abreast, he nonetheless
doted on what he called his transformations. Just as afraid as Byron
of being trapped (and, incidentally, just as cavalier about his literary
vocation) he counted on omissions to keep him free: "incompleteness
stimulates," he said, and he always preferred to think of "coming into
existence" rather than of existence achieved. He ceaselessly recon-
ceived and modified the characters in his plays and novels (especially
in *Faust,* one of the most baffling masterpieces ever). So nothing got
really finished: there was always a revisionary rendezvous for later, a
restyling of the brain-children's faces. And this has tempted us to
exchange the protean, elusive, over-maneuvering Goethe for the de-
pendable monolith who, in fact, was never there.

If we are to see him plain, we have to acknowledge a few not
very exciting but vital truths. He was always getting something out of
the way—shelving it: for two whole decades he wrote nothing of
consequence; he assumed Napoleon would win and, with that settled,
devoted his mind to the serenities of geology and Chinese history; he
rejected deposed monarchs and mass movements equally; he imper-
sonalized his companions into walking encyclopedias; he couldn't bear
the company of any but his mental inferiors and his social superiors
(the two faces of sycophancy); he was callous, snobbish, smug, deceit-
ful, disloyal, envious and quarrelsome. Friedenthal skins him alive.

Well, we always knew something of this: that Goethe was a bit
of a monster but, being a genius . . . and so forth. The main truth
(which now includes other truths—he was guarded with Schiller;
Weimar was really a shabby little town presided over by a nit-wit) is
larger. The monster was, in fact, a perpetual alien altogether more up-
to-date (for us) than Byron's Childe Harold; a sort of Johann Landless
or Wandering Aryan; an outsider, a refusing captious stranger akin to

Camus's Meursault. His mind exceeded the resources of his personality. It was his mind that led him against his will into situations in which the mind is not enough: he debauched, he married, he begot a son who died ("I knew I had begotten a mortal"). He fought his mind. He mocked the German passion for abstract ideas. He came out against Kant, against Goethe. He even lauded British heartiness and British empiricism.

But it was no use. The mind still led. In 1816 he noted in his journal, "At midnight my wife taken to the mortuary. Myself in bed the whole day" (a convenient catarrh while she screamed with uremia). Only hours later he was planning new experiments with light. Lang, the Bavarian, called him the "old, ice-cold Imperial City Syndic" and others called him worse. The explanation, I think, assumes its most concise form in a letter to Zelter, the confidant of Goethe's later years. "There is," he writes, "something oppressive, limiting and often hurtful about presence—absence on the other hand induces freedom and naturalness. . . . The absent person is an ideal person, in each other's company people appear trivial to one another." It cuts both ways, as Friedenthal ably proves, making Goethe present and more trivial, limiting and hurting the ideal demi-god in the process.

Present, Goethe hurt almost everyone he got to know, benefiting only those pathetic frigid women, his "abbesses," who welcomed the lyrical idling of his gonads, or those others, such as Christiane Vulpius, who served without demand his intermittent, late-blooming lusts. Everyone was less present to him than such cumbersome mental furniture as *Gott-Natur,* entelechy, transformations, *Das Ewig-Weibliche* (in the neuter), the *Urs*—the *Ur*-plant (whose root he despised), the *Ur*-stone, the *Ur-Pferd* (the primal horse)—and the little bone, *os intermaxillare* he dubbed "the human keystone." He dubbed himself Columbus and Hercules. Byron was "Euphorion." Christiane was "Erotikon." For a psychological principle, his "elective affinities," he went to chemistry. The Weimar courtiers were toads and basilisks— "nothing but dung." The menopausal Charlotte von Stein's distress on being dropped in favor of "Mamsell" Vulpius he attributed to too much coffee. All of which, I think, we can attribute to too much mind on Goethe's part.

Inhuman then? Yes: more so than somewhat, but not entirely so.

Erysipelas, kidney trouble, angina, pericarditis took their toll, as did his impossible daughter-in-law. It is amazing he survived so long, almost as if he thought death into non-existence. As if he was spared for being not all bad: while Christiane sleeps he sets roses and two oranges for her to find on waking; he sends her candy from Verdun, feels the heartbeats of his unborn child, finds a chocolate for a little girl, is deeply affected by columns of refugees from the Revolutionary wars.

But mostly bad all the same. The great brain zooms on, stagnates, then zooms again; and, here at hand in dozens, out there chattering and loving and bleeding and being nervous by the thousand, are the homuncles who admire. The guilt is all in *Faust* which it will be impossible to read from now on without recalling the image Friedenthal has painstakingly built. And, because the image shows Goethe, Faust-like, promoting himself out of the human condition, the image will endure.

Bismarck said Goethe had a tailor's soul: what kind of man, he asked, could say "Blessed the man who stands aloof, unhating, from the world, clasping to his breast a friend with whom to share his joy?" What, he scoffs, "no hatred!" Goethe himself, ridiculed by Herder for being Director of Roads and Services ("in plain German road-inspector and crossing-sweeper") commented: "In our youth we think ourselves capable of building palaces for people, and when it comes to the point we find we have our hands full merely disposing of their excrement." Friedenthal has built a glass palace for the old *Vollendete,* the philosophe-god, and left him with both hands full.

A. Alvarez
Beyond All This Fiddle

IN ONE OF HIS STORIES, Borges identifies the Englishman's character-istic flaw as a sense of his own unreality; and from what I know of the matter, he is right. He means the thinking Englishman, the man who at home finds the class system and the manners inane, yet when abroad finds himself helplessly thinking along class lines. Where does he belong? Some have found Canada the answer; some have stopped wondering and have gone home or have become professional Americans. And others, like A. Alvarez, somehow transform their insularity into peninsularity, and then feel more unreal than ever.

Alvarez goes a step further; he finds himself, almost by accident, in a position that prompts him to select his title form Marianne Moore's admission about poetry: "I, too, dislike it: there are things that are important beyond all this fiddle." There are: in Alvarez's case a pro-found humanitarian concern. He is torn between wanting it expressed in an "Extremist" literature (concerned with madness, illness, suicide, the death-camps, and other disasters), and wanting it dismissed from literature altogether (on grounds of what he calls "an utter boredom with literature as the beginning and end of wisdom"). These are strange thoughts to come from an Englishman. No longer to want art, not only as art has been but art at all, seems hardly human. But then, Alvarez seems to imply, it's time we revised our notion of what "human" is.

What enables him to achieve this nauseated, almost agonizing condition is the sense of human destiny which the least English-minded Englishmen usually have: Schooled for suffocation, they break out and breathe the air of the Territory with a special gusto. Alvarez, for instance, finds English gentility insufferable, but has also objected to the "insulting" nature of American life. An English Jew, educated at a public school and Oxford, he has stuck it out in London (denying himself the mediocre sinecure of an English university job) and has made only brief forays to lecture in the United States. Trapped is what he seems to be, especially in view of his passion for American poetry and for writing that tackles unseemly extremes. His compensation has been to apply a Jewish sense of secular responsibility to the chore of literary journalism, attempting to introduce English readers to international standards and experience. He is that rarity in England, a practitioner of "comparative literature."

Not that this book has a thesis. Simply, whatever he is reviewing or retrieving—Mailer's *An American Dream,* a biography of D.H. Lawrence, Donne's *Holy Sonnets,* Strindberg's plays—he seems to read it always in the presence of books that are truly great or largely true. The currents of his mind run over a bizarre variety of topics, but they run at a constant speed and exert a constant pressure, so that even when he doesn't explicitly link one essay with another, you can usually see how they bear on each other: Keats on Yvor Winters, Sontag on Dryden.

Nothing flip, no gush, just a bony integrity raised to its highest power by two things: a sense of the moral-metaphysical hangover of World War II and of what it really is like to write creatively. The two senses come together when he suggests that art is not therapeutic and serves not to get something out of the artist's system, but only to make it even more present to him, often unendurably so. There is truth in this; but surely then the "fiddle" stands vindicated after all. If my art brings first and last things inescapably home to me, then what "important" things can be beyond it? Only God, it seems to me, and maybe harmony, and (something Alvarez doesn't say much about) what we call love.

This is my main reservation about his book, and it comes out of sympathy with his position of Extremism. I too succumb often enough to a European grimness and am willing to blame poems that aren't primarily concerned with Auschwitz. But it is one thing to be serious about grave matters and not to take other matters so seriously; it is something else to omit the others altogether. In the long run we have to admit that life is a bewildering mixture and that, as Eliot wrote, "human kind cannot bear very much reality." I suppose that is why such activities as stamp collecting and flower arranging help to save us, even from the harshest reality of all: the reality in which stamp collecting thrives alongside Auschwitz, flower arranging goes on before and after Hiroshima.

I do not mock Alvarez's seriousness; I too wish life were less discordant and shoddy and that art were less the compensatory game it seems to be. But the game is surely inevitable, and there is a sense in which even the most relentless preference for the tragic is merely another literary mannerism, another sort of fiddling. Indeed, the only utterance we cannot fault is that which is never made—which explains, no doubt, why "silence" has become one of the cult words. We are, as I think Alvarez suspects, beginning to lose faith in the ways we have of notifying one another about what upsets us most.

Who can establish at what point Josef Bor's *Terezin Requiem* or Elie Wiesel's *Night* (about both of which Alvarez writes movingly) must be seen not as almost unbearable accounts of Nazi atrocity but as failures as works of art? Alvarez insists that anyone writing about the extermination camps

> must exercise his imagination on situations which, in proved, lived fact, were beyond the imagination, and on circumstances where the imagination, with its power of making things come nervously close, was potentially the most dangerous and destructive of all qualities. He has to take the utterly psychopathic as his norm, and rake art out of the forces of anti-art.

At this, he says, Bor and Wiesel fail, and he goes on to specify how Tadeus Borowski surpasses them through a style "curt, icy, and brutally direct." Maybe so, but I think that here he is returning us to that familiar point at which imagination is no longer needed or even useful.

Imagination's role, if it still has one, is surely not to make fictions about concentration camps, but to remind us of the total context in which the camps existed. Alternatively, imagination will bring into being what did not exist—thus adding to the sum of created things—while the mind will assemble documentary epitomes from clippings and photographs, ads and tickets, catalogues and canceled checks.

Such is the point Alvarez at his most searching conducts us to, leaving many questions open. He knows the mind's duplicity, especially when it looks to the future. "Americanism is a quality of the future," he says. "You take to it only the most portable personal baggage: energy, ambition, passion, nothing as cumbersome as a set morality or accustomed habits of life." In exactly that spirit Alvarez here engages the literature and the future of many countries, and his mortified openness will make the complacent wince and give the uncertain nothing glib to hold on to—nothing at all, in fact, which they won't earn for themselves, once exhorted.

Jiri Weil
Mendelssohn Is On the Roof

IF ONLY HIS AMERICAN PUBLISHER, retrieving Jiri Weil's 1960 novel, *Mendelssohn Is On the Roof,* had told us how to say his first name! It remains easier to refer to Simone Weil than to him, and this is to subject him to a burden he doesn't need. Try to look Jiri Weil up at random, as I did, in George Theiner's Penguin anthology of Czech "New Writing" (which includes Holub, Kundera, and Lustig) or *World Authors: 1950-70,* or the admittedly spotty *Britannica,* and you find no mention of him. It is possible to rise without a trace, leaving fine novels behind you, scattered somewhere in the warehouse of literature until, if you are lucky, some Philip Roth comes along and writes a preface to a reissue of your work, pointing out how you rose to fame—as Jiri Weil did—between 1930 and 1950. In 1942 he feigned suicide and so managed to avoid deportation with the Jews of Prague: in fact, he hid out for the remainder of the war and died at fifty-nine of cancer, in 1959.

A preface to *Mendelssohn,* providing more facts than these, would have been welcome and useful. Readers forget, and none faster than American ones, who clearly are going to have trouble seeing the Weils for the Kunderas. As it is, *Mendelssohn* arrives on the doorstep like a recently written novel, only the second of Weil's to be translated into English, deserving serious attention but thrust into the hurly-burly of the Post-Wall world without introductory entrée, a favoring hand that tells review editors what we have here, who Weil was, and why his art endures. Perhaps I am dreaming and cynical, but I wonder in how many homes parents are recommending the all-but-forgotten Weil to their college-age children. I wonder how many professors of Slavic or Comparative Literature have perked up at seeing his name again, in an exquisite translation. Certainly he should be taught and heralded and his peculiar (peculiarly Czech) mix of emphatic imagism and narrative minimalism explored. I don't read Czech, but Weil feels different: his touch unnerves, his way of almost looking past what he narrates makes you wonder if you are misreading him and if you should go back and try to get straight what he is doing (in *Mendelssohn* he often gives an event and follows it with what led up to it: an anti-etiology, if you like, making the past not prologue but postscript).

Weil's previous novel, *Life With a Star,* also about Prague during the Holocaust, is a more ferocious work than *Mendelssohn,* more supplely and abundantly written, both catlike and obtusely serene. It is not a better novel, but a less oblique one: arithmetic rather than algebra. *Mendelssohn* implicitly honors Kafka without being Kafkaesque. It takes you all the way from Nazi buffoonery to the torturing of children and is bound to distress even while it condemns.

The core of its cry is how the Nazis contrive to deal with a statue of the composer Mendelssohn on the roof of Prague's concert hall. There are other statues there too. Well, which one is Mendelssohn's? The ignorant Nazis have no idea, so they send for a learned Jew, who is bound to know; but Rabinovich knows too much, reminding himself like a sleepwalker that Jews "never carved any statues" and that all bad things began with Moses Mendelssohn, founder of the Reform Movement:

> He wasn't an artist, after all, but a religious reformer. He did have descendants, but they weren't Jews. They had themselves christened and married Christians, and so nobody cared about those descendants. One of them was a composer and he had two names. Of course, he must be the one the Municipal officials were looking for.

Then he tells the Nazis he can't identify the statue because this particular composer was not a Jew. They bash him and send him away, back to what he supervises, as *Dr*. Rabinovich: a museum of objects confiscated from synagogues, a Reich "storehouse of trophies"—prayer robes, ark curtains, Torah crowns and pointers, shipped in from the provinces. A massive, desperate souvenir, this museum is also "a victory memorial, for the objects displayed here belonged to a race scheduled for annihilation." All the visiting Nazi high-ups see in it, however, is an unfamiliar arrangement of familiar merchandise—silver and wood—in spite of special lighting intended to communicate the mystery of ancient ritual.

One is reminded of T.S. Eliot's caricature of unbelievers' response to Catholic paraphernalia; "rugs and jugs and candlelights." I am not sure that Weil's explanation of the museum's nature and effects is complete; what he creates is a dense, centrifugal image, material at first glance, but drenched in emotion and functioning as a disastrous emblem: a ghetto of the defunct, a cemetery of stuff, a prophetic and surrogate clamming house. As you read on from page sixty-nine, the museum—and your memory of it—begins to work upon you like a morality play embedded in the novel. Up on the roof, it is the statue of Wagner that Nazi ignoramuses begin to topple; down in the museum, a specially commissioned life-size exhibit of a family celebrating the Passover feast of the Seder comes together in papier-mâché piety. Dr. Rabinovich, trapped between expedience and eternity, has been obliged to design it, and he berates himself for committing such a sacrilege. The family at the table seems to despise him, and he can bear to be in the exhibition room no longer. Not far away is a warehouse-museum of a different kind, full of secular Jewish property: not tidy and orderly like the so-called Collection agency (yet *another* repository, containing similar items), "where . . . every type of object had its own special stockroom: an eiderdown stockroom and a refrigerator stockroom," but higgledy-piggledy, a junk shop

> full of every possible kind of thing—furniture, chandeliers, refrigerators, radios, phonographs, clothing, vacuum cleaners, paintings, framed photographs, pots and pans, serving platters, toys, binoculars, typewriters, irons, tennis rackets, oars, kayaks, footballs, a garden ornament in the shape of a dwarf.

A diaspora sealed into a test tube. Impossible to read the above and not think of atoms swirling, of rubble, of detritus, the families of course having gone before, deported to execution.

So: we have the museum of religious articles; the Collection Agency; and, third, this grotesque room run by a self-styled "baroness," a Baltic German who used to run a brothel in Riga. Weil limns an evil trinity that juxtaposes holy relics, classified relics, and relics briefly arrested in their useful migration into the hands of Reich relief societies, dealers who used to buy from pawn shops, and bombed-out families. The author weaves history past this trinity and its analogues in the novel, sometimes letting one collection or the other blur and obstruct the narrative, as if the conglomerate love attached to ownerless objects had paralyzed his mind, sometimes letting the narrative surge didactically right through, like a tank.

Jangling her necklaces, the fake baroness insists that one of her regular dealers, Mr. Smutny (who retrieves things he recognizes on behalf of their owners), buy a half-meter statue of justice—a copy of a statue that stands in the main courtroom at Pankrac. Three weeks later, the statue reappears in the baroness's storeroom and she has it hammered to pieces. Weil ends that chapter with the unnecessary remark "Justice would no longer stand in anyone's way" and, on the next page, noting the route taken by the gun carriage that bears the body of the assassinated Acting Reich Protector, Reinhard Heydrich, mentions the statue of Roland. There are many other references to statues and public emblems, such as the last page of the Prague newspaper, covered with military crosses representing the deaths in action of Nazi soldiers, and the T-shaped gallows that Schoenbaum, who made the papier-mâché Passover Seder, has to build. Heydrich muses on how like a statue you have to become in order to carry out harsh measures in occupied countries. The tormentors turn to stone: they do not feel. The tormented, turned to ashes, do not feel either.

You do not often get a novelist who pours concrete into his own novel, or rigs up graven images to make his point, but Weil has to because he is writing about the conversion of humanity to something inhuman. The effect is extraordinary, like a social satire staged among tank traps, and the mincing, joshing, half-amused elements in the novel keep ending up next door to something massy, dumb, and awful. It is the effect you find in Virginia Woolf's astounding *Orlando,* in which, at one point, Orlando leaves London and looks behind him/her only to see a vast unorganized geyser of London stuff rising into the sky.

To read this novel in terms of phrases from the heyday of existentialism may be going too far, but I doubt it—that was the intellectual climate Weil came from and thrived in. In *Mendelssohn* you find the *pour soi*—agonized awareness—contemplating the *en soi*—thingness unaware—and wishing not be be aware at all. This is the most grievous form of the insentient dumb ox proposed by Hemingway and the anesthetic jargon of the military: "Terminate with extreme prejudice."

In Weil's novel, you keep running into concrete mind-numb-ers that give the lie to the charm and suavity of the narrative. It is as if the author plugged on, trying to report the idiocies of Nazi thugs as material for an arcane comedy, when really, whether jocular or fiendish, they personify the anti-life. Heydrich (who "understood music") introduces a high-ranking Nazi minister to the perfect acoustics of the Rudolfinum, "a concert hall now returned to German art," and the members of a Nazi orchestra brought in "play and sing any old way" because the big shots of the SS Elite Guard and the highest officers of the Gestapo know nothing of classical music. Off the performers go to shop, running around the city for poultry, bacon, woolens. This might have been a frolic about fatheads and philistines, but Weil vitiates any such possibility, either insinuating terror and death through the small auscultations of imagery (a dummy push button instead of a doorbell) or the grand events of a finale in which, for the most trivial offenses, twenty-five members of the ghetto population are to go to the hangman: a stolen half-rotten potato, a bit of lumber filched.

First, however, a hangman must be found. *Two.* A couple of "criminal types," perhaps. Eight butchers appear. No good. Finally, a professional hangman shows up, a hunchback, who chooses one of the butchers to help him. The novel now becomes a muted shriek rather than a lump of fiction. It dare not be fiction, dare it? Would that not be pornographic? The hangman, who comes form the routine execution shed at the Small Fortress, boasts that, after he dispatches someone, he usually receives a salami, rum, and chewing tobacco—as if to return him to the zone of human conviviality after his deviation into

barbarism. Weil shoves on with bemused incredulity, making sense in
a senseless dimension:

> One of the [doomed] prisoners was guilty of not giving the
> required salute to an SS man. But if a hungry and exhausted
> person is heading home after a day of endless labor, he drags
> through the streets looking down at the ground to avoid
> stumbling.

That almost apologetic second sentence, oral in impact, begets a
third, in which we learn that the usual punishment was one or two
weeks in jail: The Nazis have swept in and grossly magnified the
feeble, limited sentences of the ghetto court. Hard concrete has dropped
from the sky. Crows, never before seen in the fortress town, fly over.
Fog envelops the sun, not symbolically, but allusively. The prisoners
muster their courage and sing a song from a famous play. The executions begin. A rope breaks. The man rehangs. One of the hanged
begins to jerk and an SS chauffeur shoots five bullets into the body.
Nine men have died, but the carpentry workshop had been told to
make twenty-five coffins overnight. A final joke, not without effect.

Such horror would have been enough, but Weil, who matches the
earlier search for a learned Jew with a search for a hangman, doubles
his theme by having two Jewish girls, who have hidden out in a
cubbyhole all through the novel, wander out into the hands of the
police. So Weil underlines, you might say, to show the difference
between representative, literary horror and horror that can happen in
each and every life.

He goes farther, though; from the book's beginning, Jews have
been herded into the Radio Mart, ready for the train. No wonder Jiri
Weil supplements narration with optional obligato: algebra for when
the arithmetic of common sense fails. At the novel's outset, Schlesinger,
the aspiring SS officer assigned to remove Mendelssohn, also removes
the remains of the Unknown Soldier. Almost two hundred pages later,
an "exquisite figurine" of *The Judgment of Paris* falls victim to a
bomb. And, on the next-to-last page, we read how, as the Soviet Army
at last rolls into Berlin, "The proud statues that lined the Alley of
Triumph collapsed and their broken limbs lay on the ground. The

Arch of Triumph caved in. The people who survived crept by the fallen, gaping heads and looked down at the ground. But the ground was a desert of stone." No trace here of those whom Weil, earlier on, calls "the millions who go against the wind."

It is amazing how well the novel works, considering how didactic it becomes, rather like early Bertolucci (before the director underwent psychoanalysis). Even the Nazis are prop Nazis, crying *"Los, los, schnell, schnell."* I attribute its success to some empathy of the numb. You put yourself in the position of the victims in the novel, and there is no need for deep psychological inspection: you are the horror while the horror lasts, and whatever rises to the surface of your mind rises in the context of imminent death. The book could have survived in-depth portraits, which would have made it seem more casual, less of a blueprint. Weil is an excruciated witness, almost too appalled to create. He deals in pellucid extremes; iteration of the demonic, the banal; personifications whose profundities have burned away long before they reach the furnaces. He does not have a rich, harmonic plenty to be ironic about: only some extremes that do not belong on the planet but have not yet been sent elsewhere.

The Book of Alfred Kantor

THE ONE-HUNDRED-AND-TWENTY-SEVEN drawings in this album of hell come out of an intensely creative two-month period which Alfred Kantor spent in a displaced-persons camp in Deggendorf. Thematically, they come out of three-and-a-half years spent in three Nazi detention camps. Born in Prague in 1923, "Fredy" Kantor was deported in 1941 to the "model ghetto" of Terezín (Theresienstadt), transferred in 1943 to the death-camp at Auschwitz (cover name Labor Camp Birkenau), and thence—virtually from the threshold of the gas chamber—to the slave labor compound of Schwarzheide. Just before liberation, he took part in a death march back to Terezín, one of two hundred who survived it out of one thousand.

Ironically, on the great wall in Prague's synagogue, Fredy Kantor is listed among the 77,297 people who perished: he just, as he told John Wykert, forgot to notify the authorities. He supplements his drawings, captioned as they are in what he calls his "best Prague high-school English" (a curiously affecting, laconic idiom), with an introduction that fills in the spaces between them and this is expansive whereas they are definitive. Even more telling, however, are the photographs, postcards, and mementoes, here reproduced, including a cheap cloth yellow star saying *"Jude,"* a ticket for Terezín café (one two-hour visit allowed per year), an Auschwitz number patch, an invoice that accompanied a food parcel from his sister (married to a non-Jew), and a map of the death march.

The mind reels at this teenaged art student's composure in the face of annihilation, not to mention daily physical abuse, and the gassing of his mother and girl friend, as well at the precision of his visual recall. No Goya or Bosch, he delineates horror with an almost innocent painstakingness which, far from expressionist, sedulously covers all the the paper, complementing the unspeakable with whatever else happened to be visible round it: trees, snow, cloud, or the vestigial dignity in grouped faces. And that is the key to his overall attitude: an ability to see and record—to accept as an abiding principle—the mixedness of things. It is almost as if, true to Beckett's maxim, "Death has not required us to keep a day free," he buries death's imminence in the passion to be a thorough witness.

Reading his introduction, we find that, despite the cold and the appalling overcrowding, Terezín had its brighter side, so to speak: no barbed wire, few SS, frequent plays and operas, string quartets, and soccer matches. But, of course, it was a propaganda showplace. These Machiavellian amenities were organically part of the code that hanged nine inmates for smuggling letters out.

Then comes, in much the same vein of antinomies that threaten to tear the mind apart, the insane decorum of Auschwitz, by which Fredy Kantor was fitted out with clothes from the dead: an enormous shirt minus collar, an elegant black vest, a Dutch coat with silk lining. Somehow, he came into possession of a tiny watercolor set, but had to tear up his sketches as soon as made. He was allowed the food parcels from his sister—his tenuous Aryan connection entitled him to that: his jailers, it seems, were working bureaucratically to the exact letter of the genocide law.

At Schwarzheide, helping to rebuild a bombed-out factory that made aviation fuel, he still received food packages. Allied bombs killed many prisoners; the Russian front line kept coming closer; and soon he was building tank traps and digging foxholes. Then the march to the Czech border, during which the prisoners ate dandelions. At the Elbe the SS guards turned back, and the surviving slave-laborers dragged on to a Terezín ablaze with lights, where they were billeted in the morgue, grateful to be anywhere without overseers.

The drawings depict this ghastly round with chronological impersonality, and readers must make their own shocked connections between the cheerfulness of Fredy Kantor the recapitulating survivor and such items as these, done in a sort of drypoint Dufy, the captions providing the punch, the insider's voice:

In Terezín: "Girls working in the SS-Garden were not allowed to pick up even a single potato . . . Charge was usually: sabotage on the German Empire—penalty often death"; "one toilet for 1000 people"; "'Uncle SS Sturmfürher' distributing candies in front of Swiss newsreporter."

In Auschwitz: "first thought," on arrival, "what are all the spot-lights for, a movie?"; "a 'greenhorn' asks, 'What the hell is the meaning of this awful smoke!'"; "Try to climb up this fence! Voltage 500"; "30 prisoners on one triple deck bunk"; "18 year olds looked like 80 year olds"; "crematories going on full blast . . . facilities for slaughter 1000 in 15 mins"; "babies still alive into the fire"; "Toilets are behind dead corpses."

In Schwarzheide: "jumping on a man's intestines makes him [an SS Unterscharfürher] feel merry"; "110 lbs of cement on your back and 800 calories per day is a shortcut to the crematory"; "in the air shelter Man in front directs us to duck (as if it would help) as new wave of B-17s approaches"; "Garbage—Our Treasure"; "Fleeing Germans"; "Girls, who have been in luck's way during wartime and could stay in T. care for us affectingly. Many of our old friends cannot recognize us"; "Happy End," with flags, the survivors still in blue-and-white-striped camp attire.

Shortly after his arrival in the United States in 1945, Fredy Kantor was drafted into the Army, where he played glockenspiel in a band. Such is vicissitude. Now an artist with an advertising agency, he plays the piano in his spare time. "Careful and steady," as John Wykert almost incredulously observes, "the adult has achieved a life he finds both comfortable and satisfying." Such is resilience and such the almost numbed, understating response to it. Fredy Kantor may have neglected to inform the Czech authorities that he had survived, but, in this colorful, restrained testament of a defiant young artist in limbo, he has certainly informed us. It is not often that the mind's eye functions as a talisman so steadily and with such command.

Hitler and Canaris

H ITLER, WHO HAD FEW FRIENDS, but killed by the million and besotted millions more, enters the demonlogy of our times as a figure both awful and oddly familiar. He stands, of course, for what he and his accomplices did; the historical Hitler has become historic. But infamy so vile also supplies a personification of evil the 20th century didn't find in Franco, say, or even Stalin. Had Hitler never existed, we might not have dreamed him up; but, existing, he worked so much atrocity he seemed like Satan in the flesh, not a remote and smokey Gothic figment, but an ungovernable bloodsucker who lived 56 years among us and remains, a gruesome mnemonic for what is foul. Thirty-four years after his death, readers the world over reach for and compulsively buy—in trances of fixated, near-pornographic aversion—books bearing his face, his swastika or the twin zig-zag flashes worn by his SS. No one in recent history transcended himself more; the worst done by other dictators is already "Hitlerian"; and the Hitler industry goes full tilt, making us learn and choke and even, perhaps, form a vicarious taste for the infernal itself.

Sebastian Haffner's pithily colloquial essay, *The Meaning of Hitler,* differs from such works as those by Joachim Fest and John Toland in being much less voluminous and spurning the chronological

approach. An historical and intellectual book rather than a biographi-
cal one, a distillery rather than a reservoir, it reveals Hitler thematically in order to sum him up and lock him into a perspective which
anecdotes cannot prettify or guesswork blur. The private life of the
master-racist gets short-shrift, therefore, not only because it was empty,
as Haffner says, of "everything that normally lends weight, warmth
and dignity to a human life: education, love and friendship, marriage,
parenthood," but also because Hitler wanted it that way, intent on an
almost wholly political destiny. Indeed in everything but politics Hitler
was a nonentity, and throughout his career he soothed himself with the
thought of how swift his suicide would be: five minutes, he told
Goebbels in 1932, but over the years the interval shrank to "seconds"
and even "the fraction of a second." As Haffner says, it was a life
"strangely lightweight" and, in the end, "lightly discarded." Only someone that impersonal could substitute politics for privacy and then take
the giant step of substituting his own political mania for the public life
of a nation. Hitler became, in his own eyes anyway, infallible and
irreplaceable, obliged to match Germany's fate and lifespan to his own
since he and it were inseparable.

The mental and moral morass into which this notion took him is
staggering. The body politic he infested had, paradoxically, to die with
him, and in the last months of World War II he did several things to
bring that about. In December, 1944 he ordered the Ardennes offensive, removing armies from the East to blast the Allies in the West.
The Russians then poured in all the way to the Oder, the Ardennes
offensive failed, the transferred Nazi armies were pulverized, and the
postwar zonal partition of Germany was a sure thing. But, as Haffner
makes plain, Hitler really doomed Germany in March, 1945 when he
issued the two "Fuehrer orders," the first commanding all Germans in
the West to begin a death-march eastward, the second (the so-called
"Nero order") requiring destruction of the means of life in both the
interior and the East. Those marching eastward had nothing to march
to. Germany had let its Fuehrer down by not being *Herrenvolk* enough
to win the war, or suicidal enough in defeat, so he *punished* it, having
"his best horse," in Haffner's colorful image, "whipped to death because it proved unable to win the Derby."

What emerges from Haffner's book, steadily implied without

being spelled out, is that Hitler was an insatiable romantic for whom murder was manna and the German nation a humanoid blow-up of himself which he could oratorically excite whenever he chose. Imagine, Haffner writes, "a man who had reason to regard himself as impotent suddenly finding himself capable of performing miracles of potency." Imagine the effect on Hitler's private life of those successive physical unions with the regimented hordes at the Nuremberg rallies. He was Narcissus. He was Narcissus at the podium and, beyond that, Caligula, volunteering himself—the nation-self he was—for godhead. No wonder Sebastian Haffner sounds incredulous; the gruesome has no right to be so silly.

After chapters devoted to Hitler's life, achievements, successes and misconceptions, almost as if doing a report card about some feisty, pigheaded, aberrant youth, Haffner reviews the mistakes and the crimes, pointing out that Hitler's twin aims—the domination of Europe, the extermination of the Jews—were unrelated and got in each other's way. Hitler could no more extract a compromise peace, once his war was lost, from nations who saw him as a psychopathic butcher, than he could make military use of SS units or railroad cars assigned to the so-called Jewish problem. What he really wanted was an ecstasy of death, the twilight of his godliness, and that is why, in the last three years of the war, with Germany surrounded and being squeezed, he "continued in his table talk at headquarters to reveal an often unimpaired self-satisfaction and at times even robust merriment."

The death-count of Jews kept going up, and he'd been able to wipe out millions of non-Jews as well: 100,000 German invalids ("useless eaters"); half a million gypsies, and over a million members of the Polish intelligentsia. All this, says Haffner, was merely for Hitler's "personal gratifications," and it aligns him with "such killers as Crippen and Christie," except that "he accomplished on a conveyor belt basis what they did as craftsmen." Only Hitler legitimizes a compliment so sour.

Nonspecialist readers may find Haffner at times caught up in historical minutiae and a bit shy of arguing his themes right through (as distinct from sifting the casts that fit them from those that don't); but his essay adds up superbly after the halfway mark and he leaves no doubt that Hitler wanted to take Germany down with him. What we have here is the *phenomenon* of Hitler: both a valuable recap of what's been said and a tidy, ravaging sortie into things underplayed or hitherto unsaid; not a parade of mug shots, but a fiend's progress, and regress, laid bare.

Among the lieutenants and backroom confidants in Hitler's executive hierarchy, none was more baffling than Admiral Wilhelm Canaris, head of German intelligence and an accomplished polyglot spy himself. Like Hitler, he had little private life, although married with two daughters. Hitler and he respected the domestic aridity they felt in each other. They both kept on the move, if only to flee the paperwork they abhorred, and their women. They doted on dogs. And when they were closeted together they overlapped so much that they never saw each other plain; when they finally did, Canaris saw the lethal cynic Hitler really was, and Hitler the dissembling plotter Canaris had become. On April 5, 1945, Hitler was shown Canaris' private diaries and had him hanged on the 9th, only three weeks before he shot himself. Weirdly enough, Hitler's passion for pointless bloodshed had its counterpart in Canaris' passion for pointless intrigue, as if the boyish thrill of being the devious masterspy—deceiving and entrapping everybody—had never left him. Even more weirdly, when everybody else was after Canaris' blood, it was Himmler of all people who stood by him because, to Himmler, Canaris personified the romance of espionage which the SS leaders first found in the stories of the British secret service written by John Buchan.

Canaris was a Janus: he wanted power and influence and prestige, and as long as Hitler supplied them he played along; but he also thought Hitler would finish Germany off and so must be removed by a conspiracy of patriots. But his thinking was usually not so black and white: a mood, a dream, would deflect him; an exotic journey would lull his mind; a chance to complicate something already complex lured him into baroque byways of intrigue for its own sake. Such is the view of him that Heinz Höhne presents in his big, immaculate and definitive biography, *Canaris: Hitler's Master Spy,* in which, against an avalanche of information about the Nazi period, Canaris the legendary masterspy who was also the pillar and patron of the German Resistance gives way to Canaris the stylish amateur who saved Jews and hired them, but also came up with the idea that German Jews should wear a Star of David. He was less of, or with, the Resistance than within its rhetorical vicinity, lending an ear (or a desk drawer) to his more heartily motivated colleagues, but sometimes not lifting a finger to help them when the Gestapo pulled them in. "I did it for show," he cried out during his trial in the laundry room at Flossenburg camp, and that is typical; he was such a hedonistic fatalist that he took no stand, other than self-interest, until someone forced one from him. Höhne quotes one intelligence officer who said "Canaris had a pronounced sense of adventure, including the adventure of evil itself." Indeed, life with the Nazis struck Canaris as like getting involved with the gangsters in a competently written thriller. It sometimes seems that the whole Nazi bloodbath was a boyhood dream wit large and gone wrong, as befouled as the rug on which Canaris' two dachschunds gamboled in his office.

Höhne's book is quite magnificent, not merely as a piece of sustained debunking with all the evidence pinned down, all the legwork and the library-checking turned into prose of steady narrative beat, but also as a refresher course in what happened between 1918 and Hitler's death. A work of social history shot through with harsh, cumulative suspense, so it's also an exhilarating thriller, especially when Canaris's associates, Oster and Dohnanyi, and then Canaris himself, begin to sway and duck, maneuver and slide, as the Gestapo tries to pick them off. Our documents, they protest, always mean the *opposite* of what they say; we're in espionage after all. We only *pretended* to play the *Führer* false.

Canaris' intimate life was thin, but its external texture has its charms. His ancestors came from a silk-spinning village on Lake Como. As a boy he played with invisible inks and assumed false names; as a young naval officer he excelled by setting up a supply system for U-boats in the Mediterranean and floated through Spain, France, and Italy using a Chilean passport and the name "Reed Rosas." His code names for espionage purposes were "Kika" and "Guillermo." In command of a submarine, he efficiently mined Allied sea routes in 1916 and then confirmed his deviousness by thwarting justice at the court-martial of the officers involved in the murder of Rosa Luxemburg. Always accumulating informants and accomplices—kings, businessmen, diplomats, rogues and financiers—Canaris came to a halt in 1931 when the German press dug deep into the trial he'd rigged. Then he marked time until his appointment to Intelligence in 1934, as Head.

He comes through a bit forlorn, with three bronze monkeys on his desk to symbolize "see all, hear all, say nothing." White-haired, ruddy-faced, 5-feet 3-inches tall, speaking with a lisp and looking nattily frail, he was a pill-popping hypochondriac, forever phoning from enormous distances to check on the bowel movements of his dogs. He slept inordinately. One officer thought he resembled "the impresario of a worldwide music-hall agency." In fact, he played croquet with Heydrich of the SS, cooked saddle of wild boar *en croûte* for his guests, and had an Algerian butler named Mohammed. His picturesque side, which Höhne doesn't waste, includes saluting a shepherd in Spain because "You can never tell if there's a senior officer underneath" and suggesting to a colleague that, after the war, the pair of them "open a little coffee shop in Piraeus harbor. I'll make the coffee and you can wait table."

Helmuth James von Moltke
Letters to Freya 1939-1945

IN THE WEEKS BEFORE HIS TRIAL and execution by strangling, Moltke the aristocrat and lawyer used to tell fellow-prisoners while exercising in the yard at Tegel prison: "Prepare yourselves; it takes twenty minutes to die." That warning does not appear in the present collection of letters, but it is typical of this unflappable, grave intellectual who opposed Hitler without actually implicating himself in Klaus von Stauffenberg's bomb-plot, which failed on July 20, 1944. Had Moltke not been arrested in the January of that year, he would no doubt have backed the assassination. And his end would have been the same. He might not have written so many letters, however, which would have been a pity as these to Freya, his young wife, have much the same force and gossipy bite as Ciano's diaries, providing a behind-the-scenes view of the German war machine.

One of Germany's best and brightest, Moltke had a secure career ahead of him in the Foreign Ministry, at least until 1939, when he began to apply his formidable legal talents to the saving of Jews and prisoners of war. Based in Berlin, but forever scurrying off to Oslo, Warsaw, Paris, Brussels, and Vienna to intercede and confer, he became an international courier of compassion. Estimating that in 1943 Germany had nineteen guillotines "working at considerable speed," beheading fifty per day (not counting deaths in the camps), he tried to save as many non-German prisoners as he could. In these pages he reports the fatigue and frustration, but skirts the grisly facts. Only now and then does he tell Freya, home looking after the family estate, what his dear friend Harald Poelchau, the Tegel chaplain, reports to him with stoic powerlessness: five of his charges were told at 7 p.m. that they were to be executed next morning at 5 (October 9, 1941); his job is "the same always, only considerably increased in quantity. Yesterday it was the turn of 13 women" (August 6, 1943). This link with Poelchau is extraordinary since he, night after night, sits with the condemned until the hangman sends for them, while Moltke wheels and deals, often successfully, all over Europe, for lives in just as much jeopardy. In the end, with grievous appositeness, it is Poelchau who smuggles Moltke's letters out of Tegel, and Freya's in.

Of some sixteen hundred letters, this edition prints fewer than the German one, but there is enough here for us to get to know well this gentle, diagnostic spirit, surely one of the most articulate martyrs of our time. He was very tall, had a South African mother, and wrote a tiny, neat script. Freya von Moltke hid the letters in the beehives on the thousand-acre Kreisau estate, where in 1940 her husband, to cheer himself up, instituted regular gatherings of compatible leaders and intellectuals intent on rebuilding Germany after Hitler was gone. He once described those bees, and their hives, as "his favorite object of meditation," perhaps because they paralleled the steady, joint efforts of his circle of friends (later called the Kreisau Circle by the Gestapo) to see beyond Naziism. One of the things which helped him keep his aplomb to the very end was his ability to fuse disparate callings. A passionate farmer, he was always asking Freya about the weighing of pigs, the lilacs and "the little flowering *prunus,*" new fences, cherry trees, the sugar-beet harvest, ploughing, manure, and the wisdom of keeping a pair of ducks.

Rarely at Kreisau, he worked for Canaris's *Abwehr* (the German intelligence service) in its Foreign Division. As legal adviser to the High Command, he found operation orders fascinating; he had never been allowed to see such things. The fascination wore off, however, as his awareness of atrocity increased, and his English-educated sensibility recoiled. His stiff upper lip was the badge of a strict conscience which, in these letters over the war years, becomes less and less tolerant of violence. In his most characteristic outburst, he denounces France's Maginot Line for having removed thousands of square kilometers "out of useful cultivation":

> In this entire region nothing grows but thistles and other weeds, and the wind just blowing across it was carrying whole consignments of mature thistle seed, to spread like a plague over German land perhaps 100 km. away, where people will have no idea why there are so many thistles.

He was an ecologist before the word came in, regarding the planet and its rind as not only sacred but also ennobling. His soul writhes in the presence of psychotic Nazi technocrats and nerdy Nazi families buying up dry goods in Paris. Hitler's showcased Olympic Games sicken him no less than Mental Homes for SS men with nervous breakdowns from executing women and children. He can hardly believe what is happening to Europe while he goes through the standard motions, taking Phanoform for insomnia, being plagued by lumbago and sciatica, hunting a purse for Freya along Tauentzienstrasse and eyeing four volumes of "the little red leather Temple edition of Shakespeare."

Habituated to long and exhausting briefs, he sometimes compresses his thoughts into exclamatory asides: "Today I can endure the sufferings of others with an equanimity I would have found execrable a year ago"; "I love ships, and all pictures of ships in motion excite me. To me a ship is a symbol of freedom"; "every man is a special thought of the Creator's mind"; "we need a revolution, not a coup d'état." He reads the *Times* of London daily, as well as Spinoza, Kant, Voltaire, Ernst Jünger, *War and Peace* and *Vanity Fair,* and gives Freya a running commentary on what he gets to eat, from blue plums bought in Belgium to caviar, ham-in-burgundy, duck, and crêpes (he dotes, actually, on mashed potatoes).

In the end, he goes to the hangman "steadfast and calm—even with joy," as reported by the Catholic prison chaplain at Tegel. He enjoys sparring at his trial with Freisler, the loud and tyrannical hanging judge. In his alert, mellow way, he had an eye for the red flashlights of the whores on Kurfürstendamm, for the man in cell 76 at Ravensbrück named Poseidon because he was in charge of watering the flowers. He was also the world citizen who once, in Istanbul, wrote of the Black Sea "I simply can't see the water without instantly realizing that this same water laps Table Mountain, Sydney, and Shanghai." His final letters while awaiting execution address his sons and the world at large as well as Freya, and they will profoundly concentrate the mind of anyone who reads them. What a spectacle this book presents of *homo sapiens* gone to waste. Beate Ruhm von Oppen's translation is considerate and idiomatic; one sees her name and recalls Lieutenant Georg Sigismund von Oppen, who was with Stauffenberg in Berlin on the day of the bomb-plot.

The final letter is dated January 11, 1945, but Moltke's execution took place on January 23. The flap copy says he was educated at Oxford; he was educated at Breslau, Berlin, Vienna, and in London, and became *persona grata* at All Souls.

Kristallnacht

IF WE DIDN'T KNOW BETTER, we might think *"Kristallnacht"* another pious German carol, still and holy, whereas anything less still and holy than that orchestrated preview of the Holocaust would be hard to find. Events in Hanover in the late October of 1938 led to the infamous night of broken glass that began in the small hours of November 10, 1938, described by Otto Tolischus for *The New York Times* as "a wave of destruction unparalleled in Germany since the Thirty Years' War." Nationwide, with a few exceptions, the pogrom went on all day as well while fashionably dressed matrons applauded and held up their babies to watch the "fun." This was when the world should have lost its illusions and had the veils swept from its eyes; a clearer statement of racial hatred was not to be had, but the world nodded on, as if already inured.

In October 27, 1938, the family of Sendel Siegmung Grynszpan, a Jew of somewhat confused nationality (Polish Russians living in Germany) was rounded up and deported by special train to the German-Polish border where, along with some 12,000 others, they were whipped by the SS toward the fixed bayonets of the Polish border guards. The Poles fired a volley into the air and the Jews panicked into no-man's land, from which the Poles eventually removed them to Zbaszyn, forty miles southwest of Poznan, where, cold from freezing rain, they were put up in pigsties and dung-thick stables. Those who tried to escape back into Germany were shot. Not until July 1939 did the Polish authorities permit the remaining survivors to enter Poland proper. Poland had told the British Foreign Office, in fact, that it had too many Jews already and wanted to export them to Northern Rhodesia, now Zambia. The mind reels.

While the Grynszpans were still in Zbaszyn, Sendel's only daughter, Berta, had written to her brother Herschel, then in Paris, a full account of their misery, asking him for money and telling him "Since we left, we have not been able to undress" and "we won't be able to stand this much longer." Badly off, a fugitive, and only seventeen, the young man talked of suicide, but in the end went and bought a gun with which to kill the German Ambassador. What he actually managed to do, on November 7, was shoot Ernst vom Rath, the embassy's third secretary, twice, on the fifteenth anniversary of the "Beer Hall Putsch" that brought Hitler to public notoriety in 1923. Vom Rath died from his wounds. Hitler was heard to say that "The SA should be allowed to have a fling." And Goebbels made an hysterical speech, pleading for revenge. The Nazis had a perfect excuse for a night of bloodletting.

At 1:20 in the morning, Reinhard Heydrich put instructions on the teleprinters for "Measures Against the Jews This Night," spelling out—if such a thing is conceivable—the protocol of barbarism ("the burning of synagogues only to be carried out if there is no danger of the fire spreading . . ."; "Businesses and residences of Jews may be destroyed but not looted"). The resulting enthusiasm destroyed 7500 stores, 29 warehouses, 267 synagogues, 171 houses, and a dozen or so Jewish community centers. Thirty thousand Jewish men, along with seven Aryans and three foreigners, were arrested. The death toll reached 236, and more than 600 were permanently maimed. This makes bad enough reading in its merely statistical form, but the book goes on to recount scores of individual dramas, each one worth a novel in its own right. The record of rape and battery, blackmail and swindling, sadism and hooliganism, beggars belief. It is an orgy of smashed pianos, bald heads daubed with red paint, children hurled from balconies, Jews spat upon and smeared with mud, made to hop and crow like cocks, Emil Nolde watercolors and Paul Klee drawings trampled to shreds, Jews hanged in the woods and Jews self-gassed at home, throats cut in baths, mutilations, Jews thrown down their own staircases repeatedly, Jews leaping, Jews drowning, Jews taking poison. In the town of Würzburg one could even buy a board game for two to six players, to be played with dice and six little figures, its name: JUDEN RAUS! (JEWS OUT!)

Some decent Germans managed to save their Jewish neighbors, but many more turned them in. Some villages, such as Warmsried in southern Swabia, were remote enough not to have felt the national mania, and their Jews survived. Some party thugs did not have the stomach for such a pogrom, and even the Jew-baiter Julius Streicher slept through most of it, yawning "If Goebbels wants it, then that's all right by me." On August 10, Streicher had personally driven the crane that toppled the Star of David from the Nuremberg synagogue and no doubt felt he'd done his bit. The sickening thing to those who know the Holocaust better than the pogrom is that this preview is every bit as dreadful; simply, the organization improves and the racism turns into an absolute from being a merely optional barbarism. The book reveals how the pogrom energized and filled the camps, which in turn intensified the urge to clear them to fill them up again. We think we have heard it all before, from the toothbrush cleaning of latrines and the whalemeat and cabbage soup to tree-hangings and crucifixions on the main gate. But we did not know, perhaps, that Kristallnacht Jews were meant to leave the camps, if they survived, and so illustrate for others the pleasures of leaving Germany. The schizophrenic Reich had it both ways: killing or exiling, and by comparison the latter even looked wantonly generous.

Perhaps the most imagination-provoking chapter in one up-to-date book about these events, *Kristallnacht* by Anthony Read and David Fisher, is the one devoted to Herschel Grynszpan's eventual fate. After shooting Rath, he made no attempt to escape and became a world figure, always being readied for trial yet never tried, at last arriving in Sachsenhausen camp (where he probably met his end). In Fresnes prison he filled two notebooks. In a whole series of *Rashomon*-like twists devised by him and consummated by others, he claimed to have fired his gun as if asleep, then concocted an entirely new story in which he became vom Rath's male prostitute. Weirdly enough, the Nazis themselves in the end found out that vom Rath had indeed been a homosexual known in and around Paris as "the ambassadress" and "Notre Dame de Paris." Appropriately enough, Herschel the fecund liar, untried and unfound, was assigned a nominal date for his death: May 8, 1945, the day after the German surrender.

With such fascinating things to recount, the authors choose to claim, on the basis of no evidence, that Hans Oster, Canaris's chief of staff, was hanged in Flossenberg "from a piano-wire noose." If Read and Fisher had concentrated on their English instead, we wouldn't be reading sentences such as these: "Driving through the streets to Göring's apartment, the extent of the damage quickly became clear" and "Once inside, the job of destruction began." Mute participles dangle from those wire nooses.

War as a Soap

THE FIRST OF THE NIGHT AIR RAIDS on Baghdad astounded me with its swirling and green lights, of course, but mainly with its sounds: the shooting sounded slap-happy, impetuous, almost as celebratory as the machineguns fired in Kuwait City at the end of it all. Then, as the war went on, I began having bad dreams, or oneiric memories, of being Blitzed for several years in World War Two as a child. First we hid under the cellar steps, a fatal place, then in the Anderson shelter outside, cold and sleepless. After the first year, my father and I would step outside to watch the bombers as searchlights roved over them; we chewed on brisket sandwiches while braving the shrapnel. A landmine had landed about a hundred yards from us and had eaten away an entire field, so we knew we were safe. Sometimes, though, when a bomb howled close, we would leap under the table we were eating at. What a luxury, I thought this year, to have the war thousands of miles away. Just imagine that, while we were pulverizing Baghdad and Basra, the Iraqis were pulverizing New York and Pittsburgh. There is a certain luxury in being able to demolish some place and have it brought back to you at the speed of light in what seems a closed system, on a TV channel next to two others on which the commercials are unrolling smoothly. What was CNN's twenty-four newsreel a commercial for? You would think it was there to sicken you of war and bombs and the military mind. No, it was really a trumpet call for technology, an invitation to cozy smugness, and the brave in-the-thick-of-it reporters struck me as no more than opportunistic, masochistic voyeurs. Of all the Arabs filmed, the Iraqis seemed the least offended, as if they had been force-fed films of blitzed Londoners, keeping their phlegmy cool amid the V-1s and the V-2s. On the spot, or under the bomb, TV coverage makes war a vicarious commodity, less frightening than it is, less frightening than Orson Welles's famous broadcast. Now the war is over, the stuff on the other channels (43 here) looks contrived and half-baked, which most of it is. The odd thing is: there is never any need to make it anyway. All you need is forty-three channels pumping out footage of today as things happen, including, say, so-and-so's finishing his latest symphony, so-and-so's beginning a new novel, so-and-so's finding a pig in his kitchen when he got up. No version of anything will ever be complete, of course, and we will never understand war, or TV, until we are watching ourselves being bombed this very minute, here in America, home of the safe. CNN English, with its "premunitions" and its incessant "during the course of"s offered a minor diversion, but not enough to distract from the mortifying conclusion that, though we might resent being bombed, we wouldn't believe we were being bombed until we saw it on TV, if we were there to watch it. The ultimate pornography, I guess, is to have that last, frenzied appetitive look at yourself and your loved ones being blown to bits as mashed innards blur the screen.